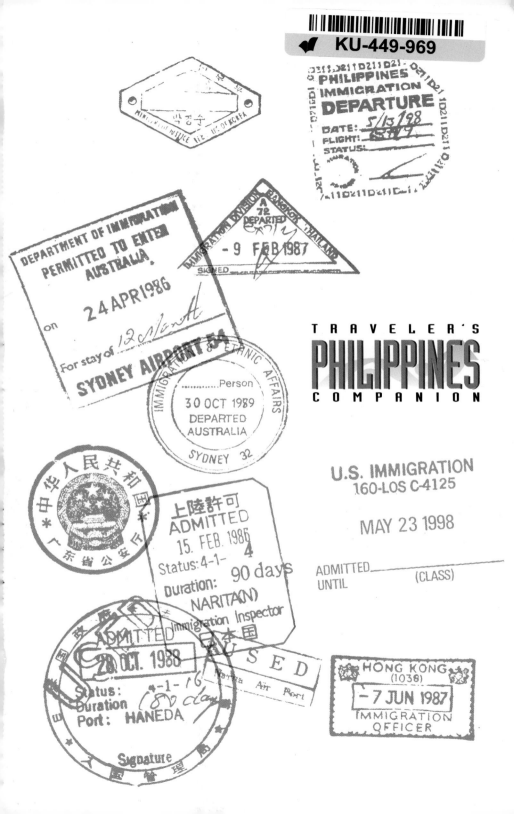

KU-449-969

PHILIPPINES
IMMIGRATION
DEPARTURE
DATE: 5/13/98
FLIGHT:
STATUS:

A 72 DEPARTED
IMMIGRATION DIVISION BANGKOK THAILAND
- 9 FEB 1987
SIGNED

DEPARTMENT OF IMMIGRATION
PERMITTED TO ENTER AUSTRALIA
24 APR 1986
on
For stay of 12 Month
SYDNEY AIRPORT 54

TRAVELER'S
PHILIPPINES
COMPANION

ETHNIC AFFAIRS
......Person
30 OCT 1989
DEPARTED
AUSTRALIA
SYDNEY 32
IMMIGRATION

U.S. IMMIGRATION
160-LOS C-4125

MAY 23 1998

ADMITTED
UNTIL _____ (CLASS)

上陸許可
ADMITTED
15. FEB. 1986
Status: 4-1- 4
Duration: 90 days
NARITA(N)
Immigration Inspector

ADMITTED
21 OCT. 1988
Status: 4-1-16
Duration: 180 days
Port: HANEDA
Signature
Narita Air Port
USED

HONG KONG
(1038)
- 7 JUN 1987
IMMIGRATION
OFFICER

The 1998–1999 Traveler's Companions
ARGENTINA • AUSTRALIA • BALI • CALIFORNIA • CANADA • CHINA • COSTA RICA • CUBA •
EASTERN CANADA • ECUADOR • FLORIDA • HAWAII • HONG KONG • INDIA • INDONESIA • JAPAN •
KENYA • MALAYSIA & SINGAPORE • MEDITERRANEAN FRANCE • MEXICO • NEPAL • NEW ENGLAND •
NEW ZEALAND • PERU • PHILIPPINES • PORTUGAL • RUSSIA • SPAIN • THAILAND • TURKEY •
VENEZUELA • VIETNAM, LAOS AND CAMBODIA • WESTERN CANADA

Traveler's PHILIPPINES Companion
First Published 1998

World Leisure Marketing Limited
9 Downing Road, West Meadows Industrial Estate
Derby, DE21 6HA, England
Web Site: http://www.map-world.co.uk
Published by arrangement with Kümmerly+Frey AG, Switzerland

ISBN: 1 89902 683 5

© 1998 Kümmerly+Frey AG, Switzerland

Created, edited and produced by
Allan Amsel Publishing, 53, rue Beaudouin
27700 Les Andelys, France. E-mail: Allan.Amsel@wanadoo.fr
Editor in Chief: Allan Amsel
Editor: Fiona Nichols
Original design concept: Hon Bing-wah
Picture editor and designer: Laura Purdom and David Henry

Printed by Samwha Printing Co. Ltd., Seoul, Korea

TRAVELER'S
PHILIPPINES
COMPANION

by Kirsten Ellis

Photographed by Nik Wheeler and Robert Holmes

Kümmerly+Frey

Contents

MAPS

The Philippines	8–9
Manila	92
One Hundred Sixty Kilometers around Manila	124–125
Central Luzon and the Mountains	144
Ilocos	152
Mindoro, Marinduque and Southeast Luzon	158–159
Cebu, Negros, Panay and Bohol	173
Leyte and Samar	192
Palawan and the Cuyo Islands	200–201
Mindanao	220–221

TOP SPOTS | **11**

Manila	11
Palawan	12
Boracay	12
The Ati-Atihan Festival	13
Colonial Architecture	13
The Chocolate Hills of Bohol	17
The Banaue Rice Terraces	17
Mindanao	18
Corregidor Island	19
Island Hopping	19

YOUR CHOICE	21
The Great Outdoors	21
Living It Up	36
The Open Road	39
Festive Flings	40
Filipino Cuisine	51
Traditional Crafts	54
Taking a Tour	59
Family Fun	60

WELCOME TO THE PHILIPPINES	63

THE COUNTRY AND ITS PEOPLE	67
Early History	69
Foreign Influences and the Rise of Islam	71
The Spanish Invade	72
The Administration Under the Spanish	76
Rebellion and Revolution	76
The Arrival of the Americans	78
The Postwar Period and Philippine Independence	83
The Marcos Era	84
The Snap Election and People Power	86
The Philippines Today	87

MANILA	91
General Information	94
What to See and Do	94
Intramuros • The Manila Hotel • The Manila Bayfront • Across the Pasig River • Santa Cruz and La Loma • Malacañang Palace • Ermita • Makati • Quezon City • Nayong Pilipino • Smoky Mountain	
Where to Stay	112
Luxury • Moderate • Inexpensive	
Where to Eat	114
Nightlife	116
Shopping	118

LUZON	121
One Hundred Sixty Kilometers Around Manila	124
General Information • Corregidor • Voyage to the Volcano's Rim • Banyan Tree • The Cavite Coast and Resorts • Batangas Province • Laguna Province • Laguna Excursions • Rizal Province • Quezon and Aurora • Mount Banahaw • North of Manila: The Luzon Heartland • Bulacan Province • Pampanga Province • Angeles • Mount Pinatubo • The Bataan Peninsula • The Zambales Coast and Olongapo	

Central Luzon and the Mountains   143
   Pangasinan Province • La Union
   Province • Cordillera Central • Baguio •
   Banaue Rice Terraces • Sagada
Ilocos Region   152
   Vigan • Laoag and Ilocos Norte
Southern Luzon Region   156
   Mindoro • Marinduque • Southeast
   Luzon

CEBU AND THE VISAYAS   **163**
Cebu and Mactan   165
   General Information • What to See
   and Do • Where to Stay • Where to Eat •
   Nightlife • How to Get There
Bohol Island   173
   General Information • What to See
   and Do • Where to Stay and Eat •
   How to Get There
Negros   177
   Bacolod • Excursions from Bacolod •
   Ilocoon Island • Dumaguete • Siquijor
   Island
Panay   182
   Iloilo • Guimaras Island • Isla Nagarao •
   Farther Afield • Kalibo

Boracay   184
   General Information • What to See
   and Do • Where to Stay • Where to Eat •
   Nightlife • How to Get There
Leyte   192
   Tacloban
Samar   194
   Sohoton Caves • Where to Stay •
   How to Get There

PALAWAN   **197**
Puerto Princesa   200
   General Information • Travel Advisory •
   What to See and Do • Where to Stay •
   Where to Eat • How to Get There •
   St. Paul Subterranean National Park
Traveling South   208
Traveling North   209
   Where to Stay
El Nido Region   210
   Where to Stay • El Nido Town
Island Hopping Through the Calamians   212
   Where to Stay • Calauit Island •
   Tubbahtaha Reefs National Marine Park
The Cuyo Islands   214
   Amanpulo

MINDANAO	**217**
Davao City and Provinces	221
General Information • What to See	
and Do • Where to Stay • Where to Eat •	
Shopping • How to Get There	
Northern Mindanao	231
Lanao Provinces • Misamis Oriental	
Province • Camiguin • Dipolog and	
Dapitan	
Zamboanga	236
General Information • What to See	
and Do • Where to Stay and Eat •	
How to Get There	

TRAVELERS' TIPS	**243**
Getting There	245
By Air • By Sea	
Visas	246
Customs and Departure Tax	247
When to Go	247
What to Take	247
Tourist Information	248
Offices of the Philippine Department	
of Tourism	
Currency and Tipping	249

Getting Around	249
By Air • By Boat • By Rail • By Bus •	
In the Cities	
Accommodation	254
Health	255
Business and Banking Hours	256
Time	256
Electricity	256
Communications	256
Mail	256
Media	256
Duty-free Shopping	257
National Holidays	257
Emergencies	257
Hospitals	
Safety	257
Etiquette	258
Language	258
Basic Expressions	
Embassies and Consulates in Manila	259
Recommended Reading	260

QUICK REFERENCE A–Z GUIDE	**262**
To Places and Topics of Interest with	
Listed Accommodation, Restaurants and	
Useful Telephone Numbers	

TRAVELER'S
PHILIPPINES
COMPANION

© Kümmerly + Frey, Bern

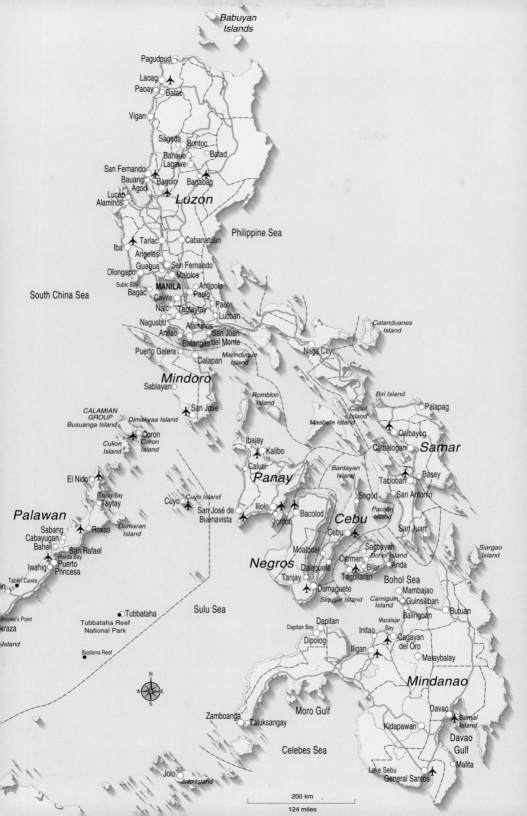

TOP SPOTS

THE PHILIPPINES HAS MANY PLACES AND EXPERIENCES TO OFFER. Do you want to be pampered in exquisite five-star luxury on the remote resort island of Amanpulo? Explore colonial backwaters and Iberian churches in rustic provinces? Or would you rather experience Filipino life, commuting from island to island by ferry or motorized banca and sleeping in native style nipa huts? It's up to you.

Here, then, are some of the country's highlights, a survey of the best — and most compelling — places and experiences to be found in the Philippines.

Manila

GATEWAY TO THE PHILIPPINES, OF COURSE, IS THE CHARMINGLY RAFFISH YET VENERABLE CITY OF MANILA. It would be misleading to suggest that visiting the capital is akin to seeing the real Philippines — it is not. Be that as it may, Manila has many attractions, some which should not be overlooked.

Don't miss a walk through the cobblestone streets and fortress walls of **Intramuros**, the restored sixteenth century citadel built by the Spanish — with its churches, reconstructed Spanish colonial houses and horse-drawn calesas. Across the city, the **Chinese Cemetery** is unique and not found on many tourist maps, perhaps understandably. Nothing except Cairo's "City of the Dead" quite matches this extraordinary suburb, which uncannily mirrors the lifestyle of the living with its fully furnished houses that serve solely as shrines to the dead.

In Manila, dining Filipino style means a meal at **Kamayan**, one of the capital's most authentically Filipino restaurants, where you eat with your fingers. Here, traditionally dressed waiters will assist you in choosing an array of dishes from a menu representing many of the nation's provinces.

Finally, no visit to Manila is complete without spending an hour or two listening to live music at the **Tap Room**, a spot beloved by veteran drinkers and new lovers, located in the grande dame of the capital city's hotels, the **Manila Hotel**, with its carved wood ceiling, chandeliers worthy of a palace and echoes of the larger-than-life Imelda Marcos.

OPPOSITE: A strong Chinese element, such as this bright temple in Cebu, is present in many Philippine cities. ABOVE: Typical wayside shop near St. Paul Subterranean National Park, Palawan.

Palawan

FAR-FLUNG PALAWAN PROVINCE, CLOSE TO BORNEO, IS THE LEAST DEVELOPED ISLAND GROUP IN THE PHILIPPINES. A fragile paradise, it is being hailed as the next great Southeast Asian Eden. Many hope that the Philippines government will take special care to preserve its beautiful seascapes and primeval, jungle-clad, ancient limestone mountains, home to wild monkeys, enormous and rare butterflies and gorgeous blossoms. Palawan has the country's biggest wildlife reservation and the offshore marine sanctuary of **Tubbataha Reefs National Marine Park**, described by diving legend Jacques Cousteau as the most beautiful seascape he had ever seen.

Tourism is still relatively small scale and built in harmony with nature: in the northern **El Nido** region, the Miniloc and Pangulasian resorts — jointly owned by Manila's elite Soriano family and a Japanese corporation — are run along ecotourism principles and are often booked a year in advance by Japanese, European and American vacationers.

Equally dramatic, on the other side of Palawan, close to the capital of Puerto Princesa, the **St. Paul Subterranean River National Park**, with its eight-kilometer (five-mile)-long underground river beneath limestone mountains, is

another natural wonder. Visitors are ferried by a small boat to explore the hushed stillness of the river's marbled caverns, accompanied by a park guide.

Boracay

BELOVED BY OLD ASIA HANDS, THIS LITTLE ISLAND OFF THE COAST OF PANAY, IN THE VISAYAS, IS AT FIRST GLANCE, one of the archipelago's loveliest beach sanctuaries. Boracay's stretch of fine white sugar-like sand has been called the most beautiful beach in the world. Tourists discovered it after it became a backpacker's mecca in the early 1980s. In those days travelers slept on its legendary soft white sands or rented out tiny native huts. There were no hotels, electricity, roads, discos or hot water. Now, it has sprouted a strip of hotels, resorts, restaurants and is one of the most popular tourist destinations in the archipelago.

While it is still worth visiting, especially to appreciate the pristine tip of the island, lapped by clear, turquoise

waters, it seems that Boracay us facing an onslaught of haphazard, greed-driven development by Manila-based real estate moguls. This includes the construction of a hotel and condominium complex, an 18-hole championship golf course, a theme park, a modern airport and port for cruise ships. The bulldozers have already been sent in. Go before what is left of the island's natural beauty is ruined forever.

The Ati-Atihan Festival

THE ATI-ATIHAN FESTIVAL IS HELD ON THE THIRD WEEKEND OF JANUARY ON PANAY, in the Visayas, principally in Kalibo, close to Boracay island. Despite the crowds this exuberant, Carnaval-like celebration should not be missed. The week-long fiesta culminates in a Mardi-Gras street parade, in which participants don outlandish, idiosyncratic costumes portraying ancient tribal warriors and kings. Since this is the country's most popular festival, make your travel

arrangements well in advance — package tours are offered by travel agents and tour operators.

Colonial Architecture

LIKE GHOSTS OF THE DEPARTED SPANIARDS, GRAND BALUSTRADED HOUSES, ELEGANT PLAZAS AND STALWART CHURCHES ARE SCATTERED THROUGHOUT THE ARCHIPELAGO, clustered in the historic city of **Cebu**, as well as the old walled city of **Intramuros** in Manila.

Only one city, however, has remained a virtual shrine to the era when Spanish conquistadors, merchants and friars roamed its cobblestone streets. This is **Vigan**, a small city in the province of Ilocos Sur, in northern Luzon. Although well known to Filipinos, it is still relatively undiscovered by foreign tourists.

OPPOSITE: Outrigged *bancas* are the usual form of sea transport around the islands. ABOVE: Boracay beaches are usually voted the best in the archipelago. OVERLEAF: Celebrating Ati-Atihan, on Sikogon.

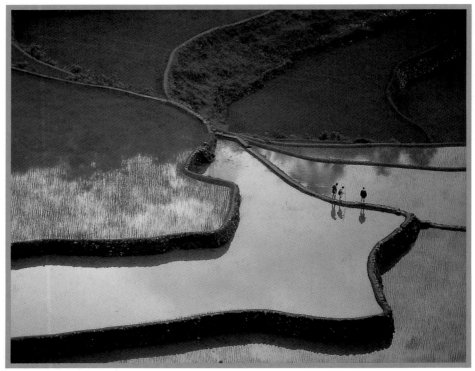

Vigan is crammed with pleasantly dissolute antiquity — its rows of nineteenth-century paint-peeling houses with their labyrinths of tiled courtyards and neat square plazas are strongly reminiscent of faraway places — San Miguel de Allende in Mexico, perhaps, or Antigua in Guatemala. Although somewhat out of the way, the detour is worth your while. Vigan is permeated with languid charm and has a few colonial-era hotels to make a stay of several days quite comfortable. There are also a number of interesting museums, since this was the birthplace of several Filipino national heroes.

The Chocolate Hills of Bohol

IMAGINE AN UNDULATING LANDSCAPE STREWN WITH GIANT TUSSOCK-COVERED MARBLES AND YOU WILL GRASP SOMETHING OF THE PECULIAR AND MYSTERIOUS SPECTACLE presented by Bohol's Chocolate Hills.

No one is quite sure how they formed and you may be inspired to speculate yourself — the main attraction of the Chocolate Hills is simply to witness the miracle of their existence — for there are over a thousand of them. You can wander amongst them and stay overnight to observe the hills' ever-changing moods as the light changes —especially dramatic at sunset and sunrise.

Easily reached by ferry, the island of Bohol lies off Cebu Island, in the Visayas.

The Banaue Rice Terraces

THE PHILIPPINE TOURISM DEPARTMENT LIKES TO DESCRIBE THE FAMOUS, PEA-GREEN RICE TERRACES OF BANAUE AS THE EIGHTH WONDER OF THE WORLD. They are nothing short of spectacular: a broad patchwork of variegated colors and glittering pools threaded across an accordion-like landscape. It is even more impressive to consider that these terraces — within the Cordillera Central in the province of Ifugao, Northern Luzon — were carved out of the mountain sides beginning some 2,000 years ago by the ancestors of the formerly-headhunting Ifugao tribe, who live across this region.

Nowhere else in the world is it possible to see rice cultivation on such a grand scale. Banaue's terraces are as monumental as China's Great Wall or Egypt's Pyramids. There is some fear that as more and more young Ifugao are lured away to look for jobs in nearby towns or cities, the terraces — which

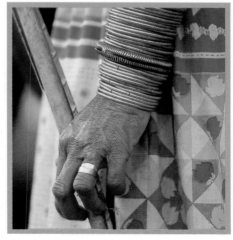

OPPOSITE TOP: From dawn to dusk the mood, and the hue, of the extraordinary Chocolate Hills of Bohol changes. BOTTOM: These Banaue rice terraces were made by hand over 2,000 years ago. ABOVE: The Ifugao tribespeople, Banaue, are known for their brilliant tribal wear. RIGHT: Tribal ornament from Bukidnon, Mindanao.

must be carefully tended — will be left untilled to dry out and crumble away. Another concern is increasing erosion caused by illegal logging of the surrounding forest. Worry that this might lead to irreversible damage has resulted in government efforts to protect the terraces. The rice terraces have been declared a national park reserve.

You can combine a visit to Banaue with stops at several other intriguing destinations, such as nearby **Sagada**, with its hanging coffins. Despite its somewhat morbid attractions, it is a preferable place to stay with its tranquil hill station atmosphere.

Mindanao

MUSLIM SEPARATISTS' ACTIVITIES HAVE CAST A PALL FOR SOME TIME ON THE SUN-DAPPLED RAIN FOREST-CLAD SOUTHERN ISLAND OF MINDANAO. Yet in many ways this region is the most interesting and rewarding to visit in the Philippines. Rich in tribal culture, ethnic wares and handicrafts and exotic festivals — as well as blessed by an abundance of tropical mangoes and pineapples which it exports — the island of Mindanao remains relatively free from from development and incursions from the outside world.

Mindanao is the home of the archipelago's highest peak, **Mount Apo** (set in one of the most spectacular national parks in Asia). The island also harbors the beautiful, endangered Philippine eagle, luscious orchids and startling butterflies. There are large tracts of barely accessible wilderness here — and a smattering of nomadic sea gypsies, contemporary pirates and renegade revolutionaries. If you are looking for the Wild West of the Philippines, then Mindanao will suit you perfectly.

Civilization strikes the island in the form of a few well-situated, rarefied resorts, such as the **Dakak Beach Resort** and the **Pearl Farm Beach Resort.** Otherwise, this is a destination to savor for its unadulterated authenticity.

Next door, the tiny island of **Camiguin** is slowly acquiring a name for itself as the latest Asian "paradise." Though it has beautiful beaches, volcanic hot springs and perfect white sand — accommodation is still rugged and tourists few.

Corregidor Island

EASILY REACHED FROM MANILA, CORREGIDOR ISLAND IS A MUST FOR ANYONE REMOTELY INTERESTED IN WARTIME HEROISM — the island is braced and buffeted by history. This is where General Douglas MacArthur along with American and Filipino troops made a valiant last stand against the encroaching Japanese forces.

As you wander across the island, exploring the extant tunnels and fortifications and examining documentary footage in the island's museum, you gain a strong sense of each stage of the unfolding drama.

It is possible to stay overnight on the island — in a hotel with a dramatic sea view — a tranquil alternative to Manila.

Island Hopping

IF YOU WISH TO ESCAPE THE RESORT VERSION OF TROPICAL PARADISE AND FIND TRUE SECLUSION, THE PHILIPPINES OFFERS MANY OPPORTUNITIES. After all, more than 60 percent of the archipelago's 7,107 islands are deserted — although many are too stark or remote to be considered idyllic. Nevertheless, you may want, for example, to avoid the tourist-filled islands of Cebu and Boracay. A beautiful and relatively accessible group are found between Luzon and the Visayas — a slew of islands that together make up five provinces: **Mindoro Occidental and Oriental**, **Romblon**, **Marinduque** and **Masbate**. Travelers with fairly hardy constitutions and time to linger for several weeks will enjoy magnificent scenery, rugged beaches and village life at its most authentic. All of these islands are served by Philippine Airlines and a regular ferry service links them with Manila.

Corregidor Island — OPPOSITE: Heavy artillery still stands sentinel, a legacy of the days when General MacArthur made a last, and in vain, stand against the Japanese. ABOVE: Beating the heat, a trolley bus ride takes visitors on a guided tour around the island's main sites.

YOUR CHOICE

The Great Outdoors

Many deem adventure essential to a holiday. You may have come to the Philippines especially to explore its spectacular diving destinations or to experience the rigors and rewards of hiking through its high, mountainous forests. Whatever appeals, be assured that, away from the cities or beaches, the Philippines is more likely to suit rugged individualists than those who expect brochure travel — and this is one of its greatest attractions.

Perhaps, however, you are more intent on a siesta style holiday that allows you to discover some of the archipelago's natural wonders, without having to rough it much. If you are looking for a place where there isn't much to do — except SCUBA dive, fish, swim, snorkel and explore nature that is — then here it is.

SCUBA DIVING AND SNORKELING
With its multitude of islands, beautiful beaches and reefs — with innumerable diving and snorkeling locations throughout — the Philippines can be considered among the best water sports destinations the world has to offer. SCUBA diving, game fishing, sailing and windsurfing enthusiasts all have an organized presence in the Philippines.

As a SCUBA diving and snorkeling destination, the Philippines has been steadily growing in popularity, and the SCUBA diving industry is particularly well-established, reflected in a growing number of resorts and on-site dive shops that cater for serious divers.

The warm, crystalline waters that lap the archipelago's coastlines host a vast world of colorful corals, sea grass, algae and fish species — not to mention sunken galleons — while the clarity of the water allows visibility of up to 60 m (200 ft). With currents flowing in from Japan, the South China Sea, the Indian Ocean and the Celebes Sea, it is no wonder that Philippine waters are rich in species of underwater flora and

OPPOSITE: Remote and beautiful, El Nido, attracts water sports enthusiasts. ABOVE: Local kids learn to swim almost as soon as they can walk.

fauna. Like undersea rain forests, coral reefs are one of the nation's most precious — and threatened — natural resources. They span some 40,000 sq km (15,444 sq miles) and team with no fewer than 2,000 identified species of fish and 800 species of soft and hard coral.

The beauty, abundance and variety of the archipelago's coral reefs and underwater topography — with its dramatic submarine cliffs and drop-offs — has to be experienced to be believed. Although you will see more if you go diving, snorkelers are able to observe a great deal, especially at the crest of the reefs near the drop-off. Even experienced divers, taking their first Philippine plunge, are amazed by the beauty of the reefs and the astonishing variety of fish. For some people this leads to an obsession, turning otherwise reasoning individuals into "dive junkies" who spend six months or more of the year pursuing the sport. You have been warned.

It is important to be aware that the coral reefs in the Philippines have become significantly threatened. Overfishing is becoming a problem; meanwhile 50 percent of the archipelago's coral reefs are in poor condition with only 30 percent left undamaged. A range of illegal fishing practices are causing some of the damage: freelance fishermen using dynamite, cyanide and spears, as well as foreign vessels using trawling nets. Collectively, these practices have had a devastating effect on the underwater environment, depopulating fish colonies and obliterating coral reefs, which have taken centuries — sometimes even thousands of years — to build up. It is also staggering to consider that some 80 percent of the world's aquarium fish come from the Philippines.

While it is clear that the Philippines has a tremendously large natural resource in its reefs and seas, it is also evident that it is being damaged at an alarming rate.

The Philippine government and international and local environmental

agencies have been making efforts to stamp out harmful practices and to promote sustainable fishing as well as ecologically sound management of the SCUBA diving industry. Changes for the better — in sustainable fishing and tourism — cannot be introduced too quickly in the Philippines. One hopes the example being set by the El Nido, Miniloc and Pangulasian resorts will catch on elsewhere. These Palawan Island resorts are the nation's most successful models of ecotourism, with their coral reef and marine life conservation programs.

Your priority when making arrangements is to decide whether you wish to base yourself aboard a specialized boat or at a diving resort. Full equipment hire is usually quite affordable. Diving in the Philippines is generally markedly cheaper than in other parts of the world. Sharing the expense of hiring a boat and divemaster with a group of other divers is sensible and dive shops should be able to help you organize a group for the adventure.

Diving resorts — such as Anilao in Batangas province (Southern Luzon) and Moalboal on Mactan Island in Cebu (Visayas) — provide comprehensive diving facilities and may offer packages that include diving trips, accommodation

OPPOSITE: El Nido is known for its extraordinary limestone formations, which prove a haven for snorkelers and divers. ABOVE: Little Lagoon.

and meals. Major resorts have experienced diving instructors and guides, as well as all the necessary equipment. While packages may range from expensive and luxurious to cheap and spartan, the underwater experience will be pretty much the same. Nonetheless, it is wise to be very attentive to the quality and state of repair of equipment. If you are diving on a budget, bringing your own familiar and trustworthy equipment is preferable to renting second-rate equipment on the cheap. While the quality of gear should never be compromised, accommodation and transport can be. On the other end of the scale, if you are intent on diving in style, most of the more exclusive resorts within the Philippines can provide a luxurious backdrop to your diving experience.

The main diving areas in the Philippines are found within the Batangas, Mindoro, Palawan and the Visayas island groups. World-class marine sanctuaries lie within these waters: the **Apo Reef National Marine Park** off Mindoro and the **Tubbataha Reefs National Marine Park** located near Palawan are the best known. At these and the archipelago's other marine reserves, an abundance and variety of tropical fish, large pelagics and colorful corals are generally assured, even when you are diving in shallow waters.

Batangas and Mindoro

The Batangas and Mindoro regions are the most accessible from Manila. The destinations can also be combined: It is possible to take a ferry from Batangas on the southern tip of Luzon to **Calapan** on Mindoro. Batangas is the unofficial capital for diving in the Philippines. Because of its close proximity to Manila and beautiful beaches, it is very popular and offers many diving tours. For many people it has been an excellent place to experience diving for the first time in the Philippines. The main diving locations are **Balayan Bay** and **Nasugbu** and the man-made **Cathedral Marine Park Sanctuary**. Other locations which

merit exploration include **Sombrero Island, Layaglang Point, Sepok Point** and **Mapating Rock;** these spots are more suitable for experienced divers and are good for observing sharks (called locally *pating*) and numerous large pelagic fish. **Culebra Island**, also called Bonito, and **Malahibong Manok Island**, both of which are marine sanctuaries, are excellent diving locations.

Best known of Mindoro's diving locations is the **Apo Reef National Marine Park** — an atoll-like reef which lies 32 km (20 miles) off Mindoro. Split into two large lagoons, the area is flush with coral species, large colorful fish, sharks, manta rays, crevice dwelling morays and tropical aquarium fish. **Puerto Galera** is the diving epicenter of Mindoro, with its bevy of bays, islands and lagoons all located within a 10-km (six-mile) radius of the town. Hundreds of years ago Spanish galleons sheltered here — today the bays harbor many diving operators and beach resorts, eager to cater to tourist demands.

Visayas: Cebu and Bohol

Within the Visayas island group, Cebu and Bohol offer many good diving sites.

Cebu is famous for its white, sandy beaches and the many resorts which complement them. Off Cebu, **Mactan Island** and **Moalboal**, Cebu's diving capital, are recommended destinations, each with clusters of resorts offering diving programs. This is a good site for both beginners and advanced divers, who can descend 50 m (164 ft) down a perpendicular drop-off into the ocean depths. Close by, the **Olongo island group** has beautiful coral gardens and game fish, although the strong currents here make it more suitable for advanced divers. Other dive sites around Cebu include **Pescador Island, Badian Island** (ideal for drift diving) and **Bantayan Island**, fringed with coves and lagoons.

Bohol Island is a good destination for all types of divers, with diving centers around nearby **Cabilao Island, Panglao Island** and **Balicasag Island**.

Palawan

Experienced divers will enjoy the challenges offered by the remote, largely undeveloped islands of Palawan, which have earned superlatives from diving guru Jacques Cousteau. In the El Nido region, the **Miniloc** and **Pangulasian** island resorts provide ideal accommodation in this isolated region and offer basic diving instruction as well as advanced tours into deeper waters where the truly incredible lies unseen and unspoiled. The Palawan islands are a sanctuary for many rare and endangered species, such as giant sea turtles, manta rays and *dugongs*, or sea cows. White-tipped and grey reef sharks can be seen on most dives. Both the **Tubbataha Reefs National Marine Park** and the **Basterra Reef** in this region are acknowledged as premier diving destinations.

Specialized Diving Boats

Another possibility is to hire a dive boat. The **MV *Nautika***, based in Manila, is a well-equipped, extremely comfortable dive boat which visits otherwise difficult

to reach dive spots in the Sulu Sea, including Tubbataha Reefs east of central Palawan, the Visayas and wreck sites around Coron and Busuanga islands in the Calamian group. Depending on the time of year and the requirements of the charter, the *Nautika* caters for up to 18 people. It has eight air-conditioned cabins with private baths, excellent diving equipment and a ratio of one instructor and dive master to every six people. Prices vary seasonally, ranging from US$155 to US$190 per person per night. For *Nautika* reservations, contact **Eagle Trek Adventures (** (2) 521-9168 FAX (2) 521-7358.

The best time of year for diving is during the dry season, February to June, when the weather is calm and plankton bloom, which makes the water cloudy, is minimal. Visibility differs from place to place, however, and in some areas the water can be clear during the typhoon season. Local divers divide the season into

Underwater, the Philippines are also a photographer's dream. ABOVE: Divers adjust flash units of a camera before taking the plunge in Moalboal, Cebu.

two parts — the southwest monsoon, *habagat*, from June to October and the northeast monsoon, *amihan*, from November to March.

Shipwreck Diving

Searching for treasure and shipwreck diving have become an exciting new addition to the adventure holidays being offered in the Philippines. Ancient Chinese junks, Spanish galleons and American and Japanese World War II vessels can all be found, coral-encrusted on the ocean floor. Many treasure hunters operate in the Philippines, where the promise of lifting gold from an ancient galleon is probably more likely than anywhere else in the world. For 250 years Spanish galleons laden with gold, ivory, coins, pearls and precious stones traveled between Manila and Acapulco in Mexico, and many did not survive the journey.

Of the many wrecks which have been located, quite a number are used for diving. The two main areas of interest are Coron Bay, off Palawan, and Subic Bay, Luzon. In Coron Bay, a 24-strong convoy of Japanese warships and freighters were sunk by an American bombing attack during World War II. In Subic Bay, which was originally a Spanish naval base, some 19 ships — including a wooden gunboat scuttled in 1898 — have been located and are divable. A number of live-aboard vessels and charter dive boats make trips to Coron, while in Subic Bay, the only dive operation exploring wrecks is **Subic Bay Aqua Sports** ((2) 384-3005 FAX (2) 384-2343.

Treasure hunters in the Philippines are treated quite generously. If you find something of importance, you are obligated to notify the National Museum in Manila, but you are usually allowed to keep a share of your findings.

The Australian based group **MV Discovery Charters** (/FAX (61-47) 586220 offers punters a chance to take part on a treasure hunting mission led by Brian Homan, one of the most famous treasure hunters in the Philippines. You'll be given the chance to use proton magnometers (metal detectors), to dive

and photograph wrecks and, perhaps, to discover treasure. The company which conducts the explorations, Archipelago Search and Recovery, has in the past undertaken projects in cooperation with the National Museum of the Philippines and has successfully located and excavated wrecks, including Chinese junks and Spanish galleons. The company is trying to locate two 1542 European vessels which were lost in the waters around Mindanao on one of the first European voyages to the Philippines. Only four passengers can be accepted on each 10-day charter trip. The voyage takes the form of a working cruise, with living conditions onboard the 15-meter (50-ft) Filipino parau survey boat basic, although the ship's cots are reportedly comfortable, and the diving equipment is first-class.

Safety

Obviously, diving requires careful attention to safety. First, it is important to ensure that you are in the company of a skilled and trustworthy guide. Professional dive boat and shore based operators should ensure that you see the best spots and should be capable of guiding you through potentially dangerous currents and riptides; they should also have an established emergency procedure.

Don't dive without certification. Dive operators are legally required to check the qualifications of anyone renting equipment or hiring guides. SCUBA instruction courses — through both the Professional Association of Dive Instructors (PADI) and the National Association of Underwater Instructors (NAUI) — are offered throughout the archipelago. Costs for these courses vary from US$200 to US$400.

It is not wise to attempt drift dives on your own. This method, which exploits underwater currents and allows you to move effortlessly through canyons, ravines and along walls, is regarded, along with wreck diving, as one of the most dangerous underwater situations, with a high potential for fatalities.

Whatever region you find yourself in, local fisherman are usually experts about wrecks, water clarity, beautiful reefs, dangerous currents and any other possible dangers to be aware of. These men, who spend their lives at sea, easily recognize signs of a threatening storm. Local knowledge of an area and its currents is essential, particularly when swimming in tidal waters in which currents can quickly become powerful and dangerous. Shark attacks are rare, however.

If you are snorkeling, strong currents will be your main concern. Avoid touching coral without gloves, as any cuts or scrapes can easily become infected. Also, make sure your feet are protected against stonefish, sea urchins and stingrays — if you aren't wearing flippers, sneakers are better than nothing. Walking on coral will contribute to the reef's destruction and should be avoided. It is a good idea to go snorkeling with a hired banca, since many of the coral reefs are too far from the shore to make them easily accessible by swimming.

General Information

The Department of Tourism has useful brochures, booklets and a diving map of the Philippines. You can also contact the **Philippine Commission on Sports Scuba Diving (PCSSD)** ((2) 503735, Department of Tourism Building, T.M. Kalaw Street, Rizal Park, Manila, the organization responsible for developing and regulating all diving related activities in the Philippines. A good source of detailed information is the excellent *Diver's Guide to the Philippines* by David Smith, Michael Westlake and Portfirio Castaneda (Unicorn Books Ltd., Hong Kong, 1982) It's available in Manila bookstores, although it is probably due for an update. *Action Asia* magazine is also useful, with current information on resorts, dive shops and charter operators. The free *Philippine Diver* magazine is another good reference with a listing of registered dive establishments and recommendations.

LEISURE CRUISES

The chant of "Heave, heave, ho!" strengthens the arms of those hoisting the sails on board the *Mariposa*, a restored Vietnamese sailing junk, which cruises from Boracay through the islands of the Visayas. The *Mariposa* junk tour is your opportunity to sail through tropical waters and leave your footprints on the Semirara group of islands, some 30 km (19 miles) west of Boracay and 25 km (16 miles) south of the large island of Mindoro. The creaking rigging and furling red sails are reminiscent of another era, and daily stops on lonely islands allow you time to beachcomb, snorkel, explore caves and even mountain bike. Scuba **diving** and equipment can also be provided. Dinner is taken onshore, where friendly locals might be persuaded to share stories, drinks and a meal around the bonfire. For reservations, contact Andy Haberl at **Aquarius Diving** (/FAX (36) 288-2132, in Boracay. Standard cruises include day trips for up to 20 people, or seven-day expeditions for up to six people.

GAME FISHING

With so many islands and so much coastline, the tropical Philippine waters provide th perfect breeding ground for game fish. Of the 2,400 species of fish in the Philippines, many are ideal for game fishing. Anglers can expect to encounter fish such as giant yellowfin tuna, king mackerel, great barracuda, marlin, Pacific sailfish and snapper. The cost of sport fishing in the Philippines is inexpensive by international standards.

Fishing expeditions are usually made with outrigger bancas of up to five meters (16 ft) long, powered by outboard motors, although increasingly a larger vessel known as the superbanca, which offers greater speed and maneuverability, is being used as well as specialized sport fishing boats outfitted with diesel engines, depth finders, outriggers and fighting chairs.

OVERLEAF: Pangulasian, El Nido. Palawan is a rich, natural treasure trove and El Nido, its crown jewel.

Well-known starting points for sport fishing include **Naic** in Cavite, **San José** in Mindoro, **Puerto Princesa** in Palawan and **Bagac** in Bataan.

Given the large number of both leisure and professional fishermen around the Philippines, it should be easy to find a friendly fishing partner with a good boat at an agreeable price. Bringing or buying your own fishing rod and tackle is wise; once you are equipped with these, fishing opportunities should be plentiful. You can contact the **Philippine Game Fishing Foundation** ((2) 530-1414 FAX (2) 530-1415, at 1055 Ongpin Street, Santa Cruz, Manila, for advice and information.

WINDSURFING AND SURFING

While not yet internationally renowned for its waves, the Philippines will not disappoint even dedicated surfers. And though there are no local legends concerning the first surf board riding king, as in Hawaii, Philippine beaches should be every bit as appealing as those in Hawaii, particularly since there are fewer enthusiasts to surf them.

There are two world-class surfing locations in the Philippine Archipelago: **Catanduanes Island**, off southeast

Luzon and **Siargao Island**, off the northern tip of Mindanao. Being on the eastern coast of the Philippines, these islands get hit by large surfable swells during the typhoon season. Since surfing is relatively new to the Philippines, not many tourist guide maps feature wave riding locations on them. But generally speaking, the whole of the exposed east coast should potentially offer good surf and clean large swells between July and December.

Siargao Island has come into vogue as a surfing destination only recently and held its first trial Cloud Nine Surfing Competition in 1995, an impromptu event in which competitors braved the massive swells, some breaking their boards in the process. Images of snapped boards, broken leg ropes and coral scrapes might deter some, but serious surfers have not been discouraged. Surf photographer John Callahan took a team of hot American surfers to Siargao Island in 1993 and his fantastic photographs have lured many more. Somewhere on the island there will be a break suited to your style of surfing, whether you are a wave guru or a tea bag. For a non-surfing holiday, as well, the island is idyllic, with dozens of excellent beaches.

A number of beach resorts around Siargao Island cater to surfers. The Australian tour company **Surf Express** ((61-2) 262-3355 FAX (61-2) 262-3210 organizes specialized vacation tours to the Philippines out of Australia.

TREKKING AND MOUNTAINEERING

VIsitors to the many mountainous and wilderness regions of the Philippines will quickly find themselves enamored of the land's untamed beauty. High mountains, active volcanoes, green and lush valleys: with its variety of high terrain, low-lying jungles, swamps and rivers and indigenous flora and fauna — there is much to instill a wondrous sense of discovery.

It is important to be aware that — like the coral reefs — the nation's forests are endangered also. Forest cover across the Philippines is down to 18 percent and reforestation programs are sporadic at best. As the forests disappear, the country's exceptionally rich wildlife is increasingly threatened. Conservation International, an environmental organization in Washington DC, ranks the Philippines first in the world in terms of biodiversity — and also the most imperiled. Many of the tens of thousands of species of flora and fauna found here are found nowhere else — and their habitat is disappearing rapidly.

Nevertheless, the possibilities for ecotourism in the Philippine Archipelago are promising, and there are dozens of trekking and mountaineering clubs and associations — including the National Mountaineering Federation of the Philippines — to help you organize and carry out your trip.

Whether you go as part of a group or with the assistance of a local guide, you can expect to *bolo* (machete) your own path through thick jungles and to sleep in rustic huts. In certain regions, you may come into contact with tribespeople living in remote mountain villages.

There are 18 major mountain peaks in the Philippines, all offering challenging climbs for experienced trekkers — although it is possible to organize less demanding treks around the foothills and mountain slopes. Guides and porters can be hired at most base camps. Plan to allow at least a day for preparation. Standard equipment should include strong and comfortable boots, warm clothing, a large water canteen, sleeping bag, flashlight, adequate food and water, a sturdy tent, insect repellent and water purifying tablets. You must carry all your non-biodegradable refuse down to the base camp for disposal.

In Mindanao, **Mount Apo** — *apo* means "grandfather" — is the nation's highest peak at 2,953 m (9,688 ft). Straddling the provinces of Davao and North Cotabato, Mount Apo is part of the largest national park in the Philippines. The four-day-return climb to the peak is regarded by most as grueling, yet rewarding, passing mud pools, waterfalls, lakes, sulfur springs and thick forest. You

OPPOSITE: Cruising the Visayas on the *Mabuhay Sunshine* is a great way to discover the central Philippines. ABOVE: Gentle Mactan breezes provide benign conditions for new windsurfers.

may even get a glimpse of the rare monkey-eating eagle and will almost certainly see the waling-waling orchid. The forest is the home of the endangered Philippine eagle, which is being bred in captivity at the Philippine Eagle Research and Nature Center on the mountain's slopes. The **Department of Tourism** in **Davao** (/FAX (82) 221-0070, Regional Office Nº 11, Apo View Hotel, Davao City, can help organize your trip and will be up to date on weather conditions and local insurgencies, which are not uncommon. Additional information is available from the Mount Apo Climber Association which can be contacted through the Davao Department of Tourism (see above).

The active **Mayon Volcano**, at 2,432 m (7,979 ft), Albay, Luzon, is a popular climb when it's not erupting. The volcano is much admired for its near perfect cone shape and dramatic views. **Mount Banahaw**, at 2,177 m (7,142 ft), which dominates the landscape in Laguna and Quezon, is a challenging climb; and local legend says Banahaw has mystical powers.

Other mountain peaks include **Mount Pulog** near Baguio City, **Mount Halcon** in Mindoro Oriental, **Canlaon Volcano** in Negros Occidental, **Mount Makiling** in Laguna and **Mount Kitanglad** west of Impasugong in Bukidnon, Mindanao.

Walking the trails through the mountainous regions around **Banaue**, **Sagada** and **Bontoc** in Luzon is an

excellent way to learn about the culture of the local tribespeople, the Ifugao, the architects of Banaue's giant rice terraces. The burial caves and hanging coffins at Sagada provide an added, if somewhat macabre, attraction. Local tribes buried their dead above ground in caves or suspended halfway down a cliff face, believing this allowed the spirits of the dead to roam free.

Less than two hour's drive from Manila, **Tagaytay Ridge** offers a fascinating walk around the rim of a massive lake. By a freak of nature the lake — which is contained within the crater of an ancient dormant volcano — has another smaller active volcano within it. In turn, this smaller volcanic island, known as **Taal**, has its own lake. Contact the **Mountaineering Federation of the Philippines** ((2) 460943 or (2) 810-2422, Room 407, Citiland III Building, Esteban Street, Legazpi Village, Makati, Metro Manila. You will also find the **Philippine National Mountaineering Association**, Tours and Promotions, Philippine Airlines, 1500 Roxas Boulevard, Manila,

helpful for specific questions and assistance. If you are concerned about the safety of climbing in the vicinity of potentially dangerous volcanoes, contact the **Commission on Vulcanology**, Hizon Building, 29 Quezon Avenue, Quezon.

NATURE TOURS AND BIRD WATCHING

Nature tourism and ecotourism may be the wave of the future for the Philippines. A string of wildlife sanctuaries, conservation areas, game and bird refuges and national park reserves — both at sea and on land — have been established in recent years by the Department of Environment and Natural Resources. Conservation programs are trying to save the skimpy population of the Philippine eagle (the national bird), eastern sarus crane, *tamaraw* (a dwarf variety of water buffalo), Philippine crocodile, dugong, marine turtles and a variety of rare deer species.

Conservationists are appalled at how rapidly the nation's natural environment and ethnic culture are being eroded — mostly from widespread unsustainable logging, mining, dynamiting and pillaging of coral reefs, as well as from the impact of a burgeoning urban population and unregulated pollution.

The protection of the country's habitat is frequently at odds with government plans for rural development. Yet there does seem to be a growing awareness of ecological matters, reflected in efforts made by various nongovernmental organizations, such as the Haribon Foundation, World Ecologists, Tambuli and the Central Visayas Regional Project, to promote sustainable practices within rural communities.

If you want to see something of the Philippine wilderness, make visiting one or several national parks or wildlife sanctuaries your priority. To help decide which park is going to be of interest to you, first visit the **National Museum** and the **Ayala Museum** in Manila, not only for

OPPOSITE: Active Mayon Volcano attracts plenty of hikers. ABOVE: Lake Taal, Tagaytay. Both are in Luzon.

their displays but to get information on conservation groups, such as the Haribon Foundation, which may offer trips or programs. Working through one of these organizations can provide a shortcut for arranging trips into the wilderness. In addition, the main office of the **Bureau of Forest Development** (BFD) in the Diliman area of Quezon City, Metro Manila, is where you must apply for the necessary permits for visiting restricted national parks and protected areas. They can be organized fairly easily and quickly and, once secured, are a big bonus when you contact the BFD representative in the provinces. The time and energy spent on obtaining these permits is often repaid in offers to help organize camping equipment, supplies, local transport and guides.

Notably, Palawan is the only populated island in the Philippines that has not had most of its forests stripped or its reefs pillaged. So far, Palawan leads the way in environmental issues and education and two of its most popular resorts strive to be environmentally-friendly. **Caluit Island Wildlife Sanctuary**, in northern Palawan, is the home to both indigenous wildlife and an number of African animals; it's and a fascinating place to visit and probably the only island in Southeast Asia where you can expect to see giraffes, zebras, elands and gazelles grazing in an "open zoo" tropical setting. These animals were given a home here when the Philippines responded to an appeal by the International Union of Conservation of Nature to save endangered species. Equally at home here are some the archipelago's endangered animals, such as the Philippine mouse deer, Calamian deer, Palawan bear cat, tasier, scaly anteater, monitor lizard and the Philippine man-eating crocodile.

Elsewhere in the Philippines, indigenous animals include nocturnal flying lemurs, rare cloud rats (found in the mountains of northern Luzon, Mindoro and Marinduque), clawless otters and leopard cats. Reptiles and lizards abound in remote areas, including iguanas and monitors, king cobra and pythons.

The Philippines will delight bird lovers, yet many of its 950 species are endangered. Among them, the impressive Philippine eagle — the world's second largest, after the American happy eagle — can be seen in captivity in Davao at the **Philippine Eagle Research and Nature Center**. Not very many years ago, there was an estimated population of some 10,000 of these magnificent birds — but the destruction of their habitat through slash and burn agriculture has reduced this number to fewer than 300.

In Laguna, Mount Makiling's forested cover provides shelter to many endemic species, such as the Philippine serpent eagle, the Luzon bleeding heart (so named because of splash of red on its chest) and the shiny drongo, which is easily identified by its long, fish-like tail. The **Olango Island Migratory Bird Sanctuary** in Cebu is the seasonal home to several endangered birds, among them the Asiatic dowager and Chinese egret, while farther south in Mindanao, the **Bago Inigo Farm** in Davao City is also worth visiting.

Many of the national parks and sanctuaries offer the chance to see indigenous bird species — as well as other fauna and flora. Of note are: **Quezon National Recreation Area** (South Luzon), **Tubbataha Reefs National Marine Park** (near Palawan),

Candaba Marsh (Pampanga, Central Luzon) Pagsanjan River delta (on Laguna de Bay, Central Luzon) St. Paul Subterranean National Park (central Palawan Island) and the outlying islands of Palawan, Canlaon Volcano National Park (Negros), Pacijan Island (Cebu), Mount Apo National Park (Davao, Mindanao) and the Batanes Islands, the Philippines' northernmost province where its capital, Basco, on Batan Island, is a mere 120 km (75 miles) south of Taiwan.

GOLF

When President Ramos (an enthusiastic golfer) has guests to dinner, he has been known to give out autographed golf balls as mementos. Increasingly, it seems, Filipinos regard the sport as a symbol of the good life.

The Philippines' major international-standard golf courses are all in Manila, where golfing was introduced by colonizing Americans a century ago. With its 11 courses, Manila qualifies as the golfing capital of Asia, a fact that gives it considerable merit in Japanese eyes. Aspiring Japanese golfers travel to Manila to play their first ever game on an 18-hole course. It isn't only the Japanese who find playing golf in the Philippines appealing and inexpensive. The average greens fee is about US$32, compared with over US$100 in other Asian cities. Caddies are generally paid around US$6.

Manila's most popular course is the aptly named Wack Wack Golf and Country Club, which frequently hosts the Philippine Open. Other courses include the Villamor, a long and flat layout located close to the airport, which has also hosted the Open. There are two military courses, the Bonifacio Golf Club and the Navy Golf Club. The exclusive Manila Golf Club — whose early exclusion of Filipino players led to the creation of the Wack Wack Club — has as an impressive backdrop the Makati skyline.

New courses have sprung up outside Manila including the Alabang Golf and Country Club, Canalubang Golf and Country Club, Valley Golf Club and Capitol Hills Golf Club, all within an hour's drive of Manila. There are now over 50 courses throughout the archipelago.

Robert Trent Jones Sr. designed the Luisita in Tarlac and his son Robert Jr. designed the Calatagan Golf Club in Batangas as well as the aforementioned Canalubang Golf and Country Club. Also on the list of celebrity designed courses, the recently opened Orchard Golf Club in Dasmarinas, Cavite, was created by Gary Player and Arnold Palmer, transforming what had previously been a simple mango orchard. The course has hosted the Johnny Walker Classic in which Greg Norman and Fred Couples participated.

Full service golf resorts have also been sprouting up. The Banyan Tree Nasugbu Evercrest Golf Course, close to Tagaytay in Luzon, is considered the nation's ultimate golf resort. Its 18-hole "masterpiece" golf course was designed by Arnold Palmer. Banyan Tree has an appealing list of other facilities including a swimming pool, a kid's club and a health center.

On the island of Boracay one golf resort, including a 600-room condominium

There is an increasing awareness of, and movement to protect, the country's natural heritage — OPPOSITE: Tarsier monkey, the world's smallest primate, spotted in Bohol. ABOVE: Protected eagles at Mt. Talomo National Park.

complex, is still in the planning stages; the development has sparked an outcry from local and regional environmentalists, who point to it as an example of misuse of a fragile island ecology.

The **Philippines Golf Association** ((2) 817-1913, Second Floor, Rizal Memorial Sports Complex, Vito Cruz, Manila, can answer all your golf vacation questions and provide broad-based information on golfing in the Philippines. The Philippines Department of Tourism has published a useful and comprehensive brochure, *Golfing in the Philippines*, which includes information and contact numbers for the nation's major golf clubs and courses. Philippine Airlines offers special golf vacation packages.

Living It Up

Manila, like most other Southeast Asian capitals, offers palatial comfort at its raft of new five-star hotels. However, Manila's room rates have yet to soar to the excessive heights of Hong Kong, or even those of Singapore and Bangkok.

In Makati — Manila's wealthy financial and shopping district — you can take your pick of opulent hotels, including the **Peninsula Manila** and **Mandarin Oriental Manila**. Ostentatious chic is most in evidence at the **Shangri-La Hotel Manila**, the hotel of the moment, with its three-story atrium entrance, multitude of restaurants, shopping arcades and lounges. The most fascinating hotel in the capital, however, will always be the **Manila Hotel**, which personifies the charms of the city's past.

Away from the bright lights of Manila and the recognized hotel chains that have also begun to proliferate in the beach resort zone of Mactan in Cebu, the Philippines offers scores of resorts designed for siesta style relaxation. In island settings or tucked away in the mountains, many small, locally-owned beach resorts and popular SCUBA dive centers are renowned for having the most competitive room rates in Asia.

One of the main attractions of the Philippines is that much of the archipelago remains a seductive, undeveloped natural paradise — comparable to the Caribbean long before its explosion of tourism and resort development. Hidden island clusters and a culture still largely undisturbed and undiscovered reward the adventurous. The good news is also the bad news, for to reach these wilder shores will mean opting for skeleton ferry services and being prepared to rough it.

But not to worry. There are perhaps half a dozen resorts which rank as the country's most memorable. While they vary considerably — from luxurious to moderately priced — these are places which have created a special atmosphere and combine the natural beauty of their surroundings with stylish and sensitive management.

The most elite of all the resorts is **Amanpulo**, which means "peaceful island," on the tiny private island of Pamalican, one of a cluster of the Cuyo islands in the Sulu Sea. It can be reached only by charter plane. One of the more recent additions to the exclusive Amanresorts chain, among the most luxurious and expensive destinations in

ABOVE: Luxury at the Manila Hotel. OPPOSITE: On Samil Island, Mindanao, the Pearl Farm Resort has a deserved reputation as a luxurious hideaway.

the world, Amanpulo has 40 splendid casitas decorated with exquisite furnishings and gallery quality artifacts, and it has excellent food.

Exotic, faraway Palawan has twin resorts, located in the El Nido region, which offer both pampering and adventure. Both resorts promote themselves as ecotourism destinations: **Miniloc Island Resort**, which is designed to resemble a small fishing village, with hillside rooms and stilt casitas, is popular with serious SCUBA divers; **Pangulasian Island Resort** attracts a variety of water sports enthusiasts as well as mountain climbers. Both are set in stupendously beautiful, pristine and remote locations — Miniloc Island is more sheltered, with a tiny cove and pebbly beach; Pangulasian has a spacious stretch of sandy beach.

The **Pearl Farm Beach Resort**, on Samal Island, off Davao in southern Mindanao, has become one of the more popular, out of the way beach resorts in the Philippines. The resort's beautiful island surroundings can be enjoyed from the comfortable privacy of stilt cottages and longhouse rooms with interiors featuring colorful crafts by Mindanao's tribes. Owned by a Filipina, former Miss Universe 1973, the management's attention to detail makes this among the country's better resorts.

Situated on the dramatic north coast of Mindanao, the **Dakak Beach Resort** is another lush hideaway alongside a forested

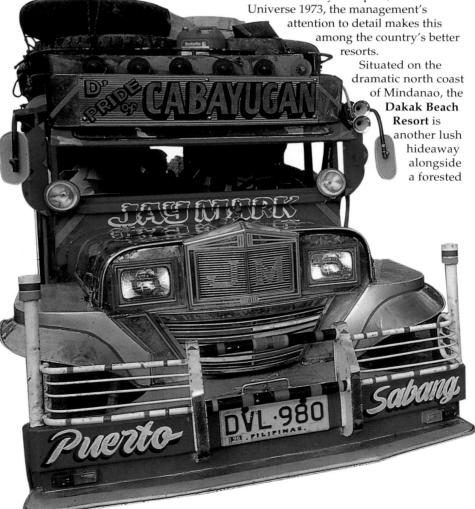

hillside in which 80 air-conditioned, marble-floor cottages rest admid carefully landscaped surroundings. The sheltered 700-m (765-yd) white sand beach is nothing less than spectacular, and plenty of water sports are offered. The resort has become very popular with wealthy Manileños, partly because it is owned by a flamboyant Filipino television producer.

Although the resort island of Boracay, in the Visayas, is already much trampled and developers look set to put an ugly stamp on it, it still has much romantic charm. Without a doubt, the best resort is **Friday's**. Its beach cottages are private and comfortable and set on the sands close to the most pleasant end of the beach.

The Open Road

Beyond the borders of Metro Manila, Luzon offers some spectacular opportunities for excursions by car, with some destinations within a two- to three- hour drive from the capital. Whether you are keen to explore for a day or wish to make a journey lasting several days, there are a number of itineraries from which to choose. These are good options if your trip to the Philippines requires you to stay in Manila and you don't have time to travel to more far-flung parts of the archipelago.

The most convenient day trip destinations from Manila are within the five provinces spreading west, east and south of the capital: Cavite, Laguna, Batangas, Rizal and Quezon. These provinces are known collectively by locals as "Calabarzon".

Calabarzon is rich in tribal culture, lushly endowed with lakes, rivers, mineral springs, waterfalls, caves and subterranean rivers. It is the market garden of the Manila area, with a brisk trade in fish from its seas and lakes, and fresh produce and flowers from its orchards and fields. Stalls and markets reveal a long tradition of artisanal work, especially in silverware, embroidery and carved furniture, much of which is exported. Rizal province in particular is notable for its artists' villages and workshops.

Good day trip options include **Tagaytay Ridge** and **Lake Taal and Volcano**, a scenically dramatic destination, reached after passing through some historic towns in Rizal and Cavite provinces; the hot mineral springs at **Los Baños** and **Hidden Valley Springs Resort**; the working plantation and hacienda museum at **Villa Escudero**, in Laguna province; and the artist villages of **Angono** and **Antipolo** in Rizal province.

If you would like to make an overnight trip or even spend several days away from Manila, look into one of the following: a stay at the **Puerto Azul Beach Resort** on the Cavite coast, a diving excursion at nearby Batangas, an adventurous trip down the rapids by banca to see the **Pagsanjan Falls in** Laguna, the star-shaped, Christmas-mad **Paskuhan Village** in Bulacan province or the eerie landscapes left in the wake of Mount Pinatubo's eruption near **Angeles** in Pampanga province.

Farther afield, the vertigo inducing roads linking the villages of **Baguio**,

OPPOSITE: The highly individualized and brightly-decorated jeepneys are labors of love for their driver-owners. ABOVE: The highest point of central Luzon.

Banaue, Sagada and Bontoc in the Cordillera Central offer some of the most spectacular scenery you are likely to see in the Philippines — although with their hairpin turns and yawning crevices, they can be a hair raising prospect.

Since hiring a car and driver is relatively cheap in the Philippines, there is little to be recommended in trying to negotiate the roads yourself, especially as you may find yourself confronted with water buffalo (*carabao*) and kamikaze jeepney drivers. Manila is the most convenient place to find a reliable car and driver, and costs by the day are negotiable with hotel drivers. However, if you are determined to be self-propelled, automobile rentals are available in Luzon province at Olongapo, Angeles and Baguio. All of these areas are favorable destinations from which to base yourself and make day trips.

Festive Flings

One salient aspect of Filipino culture is the almost daily occurrence of various festivals and holidays: Filipinos love lavish processions and spectacular displays of gaudiness. For reasons ranging from the venerable to the eccentric and for periods of a few hours to nine days to even a month, each festival or holiday is zealously celebrated in commemoration of a specific event (whether religious, political or rite of nature) or in honor of a religious or national icon. The exact times and places of these events are provided below, but whet your appetite and choose your spectacle, by considering the following summary of the most interesting celebrations.

The purely local Fiesta of St. Martha honoring the saint's rescue of a town's ducks from a crocodile and the Bamboo Organ Festival celebrating the 1975 restoration of a nineteenth century bamboo organ are as eccentric as they come. The Ati-Atihan or Dinagyang festival, based on the thirteenth century acquisition of Panay, is about as flamboyant and frenzied as they get. The nationwide, month-long Flores de Mayo (May) and the Philippine Christmas Festivities (December) are long and profoundly religious. For "pigging out", there is the sumptuous parade of roast pigs, the Parada Ng

Lechon, also known as the **Feast of St. John the Baptist**, where the zanily clad participants present their whole roasted pigs (or *lechon*) at the morning's parade only to devour them later in the day. No festival in the Philippines exhibits more colorfully spectacular costumes than the **Moriones Festival**, commemorating the Roman Longinus' conversion to Christianity after the blood of the crucified Jesus, drawn by Longinus' own sword, restored sight to his blind eye. For sheer fun, visit the **Pulilan Carabao Festival**, held for a day to honor the national beast of burden, the *carabao,* or water buffalo. The beasts are bathed, shaved, oiled, decorated and paraded through town in droves, then entered in a race where at the finish line they are all made to kneel and are blessed by the parish priest.

There are many more occasions for involvement, if not immersion, in these celebrated aspects of Filipino culture and every itinerary should include a visit to one or more of them. From January through December, they are:

JANUARY

January 9: **Feast of the Black Nazarene** (Quiapo, Metro Manila). A life-size Black Christ, made of black wood, is carried through town by barefoot men yelling, "Viva Señor," while a huge crowd tries to touch him in the hope of having their sins forgiven.

Week 3: **Ati-Atihan** (Kalibo, Panay). The first of three such festivals this month on Panay sees Kalibo run joyfully amok for three days and nights in celebration of the time when a certain people of the Negrito tribe, the Atis, bartered a portion of Panay to a group of 10 families fleeing from Borneo. The descendants of these Bornean families have been grateful ever since, holding a festival to commemorate Panay's barter which occurred in the early to mid-thirteenth century (historical accounts differ). The festival glorifies peace and camaraderie among peoples. The term

"Atihan" means to "make like the Atis," thus the revelers blacken their faces to look as the local Ati did 700 years ago. They march and brandish their spears, chanting, "*Hala bira!*" (Come on and join!). Not only the participants, but also the thousands of spectators dance and sing, round the clock, until the final night, when a procession of the participants closes the festival. Although the festival celebrates hospitality and good will, it is ironic that in the sixteenth century, the Spanish used the props of the festival — the black skin dye and the warlike clothing — to repel hostile Muslims who sought to convert the recently Christianized Kalibo to Islam. The Spanish were successful against the Muslims and attributed their victory to Jesus Christ. This has lent the festival a layer of religious significance in addition to its original purely historical import. It is the oldest and most spectacular festival in the Philippines.

OPPOSITE: The Black Nazarene Procession in January, Quiapo, Manila. ABOVE: In a devoutly Catholic country, the majority of fiestas are religious. Here an Easter parade in Manila.

Week 3: **Sinulog**, or **Santo Niño de Cebu** (Cebu City, Cebu). Commemorated on this occasion is the Christianization of Cebu and, specifically, Cebu City's patron saint, Santo Niño. Costumed, soot-covered crowds dance and march through town to the beating of drums. The dance rhythm derives from the *sulog* (river current).

Week 4: **Ati-Atihan** (Ibajay, Panay). Occurring the weekend, after the same festival in Kalibo, this fête is no less raucous but much less touristed and commercial. Ibajayans declare it is the original and authentic celebration of Panay's barter by the Atis.

Week 4: **Dinagyang** (Iloilo City, Panay). Yet another celebration of Panay's barter, this one is not anarchic and frenzied like the other two because its dances, also featuring masked, soot-covered revelers intended to look like the Atis, are choreographed and spectators observe from the sidelines.

FEBRUARY
Bamboo Organ Festival (Las Piñas Church, Metro Manila). This is known as a "movable" festival, meaning times and dates change from year to year. (Check with the Department of Tourism on Kalaw Street in Metro Manila for the exact date and time of this and other movable events.) Featured are recitals by American and European organists and the Las Piñas Boys Choir.

February 2: **Feast of Our Lady of Candelaria** (Iloilo City, Panay). The biggest religious event in the western Visayas island group, this festival honors the patron saint of Jaro, a district of Iloilo City and is marked by parades and the of blessing candles, which people take to their houses for protection against danger.

February 11: **Feast of Our Lady of Lourdes** (Canlaon Street, Quezon, Palawan; also held in San Juan del Monte, Bulacan province, Luzon). Unrelated to specifically with the Philippines (but reason enough to party), this feast celebrates the appearance of the Lady of Lourdes, in Lourdes, France.

February 22 to 25: **People Power Days** (Epifanio de los Santos, Quezon, Palawan). To commemorate the return of democracy borne by the People Power revolution, celebrants give thanks for the demise of the Marcos regime. February 25 is an official national holiday to recognize this political milestone.

MARCH
March 10 to 16: **Araw Ng Dabaw** (Davao City, Davao del Sur, Mindanao). This is a citywide fair to celebrate the founding of Davao, featuring games, various sporting tournaments and contests, including the Mutya ng Dabaw (Muse of Davao), in which natives strive to win the title of queen of the event.

MARCH/APRIL: EASTER CELEBRATIONS
Lenten Week: **Moriones Festival** (Marinduque). The island of Marinduque metamorphoses into a colossal Roman theater during this, the most colorful Lenten festival in the Philippines. Every island citizen is a cast member in this week-long drama, wearing tunics, painted masks and helmets of flowers and dramatizing the conversion of the Roman soldier Longinus. In the play, Longinus pierces the side of the crucified Jesus with his sword, regains his sight when Jesus' blood splashes on his eye, sees Jesus ascend to heaven and, as the result of telling his fellow Romans what he saw, is forced to flee for his life. The play culminates in the Romans' capture and execution of Longinus on Easter Sunday.

Maundy Thursday and Good Friday (national and official holidays). Work stops on the Thursday before Good Friday while people attend church throughout the country. The most intensively celebrated day of this holy week is Good Friday, where in almost every Philippine town religious plays and processions fill the day with both

OPPOSITE: Soot and revelry at the annual Ati-Atihan festival in Kalibo, one of the country's most popular.

solemnity and pageantry. A popular tourist attraction are the mock crucifixions. Widespread actual nailings on the cross occur, taking place in San Fernando (Pampanga province, Luzon), Antipolo (Rizal province, Luzon), Jordan (on Guimaras Island, Western Visayas) and in Manila. Throughout the country, hundreds of flagellants beat their backs to a bloody pulp with bamboo whips in processions that can become increasingly frenzied and gory. In some cases, barefoot men wearing thorn crowns stop and ask helpers to cut their skin with shards of broken glass to make the penitential rite still bloodier. Re-enactments of rituals relating to the life of Jesus also take place in numerous other locales throughout the Philippines. Contact the Department of Tourism in Manila for specific places and times of performances.

Easter Sunday: Throughout the country at dawn, church bells chime while mothers and sons march in separate processions to honor Jesus' meeting with his mother after his resurrection. Otherwise, this holiday is celebrated in traditional Catholic fashion.

APRIL

April 9: **Bataan Day** (national official holiday; Bataan province, Luzon). At Mount Samat Shrine, the 1942 World War II battle against the Japanese is remembered, in part by boy scouts re-enacting what is known as the "Death March" on Bataan Peninsula. In World War II the Japanese invaded the 15-sq-km (six-square-mile) fortress island of Corregidor, which lay at the entrance of Manila Bay, capturing the American and Filipino soldiers stationed there. They then forced them to march 184 km (114 miles) through Bataan to Capas, Tarlac, where they remained imprisoned throughout the war. Nearly 10,000 men died on the march; many more died as prisoners. The port town on the Bataan Peninsula is Mariveles. Leading north from Mariveles is the road to Mount Samat, on which stands a tall cross containing an elevator which will take you to an observation deck with spectacular views of Manila.

April 27: **Bahug-Bahugan sa Mactan** (Mactan, Mactan Island, Cebu). In a two-hour performance, Magellan's historic landing and battle here are re-enacted.

Note that the festivities commence as early as 8 AM in some years.

MAY

Month-long: **Flores de Mayo** (observed nationwide, but most elaborate in Ermita, Manila). May means flowers in the Philippines, so every day this month little girls dressed in white present flowers at the altar to the Virgin Mary. In every town, on the last day of May, a procession of *sagalas* (the most beautiful girls of the town) marks the end of the festival.

May 1: **Binirayan–Handuyan** (date varies between April 28 and May 1; place varies as well). Celebrated and re-enacted here since 1974 is the welcome accorded refugees from Borneo in the thirteenth century when they landed in Panay. In contrast to Ati-Atihan, the thirteenth century host was not the Atis but rather the chief of the Negrito tribe, Marikado. The best feature of this event is the spectacular boat landing that starts in the early morning.

Turumba Festival (movable, occuring in April, May or June; Pakil, Laguna province, Luzon). A celebration in honor of Our Lady of Sorrows, this festival commemorates the 1778 finding of the virgin's image in Laguna Lake. Colorfully dressed Pakil townsfolk, adorned with flowers and garlands, join a procession from the river to the church, holding up her image (which they believe has miraculous healing powers) and chanting "*Turumba! Turumba!*" The term *turumba* means dancing, leaping and skipping, which the revelers do in the hope of attaining lifelong health.

May 14 or 15: **Pulilan Carabao Festival** (Pulilan, Bulacan province, Luzon). The patron saint of Filipino farmers, San Isidro de Labrador, lived not in the Philippines but in Spain in the eleventh and twelfth centuries. This festival honors the saint with a presentation of the farmers' best friend, the *carabao,* or water buffalo, to the parish priest. The splendor which accompanies this presentation is perhaps unsurpassed

anywhere in the Philippines: brass bands, contests, games, displays of harvest produce and comedic stage shows, herds of carabao dressed to the nines in flowers and ribbons — culminating in the carabao race which finishes with the carabao all kneeling before the priest to be blessed.

May 15: **Pahiyas** (Lucban and Sariaya, Quezon province, Luzon). This festival also honors San Isidro de Labrador. *Pahiyas* means "precious offering," which here involves every house in entire towns lavishly decorated with all manner of agricultural products and chandelier-like floral designs made from rainbow-colored rice wafers known as *kiping*. Parades and processions for the saint are held in mid-afternoon, with homeowners throwing the fruit and other produce decorating their homes to the passing crowd.

May 17 to 19: **Obando Fertility Rites** (Obando, Bulacan province, Luzon). This is a three-day celebration in honor of the town's three patron saints — Santa Clara,

OPPOSITE: Harking back to days of Spanish rule, these elegant dresses are paraded in Zamboanga. ABOVE: A fire eater on Mindanao island.

patron saint of the childless; San Pascual Baylon, model of religious virtue; and Our Lady of Salambao, to whom fisherman pray for a bountiful harvest. For Santa Clara, the childless dance, praying for children and the unmarried dance in the hope of finding a mate (women and men dance on separate days). Parents dance in thanksgiving for finding a mate and for the blessing of children. Fishermen and farmers dance to pray for a good harvest. All of the Obando dances and processions are based on pre-Christian, ancient fertility rites.

Week 3: **Apung Iru River Festival** (Apalit, Pampanga province, Luzon). The image of St. Peter, called *Apung Iru* by the locals, is carried through town to the river, where a lavishly decorated pagoda mounted on a barge awaits. The image is placed on the pagoda and devotees dance and pray before it. The day ends with masses and prayers as the image of St. Peter is carried back to Apalit's church.

May 24: **Parada Ng Lechon** (Balayan, Batangas province, Luzon). Early in the morning, people assemble at the patio of the town church dressed in zany clothing (whatever amuses them) and present their golden-red roast pigs. Water is thrown over the pigs and people, and the parade begins, all culminating in a feast of the lechon.

JUNE
June 12: **Independence Day**. This national holiday commemorates the beginning of the First Philippine Republic (1895) and is celebrated throughout the nation with parades, firework displays, concerts and pealing church bells. A giant military parade is staged through Rizal Park, in Manila.

June 19: **Birthday of José Rizal**. The national hero's birthday is celebrated as a holiday, with a ceremony and flowers at his memorial site in Rizal Park, Manila and at his birthplace in Calamba (Laguna).

June 24: **Manila Day**. The anniversary of Manila's proclamation as capital (1571) is celebrated with a parade, film festival and concerts in Manila, as well as a proliferation of "I love Manila" T-shirts.

June 24: **Feast of St. John the Baptist**. All towns and suburbs named San Juan celebrate this festival, which involves playful "baptism" with ilang-ilang

scented water and is meant to be a coy flirtation between the sexes. It can degenerate into a free-for-all water fight with much drenching and laughter. Places to see and be drenched in include San Juan in Metro Manila; Balayan in Batangas, which stages a lechon parade; Punta Taytay, near Bacolod City, in Negros Occidental and Camiguin, Northern Mindanao.

JULY
July 5: **Pagoda Sa Wawa Festival** (Bocaue, Bulacan province, Luzon). A replica of the cross on which Jesus was crucified is paraded on a pagoda adorned with magnificent trimmings and guided by colorful bancas. Hundreds attend the procession for a nine-day novena, during which they feast and celebrate the legendary rescue of the Holy Cross from the Bocaue River.

Week 4: **Sandugo** (Tagbilaran, Bohol). This is a four-day festival honoring the treaty made between Sikatuna, a local Boholano chieftain and the Spanish conquistador, Miguel Lopez de Legazpi. There is a dramatic re-enactment of the treaty followed by dancing and festive carousing in the city streets. Sandugo

derives its name from the "blood compact" between these two warriors.

July 24 to 25: **Kinbayo Festival** (Dapitan City, Zamboanga del Norte, Mindanao). This festival features a flamboyant re-enactment of the Battle of Covadonga fought between the Spaniards and the Moors in which Spain won, supposedly through the intercession of St. James.

July 29: **Fiesta of St. Martha**, also known as the Pateros River Fiesta (Pateros, Rizal province, Luzon). This suburb of Manila is renowned for duck breeding and supplies Manila with this Filipino delicacy. On this day, townsfolk celebrate in memory of the occasion when the apparition of St. Martha saved the town's ducks from a crocodile.

AUGUST
Week 4: **Kagayhaan Festival** (Cagayan de Oro City, Misamis Oriental province, Mindanao). Legend has it that two hostile ancestral tribes were unified and

OPPOSITE: A young reveler flags after three exhausting days of Ati-Atihan celebrations.
ABOVE: Young Muslim girls, from Mindanao, participating in the National Day Parade.

then rent asunder by the marriage of Bilawin, daughter of a muslim chief, to Bagani, a Manobo warrior. The community suffered shame (*kagayhaan*) as the result of this reversal of their optimism about peaceful tribal coexistence. A reason to party lurks somewhere in this event: that reason is continued solidarity in the midst of tribal cultural diversity, which is celebrated for a week by Mardi Gras-type street dances and lyrical melodies performed by members of Cagayan de Oro's schools and organizations.

Weeks 3 and 4 (movable): **Davao Orchids and Fruits Festival**, also called the Kadayawan sa Dabaw (Davao City, Mindanao). For two weeks, residents celebrate the bountiful harvests of fruits and orchids produced by the rich and fertile Philippine soil. On display is virtually every flower, fruit and vegetable borne by the Davao earth. Specialists and enthusiasts converge at a trade fair to judge the fruit and flower competition and purchase, at bargain prices, the most exotic orchids imaginable. No Filipino festival would be complete without street dancing, parades and something a little eccentric — in this case, a horse fight.

SEPTEMBER
Week 1: **Kaamulan Festival** (Malaybalay, Bukidnon province, Mindanao). Here is another Mindanao bash in celebration of camaraderie despite tribal cultural differences. Many tribes come jubilantly together and blazon forth with fiery dancing and merrymaking.

September 10: **Sunduan** (Parañaque, Metro Manila). Sunduan means "act of courting a maiden." Here, in a festive procession, men escort women in a dance around the town square and revel in the age-old art of coquetry and flirtation.

Week 3: **Penafrancia Festival**, also known as Feast of Nuestra Señora de Penafrancia (Naga City, Camarines Sur, Luzon): This festival lasts nine days (a novena) and is based upon the belief that the Virgin Mary once healed the dying daughter of a Spanish official. Featured is a boat parade whose centerpiece, set on a pagoda, is the Blessed Virgin of Penafrancia. Hundreds of devotees occupy boats and line the riverbank to partake in prayer and song.

Week 3: **Lem-Lunay T'Boli Festival** (Lake Sebu, South Cotabato province,

Mindanao). Six South Cotabato tribes partake in a commemorative mass, horse fighting, games and dances, all in an endeavor to remember their promise to work toward the Christian paradise, Eden. Catholic rituals and ancient tribal practices combine to create a special and inspirational day.

OCTOBER

Week 2: Zamboanga Hermosa Festival (Zamboanga City, Zamboanga del Sur province, Mindanao). The reason for celebrating here, over a nine-day period, is the Virgin Mary, toward whom the peoples of this province hold a special devotion as the unifying cultural and historical symbol of the land. There are fireworks, parades, a regatta, variety shows, plenty of games, a carnival and something a little different — the Miss Zamboanga Pageant.

Second Sunday: **La Naval de Manila** (Quezon, Palawan; also in Angeles, Pampanga province, Luzon). This festival has been attributed variously to the 1646 victory at sea in a battle against a Dutch fleet and to the 1533 gift of the carved image of the Blessed Virgin of La Naval to the Dominican Fathers. It revolves around a procession from the Santo Domingo parish through Quezon's main streets in which the images of Dominican saints and that of the Virgin are borne on an elaborately decorated and lit carriage in the form of a ship.

October 6 to 19 (movable). **Masskara Festival** (Bacolod City, Negros Occidental province, Negros). No event of religious or cultural history, no saint or divine spirit serves to justify this big blowout. What we have here is fun for fun's sake. In this city, on these days, it's time to party, masked, costumed and in the streets. Even if you don't feel like dancing and singing, the pig catching and pole climbing competitions are musts. The contest for the best mask is also exciting. Of course it's not as purposeless as it may appear: this festival is meant to lift people's spirit and to benefit their means as tourists flock here

to join the merrymaking and to buy the orchids and ornate handicrafts on sale.

Week 3: **Lanzones Festival** (movable; Mambajao, Camiguin Island, Western Mindanao). The lanzones fruit is a major source of the Camiguin islanders' livelihood and it is for the annual harvest that they celebrate this thanksgiving day. Houses, carriages, street poles and even people are decorated with lanzones and lanzones leaves. Townsfolk dance in joyful abandon in commemoration of the legend

OPPOSITE: Santacruzan Festival, in Lugban Town, appeals to the music-loving Filipinos. ABOVE: Ride a buffalo? The annual Water Buffalo Festival, in Pulilan Town, Bulacan, is the place to do it.

that a beautiful, unknown maiden took from the lanzones its former bitter flavor to leave only its luscious, sweet taste.

Gigantes, also called the Feast of San Clemente (movable; Angono, Rizal province, Luzon): The party here centers around papier mâché giants, colorfully garbed and painted, surrounded by much dancing, singing and feasting. These *gigantes* (giants) lead the procession, mounted on stilts or carried by members of the community. Puppets, trailed by dolls which portray the occupation of their creators, follow as part of the entourage. At the end of the procession are small puppet children and a brightly painted papier mâché bull whose body sparks with fireworks. This festival is a thanksgiving by the fishing people of this community in honor of their patron saint, San Clemente.

NOVEMBER
November 1: **All Saints' Day** (nationwide official holiday). This holiday is observed at night and in cemeteries, where families gather with candles and flowers and do not leave until the break of dawn — an impressive spectacle.

November 10 to 30: **Baguio Arts Festival** (Baguio City, North Luzon). A grand gathering and art exhibit of works by local, national and international artists. Included are works of painting, photography, sculpture, drawing and mixed media. There are also workshops and lectures on local tribal arts.

DECEMBER
December 1 to January 6: **Baguio Christmas Festival** (Baguio City, northern Luzon). Partying continues for over a month in Baguio as various Christmas activities — dances, fireworks, agricultural exhibitions, contests, and craft demonstrations — dominate this mountain resort town.

December 1 to January 9: **Pasko sa Tanjay Christmas Festival** (Tanjay, Negros Oriental province, Negros). Like Baguio, Tanjay also becomes Christmas City for more than a month, with residents, business establishments and civic organizations offering cultural presentations and daily contests.

December 1 to 30: **Paskuhan** (Davao City, Mindanao). Paskuhan is the collective term for the fiestas celebrated throughout the Philippines during December. In Davao, as in many other Philippine cities this month, the birth of Jesus is commemorated with much enthusiasm and merrymaking, including (in Davao) a series of competitions that highlight the Christmas festivities.

December 1 to 31: **Kamundagan Festival** (Naga City, Camarines Sur province, Luzon). This is another month-long Christmas festival featuring trade fairs, parades, beauty contests and other events.

December 24 to 25: **Giant Lantern Festival** (San Fernando, Pampanga province, Luzon). The *parol*, a star-shaped lantern, is the symbol of Philippine Christmas. At this time of year, parols are everywhere in the country. But San Fernando lanterns represent the ultimate in parol art and are indisputably unique in design and grandiosity. Parols are displayed in all shapes, colors and sizes — some huge they must be mounted on flat bed trucks for the festival procession and competition. Once launched, the kaleidoscopic pattern of lights sways to the music of accompanying bands. Note that you should be at the main church by 8 PM to attend the service. At 11 PM the procession begins. After a midnight mass, the most magnificent lantern is selected.

Week 4: **Binirayan** (San José, Antique province, Panay). The year ends with a celebration of the barter of Panay, re-enacted most graphically here. In the thirteenth century, 10 *datu* (chieftain) families fled Borneo and secretly set sail in search of freedom. Their sudden arrival on the island of Panay aroused the suspicions of the native Ati whom the Borneans placated with a golden *salakot* (wide-brimmed hat worn by farmers) and necklace. In exchange, the datus were permitted to settle and live on Panay. This barter is commemorated in Antique province with a mass followed by nonstop dancing until dawn, feasting and carousing. Festivals honoring this inaugural barter of Panay continue through January.

Filipino Cuisine

Filipino food marries elements of Asian and Spanish cuisine and combines regular staples in a way that is uniquely imbued with the archipelagic culture of the Philippines. Pinoys — expatriate Filipinos — tend to be enthusiastically appreciative and nostalgic about their national cuisine, although exactly why this is can be lost on outsiders — there are few Filipino restaurants to be found in large European and American cities, despite the widespread popularity of other Asian cuisines.

In Manila, among the capital's thousands of restaurants serving cuisine from all over the world, you will find fine and authentic Filipino food. Especially noteworthy are **Kamayan** and **Islands Fishermen** restaurants (see MANILA, pages 114 and 115).

You may, while traveling throughout the Philippines — unless you are staying at top-notch resorts — find the food

OPPOSITE: An enthusiastic band at the Quiapo Fiesta, Manila. ABOVE: The myriad tropical fruits, available year round, lend themselves to exotic cocktails.

somewhat monotonous. To sophisticated palates, Filipino meals can be unexciting, dominated as it is by liberal servings of rice, fish and roasted pig. Nevertheless, the many indigenous and foreign influences that make up this cuisine provide interesting opportunities for experimentation, and you may be pleasantly surprised by the diverse array of regional dishes.

In general, emphasis is placed on fresh ingredients and light seasonings, with minimal preparation, rather than a reliance on elaborate sauces, spices or intensive cooking. Rice — served on a plate or a banana leaf — coconuts, vegetables and fish, constitute the main staples. Filipinos tend to prefer serving an array of dipping sauces, or *sawsawan*, so that dishes can be seasoned to individual taste. These vary from vinegar with minced garlic, soya sauce, ketchup, chili sauce and *patis* (mustard). Other accompaniments include *bagoong* (chopped green mangoes mixed with shrimp) and *achara* (pickled papaya). Usually, Filipinos like to serve all the dishes at once, rather than having several courses and, especially in the rural provinces, people eat in the traditional way — with their hands.

Many of the classic Filipino dishes are derived from Spain, with some Mexican influences also, mixed with Asian flair. This means that *lengua con champignon* (marinated ox tongue in cream of mushroom gravy) crosses paths with crispy *pata* (deep-fried pig's knuckles in garlic and soy sauce) and *laing* (taro leaves in spicy fresh coconut milk, flavored with shrimp paste) in what may seem somewhat surreal combinations.

Probably the most popular staple dish is *adobo*, a casserole which combines pork or chicken stewed in a mixture of vinegar, bay leafs, peppercorns and garlic over a slow fire.

The Spanish influence is also evident in such dishes as *paella Valenciana* (rice cooked with meat and seafood) and the popular stews, *cocido* and *puchero*.

Lechon (oven-baked or charcoal-broiled roast pork) is typically served at a special occasion or a fiesta. Depending on the restaurant, you can usually order single portions or even an entire whole roast pig, if your party is large enough.

Many dishes are Chinese in origin but have evolved a distinctly Filipino twist. Noodle dishes and soups can be found everywhere, and street cafés and restaurants devoted to them are called *panciterias*, named after the classic noodle dish, *pancit*. There are many regional varieties, including *pancit malabon*, made with seafood, or *pancit molo*, an adaptation of wonton soup. Dining at panciterias is a good way of experiencing Filipino life — they are always busy, with rickety little tables and chairs on the street — and usually good. Many panciterias and *carinderias* (the Filipino version of a fast food stall) serve an array of Filipino morsels which are fun to sample.

It is always useful to remember that carinderias operate on a *turo-turo* (literally, "point-point") system allowing you point to whatever looks good. *Ihaw-ihaw* (grilled or barbecued meat or seafood), *morisqueta tostada* (Yangzhou fried rice), *camaron rebozado* (shrimp fried in batter) and *siopo* (a steamed bun filled with meat) are all tasty examples of what you will encounter. The Chinese staple of rice congee has found its way into the national diet, renamed *arroz caldo*, rice porridge with slices of meat or tripe topped with spring onions. Another Chinese addition is the popular *hopia*, lightly sweet pastries filled with lotus or mashed bean paste.

Once you are familiar with a few Filipino terms, you will soon find your way around a menu. The name of each dish usually describes how it has been prepared. *Sinigang* is a hot, sour broth and uses either fish, prawns or meat and vegetables. *Prito* means fried, while *gisa*, *gisado* and *ginisa* mean sautéed. *Pakisaw*

OPPOSITE: Appetizing snacks TOP and fresh vegetables BOTTOM on display in a Laoag market, Ilocos Norte (Luzon).

52

YOUR CHOICE

indicates the dish has been stewed in vinegar; *ginataan* is a dish that has been cooked with coconut; and *ihaw-ihaw* means broiled or barbecued.

In a classic Filipino restaurant, you will generally find *adobo karekare* (beef and vegetables stewed in peanut sauce), sinigang, *rellenong bangus* (milkfish, deboned and stuffed with chopped meat and vegetables), crispy pata, fresh or fried *lumpia* (spring rolls), *tinola* (chicken stew) and *bistek* (Filipino beefsteak).

Seafood is abundant and rarely disappoints. *Lapu Lapu* (garoupa), *tanguigue* (a local species) and blue marlin are Filipino staples, while *bangus* (milkfish), lobsters, prawns, shrimps and crabs are plentiful. If you come across *tatus* (coconut crab), try it for its unusual, rich flavor.

Filipinos are great devotees of their afternoon ritual of *merienda*, a break to savor a few snacks, typically sweet and full of calories. Whether served in on a humble roadside stall or in a five-star hotel lobby, they are usually delicious. Merienda usually comprises such sweets as *bibingkas* (sweet coconut cakes), *ginataan* (glutinous, sugary concoctions), and *halo-halo* — a dessert made from crushed ice mixed with diced gelatine, candied sweets and fruit with evaporated milk poured over it.

Fruits are superb, almost always perfectly fresh and, no matter where you go, beautifully presented. Tropical fruits include mango, jackfruit, star apple and dozens of banana varieties, as well as pomelos, custard apples, rambutan and lanzones — a specialty of Camiguin Island in Western Mindanao.

As for drinks, there are many fruit concoctions which are good thirst quenchers, either on their own or mixed with water. Fresh *calamansi* (a small fruit which is a cross between an orange and lemon), mango and pineapple juices are especially good. Delicious and healthy coconut milk is served everywhere by roadside or beachside sellers, who lop off the coconut's top with a flourish. Otherwise, the national drink is San Miguel, the best known and only locally brewed beer. You may encounter various fermented creations on your travels: *tuba*, made with coconut sap, or *buri* from nipa palms, are both distilled into the powerfully inebriating *lambanog*.

Traditional Crafts

Perhaps the secret will soon be out: The Philippines offers extraordinary opportunities for serious shoppers. Fussy antique collectors, furniture hunters and aficionados of ethnic fabrics will find that the archipelago has some of the best buys in Asia. Naturally, you can expect to see a lot of mass-produced junk around but, in general, the quality of handcrafted goods is high. If you have the chance to immerse yourself in the search, it is fascinating to see native artisans in their own environment.

While you are in Manila, it is well worth browsing in some arts and crafts emporia, either to make purchases or to give you a glimpse of what to look for — at a cheaper price, with more variety and perhaps better quality — out in the provinces. The best place to begin is **Silahi's Arts and Artifacts**, Calle Real in

Intramuros. With its abundance of artifacts, crafts, fabrics and antiques as well as contemporary wares, it provides shoppers with an excellent overview of regional artistry. **Narda's Handwoven Arts and Crafts**, 578 Félipe Street, Makati, specializes in tribal fabrics with a contemporary twist.

The Philippines has a still-thriving tradition of indigenous carving, weaving, pottery and metalworking, much of it undertaken by tribes working in the manner of their ancestors.

WOODCARVING

Once in the provinces, check with the regional Department of Tourism offices for suggestions about artists workshops, village markets or factory tours that may help you find extraordinary bargains, whether you are looking for fabrics or furniture. Cebu, for example, teams with manufacturers based in its Mactan export zone and many sell directly. Other towns, such as Angono and Antipolo (Rizal), Baguio and Paete (Laguna), all on Luzon, survive largely from selling wares such as paintings, fabrics and carvings.

Carved wares are offered in many different media, ranging from mass-produced geegaws to luminous art objects imbued with much significance by their makers. In northern Luzon, you can look for statues of the Ifugao rice god, the *buhul*, who is believed to bring a good harvest and create peace within a household or community. With tourism changing some of their priorities, the Ifugao now carve bowls, platters and giant utensils and have begun to incorporate some of their sacred images into these items.

Ancestral figures and images of deities, called *latches*, are much sought after. Latches can be seen throughout the Philippines adorning churches and houses. In Palawan, the Tagbanua tribe uses soft wood to carve quirky images of birds, lizards, turtles and other animals; the images are used in rituals or given to children. In Muslim dominated Mindanao, carved fragments of beams

used in traditional noblemen's houses are being sold as curiosity pieces. They are admired for their aesthetic beauty and their distinctive linear patterns, called *okir*. The Maranao people are especially well-known for their fine workmanship, as are the woodcarvers of Paete, in Laguna, Luzon.

In your travels throughout the Philippines you are sure to see many *santos*. These are carved wooden or ivory images of saints. Santos range in their antiquity but date back to the Spanish period. The earliest and finest examples are much sought after by collectors. Genuine santos often have ivory faces, hands and feet. Some show signs of defacement, apparently because during colonial times, Filipino revolutionaries identified the santos as images of their oppressors. Be aware that clever fakes, especially of antique *likhas*, or tribal carvings, and santos abound.

Lastly, handcrafted antique furniture — made in the style popular with the early Spaniards and then with the

OPPOSITE: Food stalls everywhere will serve up dishes of spit roasted suckling pig or chicken.
ABOVE: Local markets are ideal for sourcing inexpensive but intricate baskets and woven goods.

Filipino elite — is a great find if you do not mind having to go to the trouble of exporting it out of the country. The town of Betis, in Pampanga province, Luzon, is worth visiting, because craftspeople there still make Spanish style furniture in small quantities.

BASKETRY, MATS AND WEAVING

The making of baskets and mats is a highly evolved craft in the Philippines, and there is a wonderful range of form and function using fiber from plants and reeds, including nipa, pandanus and coconut. Distinctive designs tend to indicate the region of origin. There is a basket for almost everything you could imagine (including catching locusts), and many of them have great decorative potential. In Manila, you are bound to see ox-drawn carts, filled with baskets of all shapes and sizes, from which wares are sold directly.

Probably the most inventive and eye-catching baskets come from Mindanao tribespeople: Bagaboo baskets festooned with horse hair, beads and bells; T'boli geometric patterned square baskets; and over-plaited Hanunoo baskets, to name a few. The most sophisticated baskets are made by the Ifugao in northern Luzon. These finely woven, dark-hued creations have an almost sculptural quality and are usually blackened by the smoke-filled interiors of the Ifugao's mountain huts.

Mats from Samar and Leyte, in the Visayas are altogether another story, dyed in primary colors and woven to depict scenes of bright flowers, birds and rustic landscapes; they're irresistibly cheerful. The mats woven from elaborate geometric patterns and bold colors by the Samal and Badjao tribes in the outreaches of the Sulu Archipelago are exceptional enough to stand alone as works of art in themselves.

The Philippines has a lively tradition of weaving and creating intricate fabrics with many regional styles. For several centuries, Filipinos have been adept cultivators and weavers of cotton and *abaca* (Manila hemp) often using ancient Malay style looms. Though less commonly found, some fabrics are woven from *piña* and *jusi*, pineapple and banana fibers, resulting in a semi-translucent cloth. These fabrics are used for, among other things, the national Filipino dress: the long-sleeved shirt, *barong tagalog*, as well as the short-sleeved version, the *polo barong*.

It is worth looking for variations on the barong theme fashioned by Filipino designers, some embellishing the basic model and experimenting with tie-dyed silk and dressed-up versions for women.

Luzon and Mindanao are both producers of exceptionally fine fabrics, usually created by tribeswomen and carrying motifs which have been handed down over many generations. In Luzon's central and northern mountain settlements of Banaue, Bontoc, Sagada and Baguio, you can see workshops devoted to the production of intricate cotton *lepanto* cloth, which incorporates Igorot motifs in its designs. In the southern Philippines, Mindanao's Muslim and minority ethnic tribes are renowned for their richly decorative cloths, as well as for the commonly worn

malong, a sarong-like garment. T'boli tribeswomen have created a unique style of tie-dying, called *t'nalak* and the clothes and coverings made from this are traditionally believed to attract good spirits to guard over pregnant mothers and marriages.

Across the archipelago, there are innumerable varieties of wares made from woven materials. It is possible to find dozens of varieties of leaves, fibers, grasses and vines shaped into mats, hats, purses, shoes and handbags. In addition, Philippine bamboo cane and rattan furniture is considered to be among the highest quality in the world. Large scale production of rattan furniture is centered on Cebu in the Visayas islands.

METALWORK

In Mindanao, Muslim tribes are the creators of the fine bronze and brass wares sold throughout the Philippines, especially the Maranao artisans of Lanao del Sur province. Whether authentic antiques or contemporary renditions, these pieces range from ceremonial urns (often taller than a human) to platters and betel nut containers to shields and scimitars, usually engraved with swirling Islamic okir motifs and patterns and cast through the ancient lost wax method. In other parts of Mindanao, the T'boli tribespeople use the same method to produce small figurines, usually depicted them in scenes of village life. The T'boli also cast buttons, musical instruments and jewelry in brass.

An unusual item to look for are silver *exvotos*, ecclesiastical offerings shaped into eyes, noses, lips, limbs and hearts for people who have been cured of their afflictions by divine intervention. Betel nut containers in silver and brass are also curious objet d'arts; most are rectangular in shape, but some are fashioned into animals, birds or butterflies.

JEWELRY

If you are set on finding unusual pieces of Filipino jewelry, perhaps the most distinctive items to look for are both the antique and contemporary *tamborin*, a gold filigreed necklace, as well as the

OPPOSITE: Cebu guitar-maker (and young helper).
ABOVE: Bohol and Cebu are great for handicrafts.

imposing silver disc necklaces worn by the Mandaya women in Mindanao, which are etched with geometric motifs. These designs are also used in earrings, bracelets and combs.

Pearls cultivated in Philippine waters are another unique feature of the region, and it is hard not to covet these lustrous jewels. Perfect conditions for the cultivation of *pinctada maximus*, the large pearl oyster, are found throughout the Philippines. This species produces the most beautiful varieties of pearls, ranging from 10 to 16 mm in diameter and, on occasion, reaching a staggering 40 mm in the form of the baroque pearl. And the pinctada maximus comes in a dazzling array of colors — ranging from white and gold to silver and gray. There are some

20 large and medium-size pearl farms throughout the archipelago, making the Philippines one of the world's largest pearl producers.

The Philippines has a long tradition of pearl cultivation, dating back to 1420 when Paduka Suli, a Suli *datu* (chieftain) is said to have offered the Chinese imperial court a gift of a pearl weighing nearly 200 grams (seven ounces). Badjao folk legends recount tales of datus who demanded their daughters' suitors prove their devotion by diving for pearls.

The Philippines produced the world's largest pearl, the "Pearl of Allah" — referred to as the "Pearl of Lao-Tze" in the *Guinness Book of Records*. Found in Palawan in 1934, it weighs almost six and a half kilograms (more than 14 lbs). It was given by the datu of Palawan to a group of Americans after their intervention saved his son from dying of malaria. Since then, it has been valued at over US$42 million and displayed at the Smithsonian Institute in Washington, DC.

POTTERY

The ancient routes that brought early Asian settlers to the Philippines, also resulted in a widespread appreciation for trade porcelain from China, Thailand and Indochina. Although excavated pottery points to an early tradition of shaping implements from clay, the closest contemporary examples of ethnic pottery are made today in Vigan, Luzon, where the solid storage pots, *burnays* are still being produced as they were since they were introduced by Fukienese settlers at the turn of the century.

In most of the major cities, and especially in the artisan villages of Antipolo and Angono in Rizal province near Manila, you will find craft shops seeling the wares of contemporary potters and ceramists.

CONTEMPORARY CRAFTS

Many modern handicraft manufacturers are reviving traditional processes, or adapting them to their own designs. For example, Filipina weaver Narda

Capuyan — whose fabrics are used by Issey Miyake among other international designers — has integrated weaving techniques used by mountain tribes, including the Ifugao in the Baguio and Banaue region of Luzon. Located in Makati and Baguio City, her shops showcase an interesting fusion of styles, translated into items as different as textured women's clothes and table linen.

Shell craft is another modern ware unique to the Philippines. This often takes the form of picture frames and small laminated boxes adorned with stones and shells. There are also capiz lampshades and shell-covered handbags, papier mâché toys, handcrafted guitars from Cebu and Filipino Christmas decorations from Pampanga in Luzon.

Taking a Tour

If you want to explore as much as possible within the time available, but are wary of having to organize it all yourself, a tour may provide the solution. The **Jeepney Island Adventure Campaign**

tour packages are recommended for their compact and well-managed approach, and they always stay at reputable hotels. Tours include a six-day trip taking in Baguio, Mount Data, Sagada, Bontoc and Banaue; a five-day trip combining a trek to Mount Mayon and a beach holiday in and the Catanduanes. Other excursions take in Vigan, Villa Escudero, Iloilo and Isla Naburot. All trips offer a good cross-section of places and the option to be on your own for some of the journey. Contact any of the following participating agencies: **Danfil Express** ((2) 585414, Eleventh Floor, R. Magsaysay Center, 1680 Roxas Boulevard, **Marsman Tours and Travel Corporation** ((2) 877031-49, Senator Gil Puyat Avenue, Makati or **Rajah Tours Philippines** ((2) 522-0541-48, Third Floor, Physicians' Tower Building, 533 United Nations Avenue, Ermita.

If you are on a tight time budget, you can investigate the seven day "flight-

OPPOSITE TOP and ABOVE: Craftsmen at the Crystal Corp. Glass Factory, Angeles, Clarkfield, Luzon, turning out a variety of glassware.
OPPOSITE: In the more remote regions, women still weave with the traditional backstrap loom.

seeing" tour offered by **Philippine Air Safari**. This is an island hop around the country's major attractions, allowing you to see parts of the archipelago that which would take months to visit if traveling by land, flying across active volcanoes, mountains and coral reefs. Flights usually last 90 minutes or less, and nights are spent in comfortable selected hotels or resorts with excellent food. As well as exploring and relaxing, the package includes such activities as paddling in outrigger canoes, sampling coconut wine, visiting tribal villages and even riding water buffalo.

Check with the Philippine Department of Tourism in Manila for new day tours or excursion packages they may be recommending.

Family Fun

The Philippines is not the first place most people think of as a family vacation spot. Not exactly Disneyland, the country can be adventurous even for hardy adult travelers, let alone small children. Nevertheless, recent years have seen much development in the tourism infrastructure. Hotels and resorts — especially the international chains in such places as Manila, Cebu and Boracay — are now set up to cater to the tastes of and needs of young visitors, with swimming pools, playgrounds and children's menus. When you journey off the beaten track, however, be prepared to forego child-friendly services and amenities. It is always worth calling ahead to request more room space or extra beds and to alert resort owners of your needs. In general, Filipino society is very much attuned to children and their needs.

If your idea of what makes a good family vacation is based on the sort of activities offered at Mediterranean or Caribbean resorts, then the expensive **Shangri-La Mactan Island Resort** in Cebu with its all-day child care program is clearly the best that the Philippines has to offer.

If your child is enthralled by exotic travel, then as long as you keep an open mind, you should all be able to enjoy the sort of pleasures that make the country special, whether this means visiting a deserted island by banca, spotting wildlife in nature reserves, climbing mountains, or simply fishing, lazing and swimming at the beach.

Most children will love the adventure of seeing such natural wonders as **St Paul Subterranean National Park**, the thrilling seascapes in places such as **Palawan** and the layered rice terraces and caves of **Banaue** and **Sagada**. Still, you should feel confidant that your child is ready and willing to endure long bus or jeepney rides through rugged countryside.

Places which are tailor-made for young children include **Paskuhan Christmas Village**, in Pampanga, Luzon, where Christmas is played out all year round. Jingling and tinkling with endless Christmas decorations, special Filipino snacks and sweets, with Christmas corals sung by people as well as mechanical toys, Paskuhan is worth a day visit. The best time to visit is Christmastime, when nearby San Fernando stages a beautiful **Lantern Festival**.

With great frivolity, fun and much dressing up, festivals and fiestas are a Filipino speciality that are especially likely to appeal to children (see FESTIVE FLINGS, pages 41–51). Try to see the **Ati-Atihan Festival** held during January (Kalibo, Panay) the **Moriones Festival** during Holy Week (Marinduque) and the **Gigantes Festival** held during August (Lucban, Quezon).

Finally, getting around the archipelago — especially on small propeller planes, ferries, buses and motorized bancas — involves inherent risk. You will have to make judgments about what transport seems safe and what doesn't, and never hesitate to ask questions.

Easter is a primetime for festive fun. Don't miss the Moriones Festival, in Marinduque, if in the country over Holy Week. It is one of the great festivals.

Welcome to the Philippines

FOR YEARS, the Philippines seemed the lost heart of Southeast Asia. While its neighbors Indonesia, Taiwan, Malaysia and Thailand surged forward to become the regional economic "tigers," the Philippines remained mired in economic chaos and turbulent politics. When, each Easter, devout Filipinos struggled to carry huge wooden crosses on their bare backs, it was difficult not to think of their efforts as a metaphor for the nation's burdens. Yet appearances, often at their most deceptive in Asia, can be especially misleading in the Philippines.

Unlike any other Asian nation, the Philippines is a unique mingling of Western and Eastern influences, for both Spain and America have left indelible traces of former domination, ranging from a steppingstone array of baroque churches, staunch Roman Catholicism, the Spanish *mañana* attitude and an American style legislative system as well as an openness to Western mores. An archipelago nation, the Philippines reaches up to China at one tip and Borneo and Malaysia on the other, its clustered islands numbering, at last count, 7,107 at low tide — most of them uninhabited — sprinkled like emerald confetti on the ocean. It should be the envy of many of its regional rivals for its innumerable beaches, fabled coral reefs and remarkably rich tribal and archipelagic culture.

It may well be that, long before encountering the Philippines, you have glimpsed something of the optimistic Filipino spirit, for not many other countries have so many of its citizens working abroad, while remaining so dedicated to their mother country. A huge percentage of the Philippine gross national product comes from remittances from Filipinos abroad. Within the Philippines, that spirit is all-embracing: from the high voltage Makati restaurants and pleasure dens of urban Manila, to the remotest outposts of undeveloped Palawan to the populous barrios and barangays in the provinces. "*Bahala na*," ("What will be, will be") the Filipinos say and, somehow, this philosophy is all-pervasive.

In recent years, the Philippines has made a sudden comeback. After two decades of dictatorship under Ferdinand and Imelda Marcos (credited with robbing the national treasury and crippling the country's economic growth) and a sudden incandescent expression of "People Power" under the yellow-clad presidency of Corazon Aquino, the Philippines has been working hard to transform itself into Asia's latest economic miracle and tourist playground. These days, foreign investment is evident everywhere, with a bouquet of idyllic resorts sprouting on far-flung islands. Meanwhile, Manila appears to be reinventing itself, with new buildings rising on every street corner of Makati, the capital's business and entertainment magnet.

With its dizzying abundance of islands, the Philippines can seem overwhelming when it comes to planning your travels. There are great wilderness areas and lush forests, island clusters and resorts to match those in the Caribbean and awe inspiring seascapes to explore; but, this is also a land that has until recently made news with its insurgent armies and kidnappings and press reports on unsafe airports and ferries.

While it is tempting to venture off the beaten track, you may also wish to ensure that your vacation doesn't turn out to be more of an adventure you expect. Although menaces do exist, few involve visitors. And, while an adventurous spirit is required to enjoy traveling in the Philippines, be warned: The rewards can be so spectacular and the beauty so soulful, that you may soon find that you have the country under your skin. As they say in the Philippines," *Mabuhay*!" Welcome!

OPPOSITE: Don Bosco Church in Basco Town, in the northerly Batan Islands. ABOVE: Elaborate weaving characterizes the dress of the T'boli tribespeople of the south Cotabato Province of Mindanao.

The Country and Its People

HISTORY CASTS long and varied shadows across the Philippines. Given that the nation encompasses an archipelago made up of 7,107 islands — some concentrated in highly populated clusters, others far-flung and remote — this is hardly surprising. Of these many islands, however, some 2,500 are not named, only 1,000 are inhabited and a mere 11 of them constitute 94 percent of the Philippines' total landmass. The 11 are, in order of size: Luzon, Mindanao, Palawan, Panay, Mindoro, Samar, Negros, Leyte, Cebu, Bohol and Masbate.

Any portrait of the many indigenous people of the Philippines also becomes an account of two of its most influential conquerors, the Spanish and the Americans, for it was they who profoundly shaped the politics, religion, economy and culture of the Philippines. Significantly, unlike any other nation in Asia, the Philippines is a Christian nation: 85 percent of the population is Catholic; an additional eight percent is Catholic-based and Protestant.

From this perspective, the history of the Philippines is dominated by that of a manageable 11 islands, two peoples and one religion. Some even subscribe to the boiled down version of Philippine history as stated in the oft-quoted phrase, "three centuries in a Catholic convent and 50 years in Hollywood," which refers to the Philippines' subjugation under Spanish rule from the late sixteenth to the late nineteenth centuries and to the nearly half century of American governance from 1898 to 1946.

EARLY HISTORY

Human migration to the Philippines began at least 35,000 years ago. It is unknown whether people came in large waves or in a steady trickle, but scholars are reasonably certain they settled as families which evolved into clans or tribes. The result was that during the period from about 35,000 BC until Spain laid uncontested claim to the Philippines in the late sixteenth century, this sprawling archipelago became home to numerous disparate languages and cultures without any semblance of national unity. Those who came by sea developed trading relations with their countries of origin and other countries;

those who came earlier, by land, remained land-bound nomadic hunters, the Negrito.

Approximately 65 native tribes have survived unscathed by Spanish and American subjugation and are scattered throughout the archipelago, comprising six million of the nation's 68 million inhabitants. Only about 10 percent of these surviving tribes maintain their prehistoric belief systems and behavior and speak their own dialects—in all, some 111 dialects are known to exist. They range from the Badjao sea gypsies of the Sulu Archipelago and the only recently reformed

headhunting Kalinga tribe in the mountains of northern Luzon.

In a discovery that amazed anthropologists worldwide, the Tau't Batu tribe of Palawan, was found in 1978 living as they did 20,000 years ago, dwelling exclusively in limestone caves and subsisting on birds, bats and snails. Tourism to the region where they live is barred.

The first peoples to reach the Philippines were the Australoid Negrito from Borneo. Over a 25,000 year period, from approximately 35,000 BC to roughly 10,000 BC, they followed the migrations of animals over the land bridges which then connected the Philippines with the rest of Southeast Asia until melting ice and rising sea levels submerged them 7,000 to 10,000 years ago. They were nomadic hunters armed with bows, arrows and blow guns who migrated to Luzon, Palawan, Mindoro and Mindanao. Today, principally found in eastern Luzon and governed

OPPOSITE: Jeepneys skirt the sinking tower in Laoag, Ilocos Norte. ABOVE: Bukidnon tribespeople, from Malaybalay in Mindanao.

only by family leaders, at least 15,000 Negrito survive — the same short statured, kinky-haired nomadic people, still clad in bark and living in huts built from branches and grass, still hunting by blow guns and bows and arrows. Descendants of the early Negritos are found in tribes throughout the Philippines, but they are concentrated in Luzon and the Visayas (the main island group of the Philippines) and comprise the Aeta, Agta, Ati, Baluga, Batak and Mamanuwa tribes.

Immigrants who came after the Negrito arrived by sea, each group more advanced between 800 BC and 500 BC, were from southern China and Indochina. They made many invaluable contributions to human advancement on the Philippines, including the introduction of copper and bronze tools, technologies involving the use of metals for copper mining and smelting and irrigated rice culture over landscaped terraces. These immigrants are the direct ancestors of the present-day tribes of northern Luzon and Mindanao.

The Malay Peninsula produced subsequent immigrants who were more advanced

than the last. The first group of these seafaring immigrants sailed from Indonesia 5,000 to 6,000 years ago. They were expert boat builders, carpenters of woodframe houses and skilled in dry (non-irrigated) agriculture. Anthropologists refer to them as the people of the Early New Stone Age or the Indonesian-A. The second group came about 1,500 BC to 500 BC and are referred to as the Late Neolithic or Indonesian-B. Their houses, sheltered by pyramidal roofs and raised on stilts, were protected against rains and flooding, unlike those of their predecessors, whose houses were covered with rounded roofs and were built directly on the ground or even inside meter-deep pits. The third group of migrating mariners, who came still. They are believed to have come in three waves: between 300 BC and 100 BC, between 200 AD and 1200 AD and during the fourteenth and fifteenth centuries. The first wave took two different ocean routes — from west Borneo via Palawan and Mindoro to Luzon; from east Borneo via the Celebes Strait to Mindanao and the Visayas — and eventually settled in the mountains of Luzon, Mindanao and the Visayas — which include the islands of Panay, Samar, Negros, Leyte, Cebu and Bohol. Their contributions were many and of enormous significance: the discovery and use of iron for tools, weapons and utensils, as well as for forging and smelting; the introduction of the back loom and spindle for making woven textiles for mats, baskets and clothing, which supplanted bark cloth; the further development of agriculture with their introduction of the horse and *carabao,* or water buffalo, and of improved irrigation methods; finally, their sophisticated techniques for making pottery and personal ornaments. In the mountains of Luzon and Mindanao today, tribes descended from these Malays practice the same types of iron forging and back-loom weaving.

The second wave of Malays were even more advanced in that they possessed an alphabet. Unlike their mountain-dwelling Malay predecessors, they chose to settle in lowlands, especially along coasts and rivers, which proved a natural training ground for their development into skilled sailors and traders. They also became rice farmers and devised superior irrigation methods which increased their food supply allowing rapid population growth. Thus the Malays proliferated across the flatlands of the entire archipelago and overwhelmed the interior tribes in number.

Surrounded by open space and water, the Malays, like rivers to the sea, were naturally bound to connect with the outside world — unlike their predecessors who settled and remained secluded in mountainous and backwater habitats. It was also these Malays, whose literacy endowed them with intellectual curiosity and whose involvement in trade with India, China and Indochinese states, taught them acceptance of foreign peoples and customs. No wonder then that it was these outward-gazing lowland Malays, spreading their population across the Philippines for over a millennium beginning in about 200 AD, who succumbed largely peaceably to the exploitative Spanish and became the forefathers of modern-day Filipino Christians.

The final wave of Malays are believed to be the ancestors of the current population of Mindanao's Muslims since they settled mainly in Mindanao and in nearby Sulu — an island archipelago as well as the name of a Mindanao province — during the fourteenth and fifteenth centuries. It was Mindanao, during that time, to which the Islam religion was brought and in which the Philippines' Muslims, forming around seven percent of the population, are concentrated today.

FOREIGN INFLUENCES AND THE RISE OF ISLAM

Straddling ancient sea trading routes, it was inevitable that the archipelago become a landing place and transfer station for early seafarers — Chinese, Indian, Arab, Japanese and Siamese among them. It is not known exactly when the first contact with China began, but it is certain that by the early part of the Zhou

Dynasty (1066 to 221 BC) trade links had been established with the Philippines, which were then strengthened in the period before the Ming Dynasty (1368 to 1644). Chinese traders bartered their exquisite silk textiles, porcelain, bronze, fans and beads, as well as lead sinkers for fishnets, while the Philippines offered such wares as gold, pearls, rough cotton, betel nut, hemp and tortoiseshell — and encouraged the Chinese craze for birds' nest soup. Another more subtle trade and cultural influence came from India, beginning in the late seventh century, permeating as far as Java as well as Sumatra.

OPPOSITE: Descendants of some of the islands' earliest settlers, the Negritos. ABOVE: A Muslim girl from Zamboanga, a stronghold of Philippine Islam.

By the thirteenth century, Arab merchants and missionaries were trading with and converting the inhabitants of Jolo, the capital of Sulu province. By then, Islam's sphere of influence in the region spanned from Arabia to throughout Southeast Asia to Sumatra and the Malay Peninsula. It became the dominant creed in the Sulu islands by the late fifteenth century. A generation later, the first sultanate was established in Mindanao under Sharif Mohammed Kabungsuwan. His followers and other Muslim immigrants propagated Islam in Mindoro, Southern Luzon and Manila. Islam, with its political-cum-religious structure, began to impart to converts a collective sense of identity and pride, which no doubt explains the success of their resistance to the Spanish invaders as distinct from the passive reception by non-Muslim lowlanders. Absent the Spanish incursion in the mid-sixteenth century, the Philippines today might well be an Islamic nation.

THE SPANISH INVADE

On the face of things, to a sixteenth century Roman Catholic European, life's most important duty and responsibility was Catholic worship and observance and the loftiest accomplishment was converting the ignorant to Catholicism. In 1519, Ferdinand Magellan set sail with his men and a large wooden cross on a mission for the glory of God and Spain. Their mission was to find new routes to the Orient and its spices and to convert those encountered there to Catholicism. Two years later, Magellan reached Samar in the Visayas and soon after erected his cross on nearby soil on the auspicious date of Easter Sunday, 1521. He was to make a blood pact with the island's leader, Rajah Humabon, followed by a mass conversion and baptism to Christianity.

No one knows exactly why Magellan lost his life a few weeks later on neighboring Mactan Island. He had a clear foe in Lapu Lapu, the chieftain of a nearby island who confronted the Spanish adventurer on the beaches of Mactan. It is only known that he was killed in a skirmish with natives and that, of his five ships, only one, loaded with spices, returned to Spain. Those spices more than

paid for Magellan's expedition and justified the dispatch by Spain of another four galleons between 1525 and 1542; ironically, the Philippines probably did not produce these spices, as was discovered by later Spanish explorers who found the Philippines without export-quality spices, its only native spice being an inferior type of cinnamon. No matter, though, as these explorers saw future wealth for Spain and themselves in the porcelains, silks, velvets, pearls, lacquer and other sumptuous goods pouring into the islands, as they had for centuries from China which, at that time, barred all foreign merchants except the Portuguese in Macao. Confident of Spain's eventual ownership of the islands, the captain of the last of these expeditions named Samar and Leyte after King Charles I's son, Felipe, who became King Felipe II in 1556. This name was Islas Felipinas, an imperial pendant that Spain eventually draped on the entire archipelago.

Anticipating fortunes born of the re-export of Chinese products from Manila to Mexico (a Spanish colony known then as New Spain), the Spanish began rapid colonization of the Philippines in 1565 and completed their occupation a mere decade later — a feat of conquest perhaps not entirely astonishing given that the people of the archipelago were so divided amongst themselves. At the helm of the Spanish occupation was Miguel Lopez de Legazpi, who became the colony's governor-general and founded Manila in 1571, only to die of a heart attack a year later.

During the Spanish conquest of the Philippine islands, the conquistadors brutalized the *indios*, as the natives were called. Their armed troops would enter villages and rob, rape, raze and kill indiscriminately, as the priest Francisco de Ortega described: "They first send in an interpreter, not with gifts or to speak of God, but to demand tribute. The people, never having been subjects of a king or a lord, are puzzled and shocked when forced to hand over their necklaces or bracelets, their only property. Some refuse, others submit reluctantly and still others flee to the hills, terrified by this strange new race of armed men. The Spaniards pursue them, firing their arquebuses and killing without mercy, then return to the village to slaughter all the pigs and poultry, carry off all the rice and burn all the houses." In 1570, a prelate, Diego de Herrera, wrote that the Spaniards were committing "acts of violence against people in their homes and against their wives, daughters and property."

In 1583, King Felipe II, supporting the Catholic clergy, wrote, "the natives have conceived such great hatred of the Christian name, looking upon the Spaniards as deceivers who do not practice what they preach, that whatever they do is only out of compulsion." In reforms decreed that same year, the king protected native villages against officers and troops by closing them to all Spaniards except tax collectors, inspectors and friars. He confined officials and soldiers to towns, permitting them to stay only temporarily on rotating tours of duty.

These reforms enabled the Catholic monastic orders to rule the country absolutely. There were five such orders, each of which answered to a separate leadership in Rome and each of which controlled its own zone of territory: the Augustinian, Franciscan and Dominican orders were dominant in Luzon; the Jesuit and Recollects orders occupied the Visayas and Mindanao. In Spain's campaign to subjugate the Philippines, the friars were now the troops, armed not with swords but with a knowledge of local languages and customs, which they used to ingratiate themselves to the natives and with Catholic education and rituals, which they manipulated to keep the natives servile and placated.

One of the friars' first items of business was the relocation of natives from their autonomous, scattered villages into consolidated settlements. This was not difficult: under the friars, the natives learned Catholicism and, in God's name and honor, built churches and the townships around them. Today, almost every Philippine town is dominated by a florid baroque church. As a seventeenth century Spanish official wrote, "Travel around the provinces and you will see populations of five, 10 or 20,000 indios ruled in peace by one old man who, with his doors open at all hours, sleeps secure in his dwelling." The religious orders founded colleges and universities, hospitals, museums and libraries, established printing

presses, studied and documented indigenous flora and fauna and sought to introduce the principles of European learning and culture.

For 300 years, the education offered the friars was limited to memorizing the catechism and the lives of the saints. They also refused to teach natives the Spanish language or to allow the ordination of Filipino priests. A 1903 survey done by United States missionaries found most of the Filipino population to be illiterate. To maintain the natives' passivity, the friars did not alter their indig-

enous tribal structure or its values; indeed, the friars combined pagan practices and paraphernalia with Catholic rituals to sustain their complacency. The friars also did nothing to improve the natives' subsistence economy of rice cultivation, livestock raising and fishing in local waters. It would seem that the friars — who had previously protested the more obvious rapaciousness of the Spanish conquistadors — cared for nothing except the preservation of their material comfort, colonial privileges and absolute authority over the indios.

Altar in the walls of Fort Pilar, Zamboanga, Mindanao. OVERLEAF: Many Baroque-style churches, such as this in Paoay, remain from the days of Spanish rule.

THE ADMINISTRATION UNDER THE SPANISH

Between 1565 and 1813, the colony's direct command came from the Viceroy of Mexico. Meanwhile, the real business of the Spanish presence in the Philippines was taking place in Manila. There, Spain, the monastic orders and individual traders and merchants were all cashing in on the trade of precious Oriental goods, bought with silver Mexican pesos. In Acapulco the pesos were loaded onto a

galleon, which made the four- to five-month journey to Manila, where it was unloaded and filled with goods for reshipment to Mexico. Only one galleon a year was permitted to make the trip, with the Manila-bound pesos always exceeding in value that of the returning Mexico-bound goods (this surplus constituting a subsidy). The galleon trade swelled the coffers of both church and crown and supported the colonial government in Manila (consisting of a joint post of governor and military commander and his subordinate officials, officers and troops, all of whom answered to the king's viceroy in Mexico). Just as the friars who controlled the indios of the countryside conferred nothing to them of value, so too, the bureaucrats of

Manila shared nothing of their lucrative trade with the provinces.

In the early eighteenth century, the Jesuit priest, Pedro Murillo Velarde, criticized the galleon trade and said the Spanish in Manila were like "visitors to an inn," leaving nothing of value behind. Of Manila's population of 90,000 in 1780, only three or four thousand were Spaniards — living along the spacious boulevards and plazas of the walled city of Intramuros. The rest were natives, living packed into bamboo shacks along streams and swamps.

Late in the eighteenth century, Spain's exploitative dominion over the largely passive Filipinos began to crack. Earlier, the Portuguese, the Dutch and a Chinese warlord all had made attempts to wrest away possession of the islands. This time fragmentation began with Spain's defeat by the British in 1762. Britain — as part of its Seven Years' War against Spain and France — sailed its ships into Manila Bay and captured the capital city. The British occupied Manila for nearly two years following this, during which they stopped the galleon trade and confiscated every Spanish ship in the harbor, an act which destroyed Manila's economy. The city reverted to Spain under the Treaty of Paris in 1763.

Spain's display of weakness triggered revolts and conspiracies by Filipinos and Chinese alike in Luzon and by Filipino Muslims in Mindanao and Sulu. These rebellions were quickly crushed, but the seeds of revolt were sown.

REBELLION AND REVOLUTION

To revive Manila's economy, Spain's King Charles III sent, in 1778, a new governor to Manila: José de Basco y Vargas. In a public speech condemning Spain's abuse of the archipelago, Basco announced, "The sun will rise over our islands after more than 200 years of darkness." With the galleon trade now on the decline and the Asian and Mexican markets no longer Manila's exclusive domain — Europe now traded directly with Asia, while Spain permitted foreign exporters to compete in the Mexican market — Basco demanded that commerce shift from the harbor to the countryside, where money, in the form of tobacco, could be pulled from the ground. Soon native Filipinos were forced to convert rice fields into tobacco plantations. They toiled in conditions of semi-slavery growing increasingly resentful, while the newly formed Royal Company of the Philippines exported tobacco at an immense profit for Spain.

Mexico's gain of independence in 1821 was Spain's loss. For the native Filipino laborers this meant more backbreaking work: To maintain its profit margin from its Philippine operations, Spain introduced sugar, copra, indigo and hemp as cash crops. Native Filipinos suffered: As rice fields disappeared, food shortages grew and supplies replenished at the natives' expense with costly imported staples.

Filipino hardship only grew worse with the advent of the Industrial Revolution in the early 1830s: As factories spread throughout Europe and America and foreign firms opened offices in Manila, Cebu and other towns, the need for raw materials accelerated — Filipinos labored all the harder. Collective Filipino suffering found comfort in Christian rituals, especially the Easter celebrations which re-enacted the suffering, death and resurrection of Jesus Christ. Ironically, Catholicism itself, which had been used as a tool to subjugate and pacify the natives, evolved into the source of their insurrection. They identified with the persecuted Christ. They championed insurgent leaders who, emulating Christ, promised salvation. One of the earliest examples of these heroic figures was Apolinario de la Cruz, who, in 1841 along with 200 of his disciples was executed by the Spanish for instigating rebellion in Luzon; he and his disciples had dedicated themselves to spreading the gospel and healing the sick.

Spain's eventual downfall was all but guaranteed by its educational reforms in 1863, which established a public school system making higher learning available to Filipinos. The opening of the Suez Canal in 1869 enabled children of wealthy families to study in Madrid, where they picked up many modern European ideas—including nationalism — as well as the history of Mexico's revolutions against Spain. Known as the *ilustrados*, these members of the Filipino intelligentsia — a racial mixture of Spanish, Indio, Chinese, Malay and even Japanese — grew to oppose Spanish domination. Their influence ignited the first major uprising in 1872 in Cavite province, Luzon, when 200 Filipino soldiers mutinied and murdered their Spanish officers. The government executed three Filipino priests who had joined this revolt — the friars Burgos, Gomez and Zamora—who dared to challenge the power of the Spanish officers and were publicly garoted, an act which by itself galvanized demands for reform.

From 1889 to 1895, a nationalist magazine called *La Solidaridad* was published in Spain by the Propaganda Movement led by Filipino reformers José Rizal, the Luna brothers, Marcelo H. del Pilar and Graciano Lopez Jaena. The luminary of the group was Rizal, a medical doctor and nationalist writer, who was the well-educated son of an upper class ilustrado Filipino family. Through his writings as an expatriate—*Noli Me Tangere* and *El Filibusterismo*—now both compulsory reading at Philippine schools, he depicted the abuses of the friars and the government. His vision was to see the Philippines represented in Madrid, not as a colony, but a province.

In 1892, he returned to the Philippines and founded an organization seeking peaceful reform, La Liga Filipina, which promptly got him deported to Mindanao. Four years later, in 1896, Rizal was executed in Manila on a

OPPOSITE: Statue of Lapu Lapu, in Mactan, Cebu. Cheiftain Lapu Lapu slew Magellan in 1521 for reasons still largely unclear. ABOVE: The site of the Spaniard's death is commemorated by a plaque.

conviction of "rebellion, sedition and illicit association." Today, Rizal, more than just martyred hero, is a national messiah, worshipped in his home town of Calamba, south of Manila, as the reincarnation of Christ.

In late 1896, General Emilio Aguinaldo emerged as the nation's next revolutionary leader. He fought that year against the Spanish in Luzon, as part of an eight province wide revolt instigated by Andres Bonifacio, a warehouse clerk from Tondo (now a slum suburb of Manila) and his secret society, the Katipunan. Soon, revolutionary fever spread

across the island provinces. A year later, Bonifacio and his Katipunan, considered seditious, were ousted by Aguinaldo's new revolutionary government, which then tried, convicted and executed Bonifacio. In late 1897, the Spanish and Aguinaldo negotiated a truce, whose terms included amnesty for the rebels in exchange for payment to Aguinaldo to procure his exile to Hong Kong.

Despite the agreed peace, in early 1898 battles erupted anew. Filipinos might finally have recaptured their own country but for some unfortunate timing: America was then warring with Spain over Cuba. One side effect of this Spanish-American War involved America's attack on the Spanish navy in Manila Harbor. On May 1, 1898, United States

Commodore George Dewey and his sailors demolished the Spaniards. Unlike Britain's belligerent visit to Manila Harbor nearly 125 years earlier in the Seven Years' War, the Americans stayed not a mere 20 months, but 48 years. And they did not confine themselves strictly to Manila as had the British; the Americans made the entire archipelago theirs. Another momentous chapter in Filipino history was about to begin.

THE ARRIVAL OF THE AMERICANS

"Have captured the Philippines; what shall we do with them?" cabled Commodore Dewey to President William McKinley. Fearing the loss of his job to a politically powerful expansionist such as Theodore Roosevelt, Henry Cabot Lodge or Alfred Thayer Mahan, the isolationist McKinley decided colonization was unavoidable. Not wishing to cite "job security" as the reason for seizing 300,439 sq km (116,000 sq miles) of land supporting a foreign population of seven million at a distance of 20,000 km (12,000 miles) from the White House — McKinley instead took the Spanish approach: "We'll Christianize them! It's our duty!" The problem was, the Spanish had already taken the Spanish approach 300 years earlier. (Amazingly, a mission to Christianize the Philippines really was McKinley's initial *stated* justification for annexing them.) No matter, most Americans exulted hysterically over Dewey's victory — they, like their president, knew nothing about the history of the Philippines — and felt intoxicated by the prospect of making the Philippines another part of their "manifest destiny" (a phrase coined in 1845 to promote the annexation of Texas).

The Americans established a military government in Manila and did not disband it, despite the ending of the Spanish-American War on December 10, 1898 under the Treaty of Paris, in which Spain ceded the Philippines, Guam and Puerto Rico to the United States. Less than a month later, Emilio Aguinaldo proclaimed the establishment of the First Philippine Republic, nominating

ABOVE: The Japanese ended 48 years of American rule with their long, bloody siege of Bataan and Corregidor Island, Luzon. OPPOSITE: General MacArthur's GM cabriolet on Corregidor Island.

himself as president. Only a few weeks after that event, an American shot a Filipino soldier and Aguinaldo declared war. Nearly three years, many battles and 200,000 Filipino fatalities later, Aguinaldo was captured and the First Philippine Republic fell. In 1902, President Roosevelt declared the Philippines "pacified." William Howard Taft, who became president of the United States and later Chief Justice of the Supreme Court, served as the first governor of the Philippines.

By World War I, anti-imperialists had gained considerable clout in America. Both

Roosevelt and Lodge, for example, had disavowed their original expansionist views. The winds of American politics had shifted to favor self-government for the Filipinos, as reflected by the Jones Act of 1916, which was intended to provide Filipinos substantial autonomy over internal affairs. Meanwhile in the Philippines, the Filipinos who wielded the political power to enforce the Jones Act were the native economic elite, those who were educated in Spain and in Manila during the late nineteenth century. They served on the American-created Philippine Assembly, elected because they could afford the time and money to campaign. They were also favored by the Americans, as their complacency was assured by America's re-

distribution to them of church-owned land; the United States had purchased these lands from the Vatican for US$7.2 million.

Like the friars of old whose clamoring for reforms in the 1560s and 1570s led the king to quiet them with a grant of the entire Philippine countryside, this class of elite Filipinos, who sought reforms in the late nineteenth century, forgot about reforms after they acquired that very same land. Like the friars, they did not want their positions of comfort and privilege disturbed and had no real desire to better the lot of their Filipino brethren.

In the 1920s, overt American imperialism ended and Filipino autonomy began, yet, paradoxically, it was in that decade that Filipinos "lost free will," according to the most revered Filipino writer, Nick Joaquin (who was educated in Spanish but writes only in English). The Filipino lost his sense of self, Joaquin notes, when he ceased to identify the American as alien, enemy, Yanqui or Gringo and embraced him instead as benefactor and America as "the mother culture." The old culture, whose heroes were Rizal, Bonifacio and Aguinaldo, began to look alien. "For in discarding the old culture we discarded as well the sense of identity it had achieved during its fight for freedom," Joaquin claimed.

Identifying with America made the Filipino provincial, according to Joaquin: "The cultured Filipino of the 1880s was intellectually at home in several worlds: Europe, Spanish America, the Orient (there was a special interest in Japan), not to mention the classic world of the hexameter; and his frame of reference had a latitude unthinkable in the 'educated' Filipino of the 1920s and 1930s, for whom culture had been reduced to 'knowing about the world contained between Hollywood and Manhattan.'" Writer Ian Buruma adds: "One could say that the legacy of Spanish Catholicism and secondhand Americana are the two things most Filipinos have in common. Even NPA guerrillas wear UCLA T-shirts. America is like a birthmark on the Filipino

ABOVE: Supporting the team from distant Philippines, Dennis Rodman's father in Angeles, Luzon. Corregidor Island: United States Barracks OPPOSITE TOP and Malinta Tunnel BOTTOM.

identity — no matter how hard you rub, it won't come off."

Following World War I, Americans patterned the Philippines after their own country: Church was separated from state, the legal system was modified to include courts of original and appellate jurisdiction, the country's infrastructure was dramatically improved with American dollars and technology and the market economy featured modern products used by most Americans. United States investors and businessmen flocked to the Philippines to exploit its raw materials and improve their United States market for manufactured goods. Quickly, Filipinos adapted to the American way of exploiting land and labor purely for the economic gain of the owners and their corporations.

There was a tug-of-war in the United States between those who favored overseas trade and holdings and those who urged that American workers must be protected against foreign competition. With the onset of the Great Depression, farm and labor groups successfully fought for legislation authorizing Philippine independence. In 1935, a Philippine Commonwealth was established which, in 1946, would become fully independent of the United States. Significantly, it was Americans and not Filipinos who pushed for and won Philippine independence.

The first president of the Commonwealth government, inaugurated in 1935, was Manuel Quezon. At that time, most Filipinos were impoverished while heirs of the wealthy, landowning old culture clamored for reassurance that America's "letting go" would not mean the demise of their comfortable lifestyles. Quezon instituted social programs to ameliorate the problems of the masses but at the same time promised the landed gentry, of which he (and all subsequent Filipino leaders) was a member, that their lives would not be affected.

World War II hit the Philippines on December 8, 1941, when the Japanese bombed United States aircraft based at Clark Field in Central Luzon. The Japanese quickly invaded nearby Lingayen Gulf and Lamon Bay and marched toward Manila. Although in 1941 the Filipino forces had been incorporated into the United States Army under General Douglas MacArthur, they were poorly trained and ill-equipped to defend against the Japanese. On January 2, 1942, MacArthur declared Manila an "Open City," and with his American and Filipino forces, he withdrew to the narrow Bataan Peninsula and Corregidor Island.

President Quezon implored President Roosevelt to grant immediate independence to the Philippines so that it could declare neutrality. Roosevelt, not wishing to surrender the Philippines to the Japanese, rejected Quezon's demands and promised to defend

the Philippines to the end. For the next three months, the American and Filipino forces fought the Japanese on Bataan. Finally, Roosevelt ordered MacArthur off the Philippines, prompting MacArthur to make his famous "I shall return" pledge. One month later, on April 9, 1942, the 76,000 men on Bataan surrendered to the Japanese. Starving and rife with malaria and dysentery, these men were forced to begin marching up the peninsula to boxcars in San Fernando in Pampanga, which took them to an internment camp at Capas in Tarlac province. That march is known as the "Death March"; it took 10 days and 10,000 lives were lost to exhaustion or to the horrific conditions imposed by their captors.

Japan's military ruled the Philippines from May 1942 until Japan officially surrendered on September 3, 1945. In 1944, MacArthur fulfilled his promise and returned to the Philippines, landing along the Leyte coastline — to wade ashore with his trademark pipe clenched in his jaw — with 174,000 servicemen and 700 vessels. The American forces dwarfed and decimated those of the Japanese (who defended the islands with an obstinacy bordering on the insane) with feats that quite easily overshadowed D Day, although they were never near Kiangan, in Ifugao province, Luzon, were routed.

THE POSTWAR PERIOD AND PHILIPPINE INDEPENDENCE

World War II claimed approximately one million Filipino lives. Property damage throughout the archipelago was vast. Manila was in ruins, second only to Warsaw in the damage it sustained. The Commonwealth government was not ready for independence in 1946, for it was without a

portrayed as such by the official wartime publicity machine. In two months, Leyte was cleared of the Japanese occupation. Five hundred kilometers (310 miles) to the north lay Luzon, toward which the Americans, supported by 250,000 Filipino guerrillas, began to march in late 1944. In January 1945, they landed at Lingayen Gulf, recaptured Corregidor in an 11-day battle and stormed Manila the following month. After a two-week bloodbath in Manila, the Japanese made their last stand at Intramuros, where American and Filipino forces fought hand-to-hand, street-to-street. Manila was finally liberated on February 23, 1945. Mopping up operations lasted until September 3, 1945, when the last remaining Japanese forces,

president — Quezon died in 1944 — and without the resources or facilities to reconstruct a country in shambles. In these circumstances, it was probably no accident that Filipinos, economically and psychologically dependent on America, elected a strongly pro-United States president, Manuel Roxas, to lead the Commonwealth which in 1946 became the Philippine Republic. Under Roxas, American dollars rebuilt the war ravaged Philippines and constructed the two largest military bases outside the United States, Clark Air Force Base in Pampanga province and Subic Bay Naval Base on the Bataan Peninsula.

Planting rice — the country's staple crop — at Bangaan.

The Philippine economy rebounded quickly, growing during the 1950s at a fast yearly clip of five to six percent. Its economy also grew increasingly diverse during this period. Filipinos now not only grew rice, corn, sugarcane, copra and coconuts; they had begun to build factories (which made textiles, shoes and cement), dig mines (for gold and copper) and clear forests (for mahogany and other hardwoods). There was a familiar problem, however: The production of such wealth neither bettered the lives of nor decreased the ranks of the poor masses,

but rather benefited the Philippine elite, the government (which in all practicality represented solely its own interests) and American business.

Rather than a giving-back to the Filipino people, there was a giving-to the Americans (just as there had been for centuries with the Spanish): The Laurel-Langley Treaty of 1955 gave Americans equal rights with Filipinos to exploit local resources in the operation of public utilities and in numerous other businesses. As a Philippine biographer of Imelda Marcos, Carmen Navarro Pedrosa, wrote: "The small number of families who had once enjoyed the patronage of the Spanish crown had formed economic alliances with American business and divided the spoils as if the

poor, or indeed the rest of the nation, did not exist."

Economically impoverished, yet politically free, the people expressed their will by never electing to a second term any of their presidents, who were limited to two four-year terms by their Constitution. Following Manuel Roxas, Philippine presidents were Elpidio Quirino (1949 to 1953), Ramon Magsaysay (1953 to 1957), Carlos Garcia (1957 to 1961) and Diosdado Macapagal (1961 to 1965).

Also troubling the Philippines during this postwar period were an unfair distribution of land, an exploding population and increasing violence and lawlessness in urban and rural areas. Forty percent of the agrarian populace were tenants, sharecroppers or paid plantation workers subsisting in miserable conditions. In 1950 the pro-communist Hukbalahap movement sought to end this feudal landlord–tenant system with its militia of armed guerrillas. In 1953, President Magsaysay resettled thousands of landless peasant families from Luzon in uncrowded parts of Mindanao and Palawan, thus deflating the Huks. In election year 1957, with plans on tap to limit the size of land holdings and to sell portions of large estates to tenants, Magsaysay died in a plane crash.

As for the population, it had risen from about 7.6 million in 1903 to 28 million by 1960, and it kept growing at one of the fastest rates in the world — three percent per year. Advances in modern medicine together with the Catholic Church's opposition to birth control were responsible for this population explosion. The escalating crime rate in the late 1940s through the early 1960s was the inevitable result of the Philippines government kowtowing to American interests, increasing unrest and overcrowding in the cities and fields and, as in America, the easy availability of firearms.

THE MARCOS ERA

By election year 1965, Filipinos needed a president who could solve their chronic problems. They yearned for a national strongman, brazen and daring. Enter, one Ferdinand E. Marcos, a lawyer, congressman and former World War II guerrilla against the Japanese.

He was alreay mildly notorious: In 1952 he was convicted then acquitted of murdering his father's political rival. The murder weapon came from the armory of the university Marcos then attended, where he was a national champion in small bore weapons; his father's defeat meant no income to finance Marcos' university education.

His shady past notwithstanding, Ferdinand and his young wife Imelda—a former Miss Manila who was then fresh from the provinces—campaigned tirelessly throughout the archipelago and promised to make the Philippines a great nation. They would break the power of the rich and of the Catholic Church, wipe out the communist threat and deliver Filipinos from poverty. To drive their message home, the Marcos clan hired publicity agents.

"Overnight, Filipinos were besieged by propaganda of a superhero combining the qualities of Audie Murphy and John F. Kennedy, who lived in their midst, unknown until the presidential campaign of 1965," writes Carmen Pedrosa. Meanwhile Imelda's propagandists proclaimed that she was the perfect "complement to this modern day superhero — rich, young and beautiful; an Asian Jacqueline Kennedy."

Unable initially to resist the charms of this Camelot couple, Filipinos soon learned the truth. The Marcos' interests were soley aimed at enriching themselves and their friends. This they did by making corrupt deals and embezzling from government loans and by assigning government posts to their friends who in turn practiced nepotism and embezzlement. Only during his first term in office (1965 to 1969) did Marcos do anything resembling public service (and probably only to win reelection in 1969, which he did, barely): He built irrigation systems, which increased rice production, and he introduced improvements in public health, transportation and communications.

After 1969, Marcos concentrated on staying in power. Imelda soon adjusted to her status as First Lady, transforming herself from a shy unsophisticated rural lass to the flamboyant figure who beguiled world leaders with her flirtatious beauty: the "Steel Butterfly," the international press dubbed her. Her shopaholicism became legendary; her lifestyle was a never ending round of international, celebrity packed spending sprees (ostensibly diplomatic missions), during which she also acquired exclusive real estate and priceless antiquities as effortlessly as her infamous shoes.

"Imelda's excesses were not limited to shopping. At home, she dreamed of glamorous projects that would bring her further glory even as they bled the national treasury. Indeed, Imelda discovered the wonderful world of international bank loans in her search to fund her projects. These loans

would flow to the Philippines for more than a decade, plunging the economy further into debt even as the Marcoses diverted millions of dollars to their personal assets," wrote Carmen Pedrosa.

Imelda's so-called "edifice complex" resulted in the construction of a series of grandiose concrete structures, including Manila's Cultural Center, the National Arts Center and Convention Center, as well as 14 luxury hotels — all at a time when 30 percent of the nation could barely afford the basic necessities of food and shelter; the country's per capita income was US$200.

On September 23, 1972, Marcos declared martial law — and it remained in force for most of his stay in office. His stated reason was that this was the only way to stop the threat of insurrection posed by the Communist Party of the Philippines and the New People's Army (NPA). In reality, these groups

OPPOSITE: Marcos during his 1985 Manila speech rally. ABOVE: Smoky Mountain garbage tip, in Tondo, Manila, is still a source of revenue for scavengers.

controlled no more than a thousand armed regulars, 10,000 part-time supporters and 100,000 sympathizers in a country of more than 40 million people. Marcos referred to a "state of anarchy," yet bombings and outbreaks of violence were few (some Filipinos have even charged that Marcos engineered many of them in order to create the pretext for martial law). Through martial law, Marcos got what he had wanted all along — an amended constitution allowing him to stay on indefinitely as head of state.

In the immediate aftermath of martial law, every Philippine newspaper except one owned by a Marcos crony was padlocked and placed under military guard. Six of the country's major television stations and nine radio stations were shut. Only one radio and one television station, both controlled by Marcos, were allowed to operate. The country was now controlled from the center, with the army and the security services as Marcos' main instruments of power. Hundreds and ultimately thousands of opposition leaders were imprisoned, among them Senator Benigno "Ninoy" Aquino, who was jailed for eight years, until May 1980, when he was permitted to travel to the United States for open heart surgery. Although Marcos ended martial law in January 1981, he ruled thereafter by presidential decrees.

Like Rizal before him (whose hero's homecoming to the Philippines from Spain was promptly followed by his execution), Aquino was catapulted to the status of a national messiah and roused the nation when, upon his return from the United States on August 21, 1983, he was assassinated on the tarmac at Manila Airport immediately after he was forcibly escorted off the plane by three government officials. The Marcos government claimed the assassin was a lone Communist agent, Rolando Galman, who soldiers gunned down on the spot. Later, many of the country's highest ranking military officers were tried for the assassination, but all were acquitted.

In the weeks after Aquino's murder, foreign banks withdrew their funds, and the Philippines found itself massively in debt. In 1984, inflation topped 60 percent. The economy declined by five percent that year and by another five percent in 1985. This waning economy bred violent crimes committed by armed factions on both the left (represented by the Communist Party of the Philippines and its military wing, the NPA) and the right (the army, police force, certain corporations and industrialists). By the mid-1980s, the NPA had more than 15,000 guerrilla fighters and was operating in the majority of the country's 73 provinces, mainly in the countryside but also in some cities, such as Davao in Mindanao. Also disrupting the peace were the separatist Moro National Liberation Front, representing the dissident Muslims of Mindanao and the Sulu Archipelago.

THE SNAP ELECTION AND PEOPLE POWER

Amid this chaos and growing international and national criticism, Marcos planned a snap election for February 7, 1986, expecting a disunited opposition, as had been the case in 1981. His opponent was Aquino's widow, Corazon "Cory" Aquino of the Philippine Democratic Party. To ensure victory, Marcos controlled the election results by having his thugs buy votes, steal ballot boxes and destroy voter registration records. But Marcos had underestimated the degree to which Benigno Aquino's 1983 murder had galvanized the nation against him and in favor of Cory Aquino. Although Marcos proclaimed himself the winner with 53 percent of the vote, Aquino, addressing nearly a million supporters in Rizal Park, refused to concede. The quiet widow with the gentle smile announced a peaceful program of civil disobedience, including a strike after Marcos' planned inauguration. The tide began to turn in her favor when, on February 20, 1986, many military officers denounced the election as fraudulent. Two days later, the highest ranking military officer, Chief of Staff General Fidel Ramos (Marcos' cousin) and Defense Minister Juan Ponce Enrile defected from the Marcos camp and called on him to resign and cede power to Aquino.

The following day, Sunday, February 23, thousands of Manila's citizens thronged Epifanio de los Santos Avenue (known as "EDSA") and blocked the vast intersection of EDSA outside two military camps. They brought the soldiers food and wildly celebrated the overthrow of Marcos and the birth of a new Philippine republic under Cory Aquino.

Jaime Cardinal Sin, Archbishop of Manila, played a pivotal role, urging peaceful protest on the streets. Some historians have credited the People Power revolution with inspiring a wave of popular discontent around the world in the 1980s. The sight, on live television, of a million people standing in defiance against Marcos' military regime remains one of the defining images of the era.

In the morning of February 25, Aquino took the oath of office; 12 hours later, following a White House call for Marcos to step down, four American helicopters descended on Malacañang Palace to airlift the Marcoses, their family and a close friend to Clark Air Force Base and then into exile in Hawaii, where Marcos was to die three years later. Within days, Aquino opened the opulent Malacañang Palace in Manila to the public so that Filipinos could witness the extravagant lifestyle of the autocrats who had ruled them for 21 years.

The terms "EDSA Revolution" or "EDSA," "People Power," the "February Revolt," and the "Snap Revolution" were quickly coined to describe the events that began the drive for "Filipinization." Toward this goal, in the first year of her administration, Aquino restored the rights of free speech and a free press, released hundreds of political prisoners, reformed the constitution to restrict a president to a single six-year term and ousted all Marcos loyalists serving as governors and mayors, replacing them with her own appointees.

After that first year, however — once a congress had been elected, essentially — the defiant widow's administration veered from reform to conservative politics as usual as in the pre-Marcos era. The question is, why?

"Was she pushed that way by the military, by the Americans, by business interests? Or was that her natural resting place, where she would have ended up in any case?" wrote W. Scott Thompson in his book, *The Philippines in Crisis.*

The second question is the more compelling, because Aquino was a member of the Philippines' richest landowning family and thus an aristocrat, whose family members include seven members of Congress, four of whom were serving under her stewardship (a brother, brother-in-law, cousin and uncle). She had substantial interests of her own and of her family to protect and defend. It is no accident that she chose to take the oath of office at the posh Club Filipinas, in one of Manila's richest enclaves, surrounded by her upper middle and upper class supporters?

As bluntly put by Thompson, "There was absolutely nothing in her intellectual or social preparation indicating the slightest interest in serious social reform." And indeed, during her six-year administration, no serious economic or social reforms were made. Economic problems and gross social inequity persisted throughout her presidency, which explains why no fewer than seven attempts to overthrow her government were made.

THE PHILIPPINES TODAY

The man responsible for putting down the seven rebellions that plagued Aquino's presidency became the nation's next president: Elected in 1992, Fidel V. Ramos was a former general known as "Steady Eddie," a man never seen without his trademark cigar. Born in 1928 and a 1950 graduate of West Point, Ramos' mother was Marcos' maternal aunt. Ramos was also the country's most decorated

Squatters bathe not far from Roxas Boulevard in downtown Manila.

soldier, with a reputation for getting things done. During Aquino's presidency, Ramos traveled from camp to camp, from group to group, talking her opponents down. Later, as president, he solved the country's electricity problem — which kept the main island of Luzon in darkness for up to 10 hours a day — by transferring control of the energy sector to private business; and he dismantled the monopolies and other regulations that had thwarted economic growth for decades. "In three years, Ramos achieved what Taiwan and Korea took two decades to do," said Srinivasa Madhur, an economist at the Asian Development Bank in Manila.

To revive the country's economy, Ramos has been selling off such onerous yet appealing government properties as Philippine Airlines and the Manila Hotel — loosening investment regulations, offering tax breaks and lowering interest rates. Foreign and local investors are grabbing whatever they can get, including clusters of islands, most of them uninhabited, which are up for sale. The former United States Army base in Manila is being converted to a mall and condominium complex. Meanwhile, Subic Bay Naval Base and Clark Air Force Base, back in Filipino hands, are being converted into an economic zone larger than Singapore, with ongoing construction, including two international airports, casinos, hotels, duty-free emporia and golf courses and resorts. Certainly, Manila reflects the sudden surge in affluence, with its slew of new hotels, massive malls, highrise office towers and "condotels."

To date, the Philippine economy has been growing nearly six percent each year under Ramos. "The Ramos-led reforms, which have transformed the Philippines from an inefficient inward looking country with protectionist barriers to an externally oriented and market driven economy, continue to bear fruit," says a report published in 1995 from the British-based Standard Chartered Bank.

Ramos' main instrument of economic reform has been revenue raising through taxes, which has increased the country's reserves and, in turn, has attracted more foreign investment. In 1994, Ramos won passage of an expanded value added tax, known as EVAT, intended to replace eight other taxes and contribute nearly US$500

million in revenue. The Philippine Supreme Court blocked implementation of EVAT until December 1995. On January 1, 1996, EVAT was put in operation, which instantly boosted retail prices by six percent. Since then, Ramos has been seeking to overhaul the tax code; the EVAT is not enough to raise the revenues needed to make improvements in education, ports, communication lines and roads. Ramos now wants to tax income, unpopular in a country that has traditionally relied on indirect taxes, such as duties from foreign trade. As Raul Concepcion, a

top industrialist said: "We need those tax reforms. When foreign investors see reserves begin to deteriorate, they will start to pull out. We have to take the bitter pills now, or we'll have a Mexican crisis by the end of 1998 (when presidential elections will be held)."

While Ramos has become the darling of regional investors — and the ruling class, the Spanish blooded and Filipino-Chinese elite of financiers and socialites — popular reaction to Ramos' economic reforms has been unfavorable. Because the EVAT issue had been apparently dormant since the 1994 Supreme Court injunction, millions were surprised when they were required to pay six percent more for everything starting January 1. A month later, in February 1996, Ramos raised oil prices by 10 percent without warning, in order to trim the government's US$40 million per month subsidy of petroleum products. In the midst of anti-Ramos rallies in that month, a poll was conducted in which 52 percent of those surveyed waxed nostalgic over the Marcos regime and said they would vote for Marcos today. Widespread poverty remains the reality for many Filipinos; the price of rice is crippling many families; meanwhile, the country has experienced an explosion of crime. Ramos admits that his reforms have not benefited most Filipinos, and perhaps many miss the illusion dispensed by Marcos that salvation was just around the corner.

In the Batasang Pambansa (the House of Representatives) the Honorable Imelda Marcos, hair lacquered and coifed as ever, is not only back from exile but has been elected to Congress and is a high profile representative for her home province of Leyte. Even her foes cannot be blind to the fact that her popularity was such that she won by a landslide. Only a fraction of the US$5 billion (some estimates go as high as US$10 billion) believed to have been misappropriated by the Marcos clan has ever been tracked down.

A major thorn in the body politic of the Philippines has been a violent civil war, centered in the southern island province of Mindanao where for the past 26 years Muslim separatists have waged their struggle for independence, a conflict that has left more than 150,000 dead. The guerrillas have complain that since the arrival of Moro (Muslim) settlers in the fifteenth century on the archipelago's southern islands, a succession of Spanish, American and Philippine colonists occupied the islands and have stolen their traditional lands. Certainly, since World War II, the Philippine government has enforced an aggressive settling policy that submerged the Moros and the indigenous tribal peoples of the south in a wave of northern migrants. A recent agreement brokered between Ramos and the Moro National Liberation Front (MNLF) may prove a crucial step for lasting peace. Under the agreement's terms, the MNLF's 20,000-strong rebel soldiers are to be gradually integrated into the Philippine Army; an independent executive legislature will be introduced; and Islamic education will be integrated into the school system. Other more militant Muslim groups, however, as well as the Christian majority in the region, have denounced the agreement.

These days, Ramos is spending a lot of time on the road — as he did also in the era of Aquino when his mission was to put down the various coups — landing by helicopter in remote townships and shouting his message on tax reform to wary crowds, as part of the lead up to the next elections in 1998. In the meantime, Representative

Pedro Romualdo, chairman of the committee on constitutional amendments, has filed, along with two other House members, a resolution calling for President Ramos to stay in office until the year 2000. In late May 1996, the Senate voted 17 to 0 against amending the constitution to allow Ramos to stay in office beyond 1998. This vote will not, however, stop members of the House of Representatives from endeavoring to amend the constitution. Ramos is saying nothing less cryptic than, "When my watch ends, that's it."

OPPOSITE: The Australian Go-Go Club, Ermita, Manila. The country saw many changes under "People Power" and the subsequent Ramos era, but Manila's raunchy nightlife remains untouched. ABOVE: The military contingent at the Independence Day celebrations, Manila.

Manila

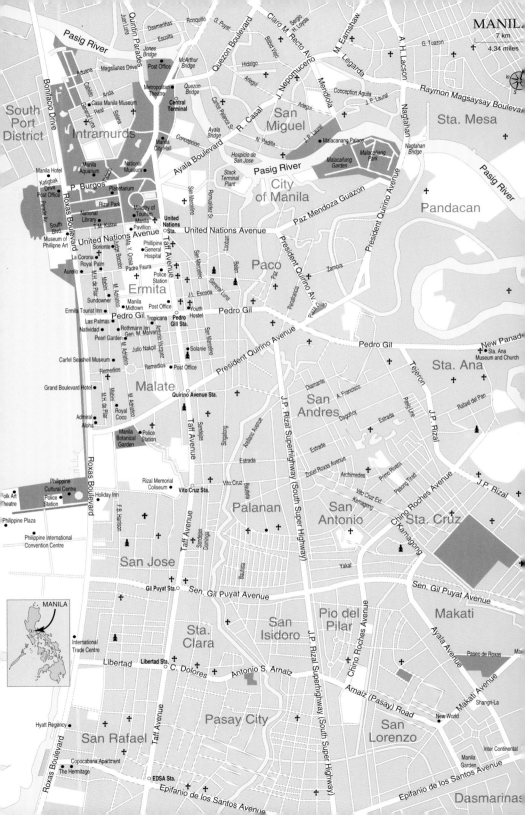

THE CITY OF MANILA wears its infamy like a badge. Home to some 10 million, this densely crowded concrete jungle has been much maligned. It has the poignant allure of a sad bar girl: excitement awaits you, but its pathos draws you in. After years of political and economic chaos, the capital also bore for some time the indignity of its somewhat clichéd yet persistent image as the brothel of Asia. This changed dramatically with the famous Snap Election and the People Power revolution in February 1986, which brought to an end the 20 years of the Marcos reign. When satellite images from Manila of almost a million determined and united citizens marching in defiance of armed tanks were beamed across the world, their spirit commanded respect and spread a wave of infectious revolutionary zeal.

James Fenton, in *The Snap Revolution*, described a scene he witnessed in the Malacañang Palace immediately after the Marcos family fled in a helicopter. On the street outside, a happy Filipino, with a whiskey glass in hand, confided in him: "You don't realize," he said, "how deep this goes. Nobody will call us cowards again. We've done it. We've had a peaceful revolution. We've beaten Poland."

Today, although not officially considered one of the Asian Tiger capitals, Manila is in hard training to fulfill that role and is the headquarters of the Asian Development Bank. The economy is booming, boasting the world's second fastest growing stock market (confounding many economists), foreign investment has been flowing in, new buildings are burgeoning in the affluent business neighborhood of Makati and the city is now liberally studded with five-star hotels to help consolidate its position as a regional leader.

Manila is in every way an extraordinary city, for all its arresting poverty and promises of wealth, a beacon for millions of rural Filipinos, dreaming of a better life from far away in the provinces. The city suffered more destruction from the ravages of World War II than even Dresden, so much so that most of the architectural legacy left by the Spanish has been obliterated. Despite its wholesale reconstruction, Manila retains a desultory aura of painful memories that it is only recently coming to terms with. It is hard not to empathize with a place that has endured so much.

Pico Iyer wrote in *Video Night In Kathmandu*: "Thus I left the Philippines. But the Philippines did not so easily leave me. For months, I could not get the country out of my head: it haunted me like a pretty, plaintive melody." Like Iyer, most visitors will remember Manila in a series of discrete, perhaps diffuse, images and moments: the luminosity of the sunset across Manila Bay, with its almost technicolor hues, melting into

the South China Sea; stumbling into a thirteenth century graveyard in the shadow of skyscrapers; society matrons with bouffant hairdos eating bibingka cakes in coffeeshops; Spanish churches with gold-encrusted icons; life in the squatter communities around the khaki-colored, poisonous Pasig River; and even CNN featured dancing traffic officers at congested intersections.

The city began as small, but prosperous hamlet alongside the banks of the Pasig River, near the mouth of Manila Bay. The settlement was surrounded by flowering mangrove plants, or *nilad,* and was thus called "Maynilad" or the place where the nilad grows. It was later called Manila by the Spanish who arrived in 1571 and established the site as the seat of their Asian empire, constructing the inner city fortress of Intramuros.

To a newcomer's eye, Manila indeed deserves the description of a "shapeless, confused and unrelievedly twentieth century mess strung out along a reeking bay," made

A taxi weaving its way through Ermita, Manila.

of it by James Hamilton-Paterson in *Playing with Water*. One of the most perceptive foreign writers on the Philippines, Hamilton-Paterson observes wryly that "the Manila which ex-President Marcos left in late February 1986, was like the man himself, a notorious mixture of wealth and decay."

Hamilton-Paterson continues: "In the late seventies and early eighties — that is to say, the declining years of the Marcos dynasty — the country appeared to be superficially in a state of stable anarchy brought about by the rigors of martial law and the untrammeled freedom of public officials to do pretty much what they liked. In this strange political half-life, Manila had some of the high, wild, *fin de saison* qualities ascribed to other famous cities under regimes in their lapsarian days, Batista's Havana, Faroukh's Cairo, even Mussolini's Salo."

Since then, Manila been trying to tighten its belt. Under the stern, reformist captaincy of President Fidel Ramos, the city is striving to put itself in the future tense. Made up of 10 cities — Manila itself, Quezon, Pasay, Makati, Pasig, Parañaque, Las Piñas, Muntinlupa, Mandaluyong and Caloocan — Metro Manila is full of contradictions. It derives much of its admirable civic order from the predominant Catholicism of its citizens, yet has a soaring crime rate with frequent kidnappings, armed robberies and commissioned murders.

On the reclaimed foreshore alongside Roxas Boulevard, the monuments created by former First Lady and now Congress member, Imelda Marcos are still regarded with pride by the average Manileño, despite having been built largely with funds earmarked for alleviating the nation's poverty. In the upper class residential enclaves of Forbes Park, Dasmarinas Village and Wack Wack, spacious villas and swimming pools are surrounded by shrub-shrouded security guards and barbed wire, while the slum dwellers who squeeze themselves into cheap concrete caverns, burned out ruins and cardboard sheeting face a future as bleak as ever.

Intramuros — TOP: Memorare Manila 1945. BOTTOM and OVERLEAF: San Augustín Church, the country's oldest stone church, dating from 1571.

GENERAL INFORMATION

Department of Tourism Head Office ((2) 599-031-048 FAX (2) 501-567, T. M. Kalaw Street, Rizal Park; **Department of Tourism Branch Office** ((2) 832-2964, Ninoy Aquino International Airport, Pasay City.

Philippine Convention and Visitor Corporation ((2) 525-9318 to 32 FAX (2) 521-6165, Fourth Floor, Units 5, 7 and 10-17, Legazpi Towers 300, Roxas Boulevard. Make sure you pick up the excellent and informative *Islands Philippines* series of maps and pamphlets published by the Philippine Convention and Visitor Corporation.

Tourist Assistance 24-Hour Hotline ((2) 501-728 or (2) 501-660.

WHAT TO SEE AND DO

INTRAMUROS

Manila's architectural layers spill out across its seams in a contradictory muddle. Formidable traces remain of the sixteenth century wall constructed by the colonizing Spanish. **Intramuros** — (literally, "within the walls") was an impregnable, five-sided bastion that contained a hive of ecclesiastical buildings, palaces, a university, schools, a printing press, government buildings, hospitals and barracks as well as grand Iberian mansions, all surrounded by *puertas* (gates), *baluartes* (battlements) and a moat. Only Spaniards and Spanish mestizos were allowed to live inside — drawbridges went up each night. Despite the ravages of earthquakes and wartime bombing, many grand husks and ramparts of the former stone citadel remain. Restoration and reconstruction work is ongoing by the Intramuros Administration, with many of the original gates — including the **Puerta Isabel II** and the **Puerta Real** gates — walls and cobblestone streets being repaired. Starting from Puerta Real, where the drained moat has been transformed into the city's golf course, you can wander for just over four kilometers (two and a half miles) around the walls of Intramuros, which are six meters (20 ft) high and 13 m (43 ft) thick.

Inside the city's walls, overlooking the mouth of the Pasig River, it's possible to ex-

plore **Fort Santiago** whose history is mired in brutality. From its bastion, Miguel Lopez de Legazpi, the mastermind of the Spanish colonization of the Philippines, surveyed the construction of Intramuros. The fort was the headquarters of the Spanish military, which was ousted by British troops in 1762 and later by Filipino Tayabas soldiers in 1843. Yet it withstood attacks by the Dutch and the Portuguese, as well as Sulu pirates. With its interrogation rooms, rat-infested hold-alls and infamous dungeons below high tide level, this was a place of terror and death through-

his legendary — or as some say, mythical — gold here. In 1988, with President Aquino's permission, American treasure hunters painstakingly searched and partially excavated Fort Santiago looking for clues, but nothing was uncovered. The fort is open between 8 AM and 10 PM — although wandering around its battlements at night is not advised.

Also within the remains of the fort, the open-air **Rajah Sulayman Theater** is a venue from December to June for staging Filipino plays in Tagalog. Beneath the theater complex, there is a quirky **museum of vintage**

out the centuries. It was here that the revolutionary hero José Rizal was incarcerated for two months on charges of rebellion and sedition before his execution by the Spanish in 1896. His cell is now the **Rizal Museum**. It is open daily from 9 AM to noon and 1 PM to 5 PM. His final poem, "Mi Ultimo Adios" (My Last Farewell) was written here and smuggled out of his cell in the base of an oil lamp.

Americans ran the fort after 1898, and it was an operational base for General MacArthur from 1936 to 1941. When the Japanese took Manila, the next violent chapter in the fort's history began. Some 600 bodies were later discovered beneath the bastion of San Lorenzo. Rumors had persisted that the Japanese General Yamashita may have hidden

cars — those used by General MacArthur and past Filipino presidents.

As you walk away from Fort Santiago, crossing General Luna Street, you will pass through **Plaza Roma**, a popular bullfighting arena during the eighteenth century and now the site for a modernist statue, by Filipino artist Solomon Saprid, in homage to the three Filipino priests, Gomez, Burgos and Zamora, who were accused of leading an anti-Spanish revolt and were publicly garroted in 1872, sparking revolution. The Plaza Roma is bounded by the **Palacio del Gobernador**, the residence of the Spanish governor-general from 1660 to 1863, which is now, despite the ravages of earthquake damage, a sturdy complex of government buildings.

Regarded as one of the most imposing church buildings in the Philippines, the **Manila Cathedral** is the sixth built on this site and was itself rebuilt between 1954 and 1958 with the assistance of Vatican funds. The original cathedral was constructed in 1571, and some original walls were incorporated from this and other past incarnations of the church. The main door holds bronze bas-relief panels depicting the cathedral's history. Inside, immediately noticeable is Filipino artist Galo Ocampo's dramatic series of stained glass windows which tell the story of the Madonna's life and portray her in various regional Filipina costumes. Beneath the main altar the remains of past Spanish and Filipino archbishops are entombed in a crypt. The Dutch organ, with its 4,500 pipes, is one of the largest in Asia. The cathedral's congregation is majestically presided over by Manila's controversial archbishop, Cardinal Jaime Sin, known for his decisive role in the People Power revolution. In 1987, Cardinal Sin set up an ecclesiastical museum to present the history of the Catholic Church in the Philippines — the **Archdiocesan Museum of Manila** is nearby at 121 Arzobispo Street.

Several blocks away on Calle Real, **San Agustín Church** is the country's oldest stone church and dates from 1571. It is built in High Renaissance, Mexican-influenced style, with Doric and Corinthian columns, while Augustinian motifs of an arrow pierced heart and a bishop's mitre decorate its grand portals, which are carved out of native molave wood. Also look for the Chinese guardian lions. Inside, a baroque pulpit and wrought-iron door are impressive. Fourteen side chapels line the nave, with a tomb and effigy of Legazpi to the left of the main altar. Here are found the remains of the great Spanish conquistadores — Legazpi, Martin de Goti, Juan de Salcedo. These and an assortment of early governors and archbishops lie in a communal vault. The ceiling, which looks like a bas-relief, is actually a *trompe l'œil*, created by a pair of Italian artists in 1875. The church was the only structure within Intramuros to survive the 1945 bombing.

Adjoining San Agustín, the **Monastery Museum** has an extraordinarily rich collection of Philippine artifacts and religious art, despite being plundered during wartime

years. It was here, in the vestry of the monastery complex, that Spain formally ceded to the United States in 1898, marking the final act of the Spanish-American War. Many prominent families in Manila's early colonial history were buried within the **Pantheon**. The peaceful, **cloistered garden** to one side was planted during the eighteenth century by the Augustinian botanist, Father Manual Blanco. One of the more dramatic incidents in the history of the monastery occurred during the battle for Manila in February 1945 — some 7,000 civilians fled here in hope of sanc-

tuary while the fierce artillery battle between Japanese and American forces raged. Intramuros was the site of the most brutal Japanese opposition and few escaped the orgy of violence that occurred here.

Just off the **Plaza San Luis**, across the road from the San Agustín Church, is the **Casa Manila**, a reconstructed nineteenth century colonial mansion, its intereior crammed with period furniture and adorned with charming archways and a stone fountain. The Casa Manila complex includes the restaurant **Barbara's Intramuros** as well as a small café and some antique and curio shops good for browsing. Casa Manila is open daily, except Monday from 9 AM to noon and 1 PM to 6 PM. Closing time during the weekend is 7 PM. Further along Calle Real is the four-story crafts complex **Silahi's Arts and Artifacts**.

Reached through the Puerta Real, the 58-hectare (143-acre) **Rizal Park** (also called Luneta Park after the crescent-shaped

Intramuros — OPPOSITE: San Agustín's Monastery Museum offering rich pickings from the days of Spanish colonial rule. ABOVE: Fort Santiago.

Manila

99

redoubt near Manila Bay) is a calm respite from traffic streamsing along Taft Avenue down to Roxas Boulevard. It has a desultory, tropical charm, dotted with acacia trees and fringed by horse-drawn calesas. During the day it is where the city stretches its limbs: a gathering place for meandering families, t'ai chi ch'uan practitioners, joggers, off-duty workers. By night it is the haunt of would-be lovers or would-be muggers. Regardless of the hour, there are always hawkers selling fresh coconuts, balloons, improbable toys or jasmine flower necklaces. During the

THE MANILA HOTEL

Bordering Rizal Park, the Manila Hotel is a mainstay of Manila life. When it first opened in 1912, the hotel was the social center of the booming industry that accompanied the Americanization of the Philippines. With its grand, California-Mission-style exterior and interior intricately paneled with warm Philippine narra mahogany, the hotel soon became a sort of exclusive club for the elite diaspora of colonizing and traveling Ameri-

People Power uprising, many thousands of protesters gathered. The most prominent landmark within the park is the **Rizal Monument**. Opposite is an **obelisk** marking the site where native priests Gomez, Burgos and Zamora were executed. On the same spot where Rizal was shot by firing squad in 1898, a sound and light show re-enacts the event with life-size statues and a recorded narrative. There are Chinese and Japanese gardens, a playground and a skating rink. Also nearby is a duck pond with the Philippine Archipelago rendered in concrete. On one side of the park, on Padre Burgos Street, is the **National Museum**, worth seeing for its archaeological exhibits, ethnological artifacts and natural history collection.

cans — entrepreneurs, politicians, military personnel and engineers among them. Much unofficial business was and continues to be, conducted at the hotel's bayside bar. Initially, social and racial barriers in the new society meant that Filipinos were neither welcomed nor made to feel comfortable here, unlike the mestizos who made up the wealthy landowning class, a divide that lingered on until the time when Manuel Quezon became President of the new Philippine Commonwealth in 1935 and instituted social policy reforms.

Ever since the Manila Hotel was reopened with great fanfare by the Marcoses in 1977 (Imelda orchestrated much of the interior design), it has continued to be the most exclusive place for private dinners, weddings and conferences — despite the mushrooming of many other, more obviously extravagant hotels in the city. Any Filipina society matron worth her salt will express profound nostalgia for the memories of the **Champagne Room** or the **Fiesta Ballroom** during the 1950s and 1960s, where lovely Filipinas clad in *ternos*, or hand-embroidered gowns, would compete for attention and dance the rigodon with partners dressed sharkskin suits or barongs and "tango shoes." The corps of international journalists who converged on Manila during the time of the Snap Elec-

ministers and dignitaries including Emperor Akihito of Japan. The Duke of Windsor, the Rockefellers, Henry Luce, Marlon Brando, Ernest Hemingway, Tyrone Power, Bob Hope and the Beatles have all been guests. All this and more is documented in the hotel's Archive Room, open daily.

The story behind the hotel's MacArthur Suite is a chapter in the history of Manila. When General MacArthur was invited by Philippine President Quezon to become military advisor and create a Philippine Army in the 1935, one of the American

tion and the People Power revolt in February 1986 have equally nostalgic memories of the heady, chaotic days spent here: at the time, the hotel was the unofficial press center, with some of the television networks taking over large sections of it. Later that year, in July, the hotel became the target of a "mini-coup" when it was taken over for several days by armed Marcos loyalists along with some 5,000 civilians.

The hotel has seen many famous people come and go. American presidents Dwight Eisenhower (then a young major in the staff of General Douglas MacArthur), Lyndon Johnson, Richard Nixon and more recently, Bill Clinton, have stayed here, among a long list of international presidents, prime

general's conditions for acceptance was that he be provided with living quarters to equal the elegance and comfort of Malacañang Palace. This request resulted in the construction of a penthouse suite for the General and his family atop the fifth floor of the old Manila Hotel. MacArthur, his wife Jean and son Arthur, lived here between 1935 and 1941. In December 1941, as the Japanese invaded, this became the command post. Unable to hold off the advancing forces, MacArthur retreated to Corregidor. In a twist of fate soon after that, when Manila was declared an

OPPOSITE: For the elite, the Champagne Room Restaurant, Manila Hotel. ABOVE: One of Imelda Marcos' premier *œuvres*, the Cultural Center, Manila.

Open City by the Japanese, the Manila Hotel became the headquarters of the Japanese army lead by the "Tiger of Malaya," General Yamashita. The next time the MacArthurs saw their old home in 1945, the hotel was a bombed-out shell.

THE MANILA BAYFRONT

Alongside Roxas Boulevard and Manila Bay are an array of some of Imelda Marcos' vast "beautification projects," financed in part by large international loans.

Theater, with an abstract Ocampo-designed curtain and the **Little Theater**, which presents chamber music and plays in Tagalog, either in their original versions by Filipino authors or as adaptations from foreign plays.

Close by, the **Philippine Convention Center**, usually a conference hall but also used for rock concerts, was inaugurated for the 1974 International Monetary Fund–World Bank Conference. The **Contemporary Art Museum of the Philippines** has a permanent collection of Philippine modern and contemporary sculpture, paintings and other

It is said that up to 10 percent of the total cost of some of these projects went into kickbacks. During the late 1970s, in her role as Governor of Metro Manila, Imelda developed an obsession with building grand status symbols, a mania that Filipino wits dubbed Imelda's "edifice complex." The **Cultural Center of the Philippines** (CCP) gathers together Philippine ethnological treasures along with works by modern artists. Its theaters, as well as the **Folk Arts Theater** nearby, are intended to provide a showcase for both Filipino and international performers. You can pick up a schedule of events. There are seven theaters and six resident companies performing dance, drama and music. The venues at the CCP Complex include the **Main**

visual arts dating back to 1910. Also on this patch of reclaimed land are the **Design Center of the Philippines** and the **Philippine Center for Trade and Exhibitions**. Here, the full spectrum of Filipino artistry is on display: weaving, woodcarving, shellcraft, jewelry making and metalwork. Next door, the **Coconut Palace** is an unusual, attractive mansion entirely inspired by and fashioned out of the coconut tree. Guided tours in English are conducted every half hour from 9 AM to 11 AM and from 1 PM to 4 PM daily except Monday.

Within the same stretch of reclaimed land is the infamous **Manila Film Center**. Conceived by Imelda in 1981, this was to be a grand Parthenon-style showcase for the first

Manila International Film Festival. Contractors were given seven months to complete the shopping-mall-size building, and the First Lady was personally in charge of the project's supervision which had a round-the-clock timetable. At 2:35 AM on November 17, 1981, the top story of the partially completed building fell through. Hasty construction had not allowed the concrete sufficient time to set. Hundreds of day shift workers were sleeping beneath the viewing theater's atrium, and night shift workers were toiling on the scaffolding above. Many were killed instantly; some were trapped and suffocated by the drying concrete; some were rescued by their fellow workers from air pockets and stairwells up to 24 hours after the accident. Orders from Malacañang insisted that the rescue operation be halted and that construction continue without delay. Security personnel cordoned off the site, and the next day newspapers reported that only a minor accident had occurred with two fatalities. Bulldozers arrived to push the mangled remains of bodies, concrete and rubble from the site, fresh concrete was poured in, and the appalling stench grew fainter. No one is sure how many died—but workers on site, who could list their missing colleagues, thought it was over 200.

The Manila International Film Festival went ahead, inaugurated with great fanfare by Imelda, but was never repeated. Within two years the Film Center was screening uncensored pornographic films in attempt recoup some of its costs. Abandoned now and rumored to be haunted, it awaits some unspecified future use.

ACROSS THE PASIG RIVER

North of the Pasig River are some of Manila's most densely populated, vibrant and historic neighborhoods, bustling with street life and encompassing some compelling detours within their limits.

Chinatown
An atmospheric, clannish Oriental warren of shops, stalls, temples and restaurants, Chinatown is not to be missed. You can spend hours wandering through its small alleys, browsing through shops selling Chinese pottery, handcrafted gold and jade jewelry and traditional medicines. Its well-stocked Chinese supermarkets, tiny teahouses, mahjong parlors, large chopstick-clattering dim sum halls, pet shops, kung fu institutes and Buddhist shrines smoky with incense create an atmosphere found nowhere else in the city.

There are several good Chinese restaurants tucked away here. In general, Chinese cuisine is predominantly Cantonese in bigger restaurants, Hokkien (where most

Chinese in the Philippines come from) in smaller ones, with a scattering of Hunan, Peking, Szechuan and Shanghai restaurants to be found as well.

Chinatown encompasses parts of the districts of Santa Cruz and Binondo and is bounded by three huge **Welcome Gates**. You can get your bearings by beginning your walk at **Ongpin Street** which runs east to west. It is the main business street, and branching off it are many beckoning alleys which snake throughout the quarter. **Binondo Church**, near the Plaza Calderon

OPPOSITE: A plethora of religious items are always on offer at Quiapo Church, Manila, one of the most important centers for Catholic pilgrimage.
ABOVE: The chaotic color of Chinatown, Manila.

de la Barca, is imposing. Built in 1596, it was severely damaged during earthquakes and wartime bombing. Only the octagonal bell tower on the present structure is original. Directly across from the church is a distinctive Chinese-style bridge, which leads across a canal, and a curious fire station contructed in the style of a pagoda.

By a twist of the city's fate, the former fashionable street of Manila's Spanish era still exists under its own name — **Escolta**. It is on the fringes of Chinatown and is a listless collection of rather dusty shops and proletar-

ian restaurants. Nevertheless, it is a segment of the city's living history in which something of an Iberian atmosphere still lingers on.

Quiapo
Named after the water lily, *klyapo*, this cramped, bustling district — a short walk from Rizal Avenue — is worth visiting to see the life that hums around the shrine of the Black Nazarene in **Quiapo Church**. Outside, pavement fakirs, hawkers, herbalists, fortunetellers and craftspeople gather daily in a swelter of makeshift stalls. It's fun to browse and hear stories about the potions, *anting-anting*, or amulets, and medicinal drinks — and you may be lucky enough to discover an unusual curio or antique bargain.

Inside the Mexican-baroque-style church, reconstructed in 1935, the famous **Shrine of the Black Nazarene** has a history immersed in Spanish lore. The life-size statue of Christ was carved in Mexico by Indians and transported, in the seventeenth century, to the Philippines by the Spaniards who fervently believed in the statue's miraculous powers. Each day, although especially on Fridays, the shrine attracts hundreds of the faithful. One of the more dramatic occasions to attend here is the procession of the Black Nazarene on January 9. This is procession is the climax of the shrine's adoration held on the Monday and Friday of Passion Week (the week before Easter between Passion Sunday and Palm Sunday).

Plaza Miranda, opposite Quiapo Church, is a popular gathering point for both entertainment and political rallies. Many large anti-Marcos rallies started at Plaza Miranda, one of which was fired upon, before ex-President Marcos declared martial law in 1972.

In the same area, you can visit the unusual, neo-Gothic-style, steel fabricated **San Sebastian Church** built on the site of three previous churches. The first was founded in 1621; all of them were destroyed by earthquakes. The current structure was built by Recollect Fathers in 1891 who, determined that this one survive, imported prefabricated steel from Belgium. The formidable structure, inspired by the fourteenth century Gothic cathedral of Burgos in Spain, has two soaring openwork towers and vaulted steel. Despite the its heavy contruction, the building has a touch of airy insubstantiality by virtue of its charming stained glass windows.

Opposite San Sebastian Church stands the **University of the East**. Also worth visiting in this area is the underpass market (Ilalim ng Tulay) below **Quezon Bridge**. Here you will find with dozens of stalls selling a wide variety of wares such as capiz lamps, rattan bags and other handicrafts.

East of Quezon Boulevard is Manila's **Muslim quarter**, which has a 60-year-old gold-domed mosque, along with a few Muslim restaurants and coffee houses. The Arab-style bazaar nearby is a good place to buy Indonesian batik, Pakistani cloth and Egyptian perfumes.

SANTA CRUZ AND LA LOMA

Sprawling, residential **Santa Cruz** and **La Loma** are vibrant neighborhoods full of streetlife and markets — with several compelling sights within their limits. **Santa Cruz Church**, originally built in 1608 by Jesuit Spaniards for Chinese converts, stands on Plaza Locsin. Within Santa Cruz, **Central Market** is full of lively stalls, with sections for textiles, cheap clothing, baskets and all kinds of foodstuffs. In La Loma, you'll see

cozy, surrounded by icons of former lives — even telephones and fax machines. Most shrines contain black and white photographs of the deceased in their youthful prime, set about with scraps of red paper, burning joss sticks and supplies of favorite food and drink for feast days and anniversaries. Often maintained by caretakers, some of whom live in the building, many of these tombs are supplied with electricity, running water and some even run to air conditioning. The old riddle, "Would you rather be a dead Chinese or a live Filipino?" to which

rows of mounted roast pigs turning on rotisserie sticks awaiting buyers on Calavite Street. Nearby, Manila's bird hustlers crowd around on the hour to watch cock fighting in the **La Loma ring**, where the unfortunate creatures fight each other to the death with razors inserted in their claws.

Like Cairo's City of the Dead, the astonishing **Chinese Cemetery** (founded in the 1850s) is an eerie replica of a well-kept suburb with tombs for the dead on a grand scale. Here, house-size — and sometimes palace-size — tombs and crypts are maintained to preserve the spirits of their inhabitants. They stand on well-swept, signposted roads; some have gardens and letter boxes. As you stroll, you'll see that tombs are often

Manileños don't really expect an answer, alludes to the juxtaposition of the superiorly appointed and serviced tombs to the largely unserviced shanty towns of the living which surround the cemetery. Society's pecking order is also evident in the range of tombs — rows of grandiose marble "mansions" contrast with eccentric, individualistic shrines. In some cases, Catholics have requested burial here. The impecunious are relegated to a sweeping bank in the cemetery's exterior walls containing thousands of tiny burial niches.

It is easy to lose yourself in the many alleys that branch through the cemetery. You may

OPPOSITE: Preparing for a furtive cockfight, Pasay City, Manila. ABOVE: Herbarium in Quiapo.

find it useful — and safer — to hire a guide to lead you through, but agree on a price beforehand. Those in a hurry can drive around the perimeters and through the main boulevards.

After this visit, you may have had enough of cemeteries. Yet **North Cemetery**, nearby in La Loma, is also interesting and historic. Many wealthy Spanish and Filipino families are buried here and there are some impressive mausoleums — one includes two pyramids and a sphinx. As with the Chinese Cemetery, it is not advisable to

come here on your own — it too has become home to a large squatter community.

Also in the area, the **University of Santo Tomas** resonates with history. Although the original Dominican university was founded in 1611 and lies within Intramuros, this private, well-regarded campus dates from 1927. Key figures in the history of the Philippine revolutionary movement were educated here: José Rizal, Marcelo H. del Pilar, A. Mabini and Emilio Aguinaldo; the three martyred priests Burgos, Gomez and Zamora and presidents Quezon, Osmena and Macapagal. During the Japanese occupation from 1942, the campus was used as an internment camp for Allied citizens, its survivors released three years later when American troops

swept through the city. Within the university, the **Museum of Natural Science** displays an extensive and rare collection that offers insights into the archaeological, anthropological and other scientific discoveries of the region — including a collection of rare and ancient pottery.

MALACAÑANG PALACE

The white and mahogany-fretted Spanish-style mansion built in the late nineteenth century has housed several previous presidents and, before them, American governors-general. But most visitors are drawn here because for 20 years this was the home of the Marcos clan. "You want to go to Malacañang?" said my taxi driver, chortling. "You want to see Imelda's shoe collection?" Like many locals and visitors to the palace, the taxi driver was not aware that, like other controversial swathes of Manila, Malacañang has been cleaned up under President Ramos. Today, a wing is dedicated to unfolding the history of the Philippine democratic tradition, with rooms displaying the personal memorabilia of each past president.

When the residence was first opened to the public in the immediate aftermath of the departure of the Marcos family, it was proclaimed an unofficial "museum of greed." It attracted thousands of curious Filipinos and foreign visitors alike. Throughout her presidential term, Corazon Aquino left the palace essentially as it was, fulfilling a campaign promise, maintaining it as a symbol of the staggering corruption associated with her predecessor.

During the Marcos era, millions of dollars were spent remodeling the palace into a passable imitation of a Disneyesque Versailles. Walls and floors were covered with Italian marble and Persian carpets. Huge French mirrors abounded. Rooms were strewn with reproduction Louis XIV period furniture, English antique furniture, Aubusson tapestries and Chinese treasures. A discotheque complete with a waterfall was created and paintings of the First Couple and their offspring — some by the same artist favored by the Reagans — were prominently displayed. Imelda's red-carpeted bedroom was the most luxurious in the palace. Designated the "Queen's Room," a carved coronet billowing with tulle topped her bed. The scope of Imelda's wardrobe and adornments — including some 3,000 pairs of shoes and 2,000 ballgowns — were reputedly enough to stock a large department store. Imelda is remembered vividly across the world's temples to fashion, from the Via Condotti in Rome and Avenue Foch in Paris to New York's Fifth Avenue and Los Angeles' Rodeo Drive, running up the nation's external debt for her wardrobe.

Because of the failing health of Ferdinand Marcos, the once gracious and airy palace was hermetically sealed — to block the wafting stench of the Pasig River and the barrios that flanked it. The palace also bore all the marks of illness — with a fully operational hospital clinic set up off the ex-President's bedroom. The equipment has since been donated to a Manila hospital. It was from Malacañang that the Marcoses fled by helicopter on February 25, 1986. Two hours later, thousands of exhilarated Filipinos stormed through the gates and gaped incredulously at the lofty rooms filled with paintings by old masters — not to mention at Imelda's gold washbasin, giant perfume bottles and naturally, the shoes.

Anyone who saw Malacañang Palace in the early days of its post-Marcos state will barely recognize it now, since so little of Imelda's fantasy palace remains. Many of Marcos' spoils — including the famous shoe collection — are stored in a semi-display state in the basement chambers awaiting adjudication. It is difficult to get permission to view this section of the palace, but it is worth persisting, for it provides a fascinating insight into the psyches of the Marcoses, especially Imelda. Ask the ticket officer or tour guide for advice about to access. The entrance to the Malacañang Palace Museum is on José P. Laurel Street, San Miguel. On official occasions the palace and the museum are closed to the public.

During the eighteenth century, San Miguel was where the Filipino gentry built their summer residences and the area — surrounded by security checkpoints — contains some buildings reminiscent of nineteenth century colonial Spain. Close to Malaca-

ñang, seek out **San Beda Chapel**, lined with paintings, murals and carved wood. Nearby **Mendiola Bridge**, which spans a small canal, became a symbol of protest when it was the scene of many clashes between riot police and demonstrators during the People Power uprising.

ERMITA

Known for years to experienced Asia travelers as "the strip," the tourist belt of Ermita was synonymous with raunchy nightlife: a

zoo of sex trade fauna, riddled with go-go bars, massage parlors, beer stalls, peep shows and, for the unlucky, venereal disease clinics. It was also the seat of the so-called "Malate Mafia" which controlled the city's underworld and trafficked in sleazy prostitution and pedophile rackets, drugs and most other known forms of vice.

Since the post-Marcos era, reformists have stepped in and Ermita has changed. Now much of its seedier and red light tinged nightlife has migrated to Pasay and Quezon City. The main force behind the clean-up of Ermita is Mayor Alberto Lim, also an influential businessman.

Ermita is colorful, far more redolent of the old Manila than Makati, and it's a haven for cheap hotels, curio shops and restaurants — most tucked around Remedios Circle and Adriatico Street — attracting tourists, expatriates and young, hip locals.

OPPOSITE: Cushy homes in Manila's smart Ermita district. ABOVE: Art on the streets. OVERLEAF: The well-tended American Cemetery, Makati, last resting place for over 17,000 World War II casualties.

MAKATI

Makati is where moneyed Manileños work by day and play by night. As the capital's expanding commercial center, it is almost a city in its own right. Megalopolis-type glass office towers, corporation headquarters, hotels and malls are rapidly consuming the teeming barrios at its outer limits. Designer shops are everywhere and the malls have an endless array of corridors bursting with opulence. For visitors, this is the place to do

business or wander in the neon-lit concrete alleys at night in search of a good meal and entertainment. Like a newly transplanted heart valve, the synthetic culture of Makati beats out a pulse that is quite different to that of, say, Intramuros or Ermita, with their heady whiffs of bygone eras. Makati glitters and beckons, a skin-deep version of Manila, with slick bars and restaurants which take cues from Bangkok and Hong Kong.

Aside from hotels, restaurants and shopping malls, there are a few places to visit in Makati of historical interest, as well as a museum and some parks and gardens. The **Church of Our Lady of Guadalupe** overlooks the Pasig River near the San Carlos Seminary and is quite lovely with its antique

stone façade, ornate interiors and shady cobbled courtyard. The **Ayala Museum of Philippine History and Iconographic Archives** on Makati Avenue contains a remarkable display of some 60 dioramas portraying key events in the nation's history — from pivotal moments in the Spanish-American War to graphic World War II scenarios and right through the tumultuous events leading up to the People Power revolution in 1986. Don't overlook the exhibition of ancient Asian boats which have sailed in Philippine seas or the museum shop, which has a good stock of ethnic crafts and art pieces. The **American Cemetery and Memorial** at Fort Bonifacio, in Makati, is the largest American burial ground outside the United States. Here, in rank and file, are buried 17,000 soldiers who died in the Philippines and surrounding Pacific during World War II. In the circular memorial are numerous photographs and montages of famous battles in the Pacific. The cemetery lies two kilometers (one and a quarter miles) from where Ayala Avenue meets Epifanio de los Santos Avenue (EDSA).

QUEZON CITY

The former capital of the Philippines, Quezon City is named after its founder, Manuel Quezon the first President of the Philippine Commonwealth. Four times the size of Manila, Quezon is a city unto itself, divided up into suburban housing estates or "projects", wealthy residential complexes and dotted with swimming pools, golf courses, hospitals and churches. Its center is **Cubao**, a maze of shopping malls and department stores, restaurants, cinemas, fast food joints as well as busy farmer's and seafood markets. This is where off-duty Manileños throng to spend their leisure hours, watching sporting events at the giant **Araneta Coliseum**. The **Museo ng Buhay Filipino** (Museum of Filipino Life), in the Central Bank building on East Avenue, is worth a visit if you are in the area, but it is not sufficiently compelling to warrant a detour.

University of the Philippines

"UP," as most Filipinos call the University of the Philippines, is considered to be the most prestigious school in the country. Located in the large campus in Diliman, Quezon City, the state university has many distinguished former alumni, including former presidents. The **University of the Philippines Museum** has an interesting display of ethnic artifacts from tribal communities.

NAYONG PILIPINO

Close to the Ninoy Aquino International Airport, the Nayong Pilipino, or Philippine Village, recreates the nation's cultural mosaic with representative architectural styles; it's is an interesting and educational visit. Nayong Pilipino more than lives up to its stated aim of being a "living museum." Set within a 46-hectare (114-acre) park are replicas of village houses from throughout the Philippines, concentrating on the six main regions — Cordillera, Ilocos, Mindanao, Visayas, Bicol and Tagalog. Each house contains examples of the region's arts and crafts. There are also well-known landmarks from each region, recreated in miniature, such as the Banaue Rice Terraces, Cebu's Magellan Cross, Bicol's Mayon Volcano and the colorfully decorated houses of Samal in Mindanao. Especially appealing, it is possible to find a range of indigenous handicrafts from all over the country — such as ikat cloth, jewelry, bags, brassware and carved wood — that you are unlikely to find in such profusion in anywhere else in the Philippines.

The Nayong Pilipino also has an aviary, an aquarium and an orchidarium (with more than 50 species of native orchids). Perhaps most interesting and unusual, at the **Philippine Museum of Ethnology** located here, actors clad in the ethnic costumes of different Philippine regions and tribes wander around and interact with visitors. You can also participate in the lectures given here and learn how to put on the Muslim garment called *malong*, beat the kulintang gongs or coax music from an Ifugao nose flute. The museum showcases a fine collection of ethnological specimens of ancient arts such as of carving, weaving, weaponry and crafted ornaments. It is well worth planning your visit to coincide with a performance of the **Nayong Pilipino Dance Troupe**. A repertoire of regional dances are offered at the

Mindanao Pavilion at 2:30 PM and 4 PM every Saturday and Sunday. Films on Philippine culture and ethnology are screened at the Philippine Museum of Ethnology from Tuesday to Friday at 10 AM and 3 PM as well as Saturday and Sunday from 10 AM and 5 PM. To get to Nayong Pilipino, take a taxi or bus from the main thoroughfare of Epifanio de los Santos Avenue (EDSA) to the main village's entrance on Ninoy Aquino Avenue. Within the premises, colorful jeepneys take you to any point in the grounds free of charge.

SMOKY MOUNTAIN

During the Marcos regime, the ultimate symbol of the dictator's callous indifference to Manila's suffering was Smoky Mountain, a fuming 21-hectare (52-acre) pile of garbage alongside Manila Bay. It is here that some 15,000 people eked out an existence — scavenging and squatting in makeshift hovels on the filthy heap. Yet Smoky Mountain continued to smolder for almost nine years after Marcos had gone. In 1994 President Fidel Ramos decided to "clean-up" Smoky Mountain — and announced that the huge

OPPOSITE: Makati, commercial and business hub of Manila. ABOVE: Nayong Pilipino, the Philippine Village, created for visitors, on the outskirts of Manila.

garbage slum would be bulldozed and transformed into a US$650 million port, factory and incinerator complex, with apartment blocks as well. Its residents would be rehoused and given training for more dignified professions, after which they would be offered permanent housing in the rehabilitated complex.

The plan has not been entirely successful, although Smoky Mountain is almost gone. When police came to relocate the squatters, they put up a battle in which one person was killed. The new housing site and

complex, complete with library, nursery and vocational centers, is all but empty. Apparently, it can be more profitable to make a living sifting and sorting through garbage than engaging in somewhat cleaner occupations, and many squatters were reluctant to give up the lifestyle. Some residents have now moved to the Payatas dump across town that is rapidly taking on Smokey's likeness. In February 1996, *Time* magazine ran an article saying that many of Smoky Mountain's former residents badly miss their old home.

WHERE TO STAY

Manila has some of Asia's finest — and in the case of the Manila Hotel, most historic

— hotels where you can be pampered in five-star luxury. There are also plenty of moderately priced and inexpensive places to stay, as well as "condotels" for longer stays.

LUXURY

The **Shangri-La Hotel Manila** ((2) 813-8888 FAX (2) 813-5499, on the corner of Ayala and Makati avenues, Makati, is the capital's slickest hotel. It's an enormous marble pile with an Italianate lobby, some excellent restaurants and facilities, including one of the better nightspots and an health club. It also connects with an impressive shopping mall with department stores, boutiques, cinemas, restaurants and bars. Arguably as glamorous is the **Peninsula Manila** ((2) 812 -3456 or (2) 819-3456 FAX (2) 815-4825 or (2) 815-3402, on the corner Ayala and Makati avenues, Makati. An affiliate of the famous Peninsula Hong Kong and in every respect it's equal, the Peninsula fully lives up to its five-star category. It has several top class restaurants and attentive service. Traditionally elegant in the Mandarin style, with all the five star amenities, the **Mandarin Oriental Manila** ((2) 893-3601 FAX (2) 817-2472, Makati Avenue and Paseo de Roxas, Makati, has a spectacular pool and excellent restaurants. There is also the **Shangri-La's Edsa Plaza** ((2) 633-8888 FAX (2) 631-1067, 1 Garden Way, Ortigas Center, Mandaluyong City.

The **Manila Hotel** ((2) 470011 FAX (2) 471124 or 482430, 1 Rizal Park, PO Box 1307, is in a class of its own — one of the aristocrats of Asia's historic hotels. Rooms , furnished with four-poster beds and Old World fabrics, look out across the medieval ruins of Intramuros or across the spectacular Manila Bay to the rocky fortress of Corregidor. There are three major suites, including the Penthouse, the Presidential and the

1555 FAX (2) 521-2674 or (63-2) 521-1118, on the corner of Roxas Boulevard and United Nations Avenue, Ermita, is opposite the United States Embassy and overlooks Manila Bay. The **Inter-Continental** ((2) 815-9711 FAX (2) 817-1330, 1 Ayala Commercial Center, Makati, has been completely refurbished and is located in the middle of Manila's busy commercial district. Among the usual facilities, it has a unique "jeepney" coffeeshop as well as a pleasant pool area.

At the high end of the mid-range, and representative of the chain, is the **Hyatt**

MacArthur. The Presidential Suite includes an indoor swimming pool, a live-in butler and as well as a helipad. The MacArthur Suite, occupying a wing of the fifth floor, includes a master bedroom with dressing room, a guest room, a formal dining, lounge and boardroom area, with a widow's walk overlooking the bay. United States President Bill Clinton and First Lady Hillary Rodham Clinton were reportedly quite taken with the suite when they stayed there during their state visit in October 1994.

MODERATE

There are two excellent choices suitable for business travelers. **Bayview Park** ((2) 526-

Regency Manila ((2) 833-1234 FAX (2) 833-5913, 2702 Roxas Boulevard, Pasay City. Both the **Nikko Manila Garden Hotel** ((2) 810-4104 FAX (2) 817-1862, 1223 Ayala Center, Makati and the **Manila Diamond** ((2) 536-2211 FAX (2) 536-2255, Roxas Boulevard, are popular with visiting Japanese, and are notable for their glittery marble lobbies, Japanese restaurants and sushi bars.

There are three other recommended international standard hotels in town, all with good facilities. The **Heritage Hotel** ((2) 891-8888 FAX (2) 891-8833, corner of Roxas Bou-

Manila boasts some of Asia's finest hotels.
OPPOSITE: The Peninsula Manila and
ABOVE the Shangri-La, both in Makati.

levard and Epifanio de los Santos Avenue, is a glossy new hotel next door to the Casino. It offers the usual amenities, including a helipad and an excellent swimming pool. The **Century Park Sheraton Hotel (** (2) 522-1011 FAX (2) 521-3414, corner Pablo Ocampo and M. Adriatico streets, Malate, and the **Westin Philippine Plaza (** (2) 551-5555 FAX (2) 832-3485, Cultural Center Complex, Roxas Boulevard, round out the moderately priced choices in Manila proper.

The **Mercure Philippine Village Airport Hotel (** (2) 833-8080 FAX (2) 831-7788, Nayong

Western La Corona Hotel ((2) 502631 FAX (2) 521-3909, 1166 M.H. del Pilar corner Aquiza Street, Ermita.

WHERE TO EAT

Unlike its neighbors, Bangkok and Hong Kong, Manila is not regarded as one of Asia's great gastronomic cities. Yet there is a profusion of good or, in some cases, excellent restaurants. One of the most popular restaurant and bar strips is found along and around **Jupiter Street** in Makati, which is a

Pilipino Park Complex, Pasay City, is a good choice if you have to catch an early flight.

INEXPENSIVE

The following recommendations are all centrally located and have basic amenities and friendly service: The **Ambassador Hotel (** (2) 506011 FAX (2) 521-5557, 2021 A. Mabini Street, Malate, is a charming hotel in the Malate tourist belt, with a busy 24-hour coffee shop that is a long-time favorite for Manila's politicians. Also in this category are the **Park Hotel (** (2) 521-2371 FAX (2) 521-2393, Belen Street, Paco, Manila. The **Hotel Las Palmas (** (2) 506661 FAX (2) 522-1699, 1616 Mabini Street, Malate, and the **Best**

good place to head if you feel like browsing for a table.

Tourist maps will offer endless dining suggestions — but the list below will assure that you experience the best of what the city has to offer. Although not always essential, it's advisable to reserve a table in Manila's more popular formal restaurants and, in some cases, to check if there is a dress code.

To sample the varied dishes that constitute Filipino cuisine, a good place to start is **Kamayan (** (2) 709-224, 523 Padre Faura corner of M. Adriatico Street, Ermita. Here, you dine, native-style with your hands, on an excellent range of traditional Filipino dishes. The atmosphere is lively here with a band performing every night as well as appearances by a group of talented blind musicians who bear a slight resemblance to the Blues Brothers. If you are looking for a more refined version of the Filipino culinary experience and want to dress up, then **Maynila** ℂ (2) 527-0011 at the Manila Hotel is the place to go. It has a turn-of-the-century ambiance and extraordinary furnishings (including capiz decorated chandeliers).

For elegant dining in an unusual setting, here are three special suggestions: Within Intramuros are two restaurants with an Iberian period atmosphere which offer ro-

mantic, candlelight dining in the walled city. **Barbara's Intramuros** ℂ (2) 527-3893 is located upstairs within the Casa Manila complex, opposite from San Agustín Church. Nearby, **Ilustrados Restaurant** ℂ (2) 527-3675, at 744 Calle Real, is elegant and formal, housed in a recreated nineteenth century mansion overlooking a courtyard. Arrange to have a taxi pick you up after dinner as the Intramuros isn't considered safe for foreigners to walk around in late at night.

In Ermita, **Chateau 1771 — The French Bistro** ℂ (2) 586932 is a good choice for a relaxed evening, and you can wander around the lively bars nearby after dinner. If it is a balmy evening, be sure you book one of the outdoor tables.

Ermita has some unusual theme restaurants. At **Islands Fisherman** ℂ (2) 582537, Aquiza Street, between Jorge Bocobo and A. Mabini streets, Ermita, diners "shop" in a little supermarket for their dinner, selecting from an array of live seafood, platters of vegetables and iced beer or wine. They are then ushered into an adjoining dining area where they are served their selections. For a similar experience, with an equally tempting array of fresh seafood as well as attentive service, try the **Seafood Market and Restaurant** ℂ (2) 505761, at 1190 Jorge Bocobo Street, Ermita. The famous **Singing Cooks and Waiters Restaurant** is a unique institution that never fails to charm. As its name suggests, at some point in the evening the "star-studded" cast of cooks and waiters break into song. There are five locations: Quezon City ℂ (2) 926 5757, West Triangle, Quezon Avenue; Pasay City ℂ 832-0658 FAX (2) 831-5015 Roxas Boulevard; Pasig ℂ (2) 645-0628 FAX (2) 645-3735 Restaurant Avenue, Marcos Highway; Makati ℂ (2) 899-7528, J.P. Rizal, corner Makati Avenue; and Mandaluyong City ℂ (2) 635-5944 FAX (2) 635-5945 SM Megamall, EDSA.

For European-style dining (outside the glossy hotels) **Le Souffle** ℂ (2) 812-3287, on Makati Avenue, with its innovative and varied menu, is regarded by many Manileños as the city's most elegant restaurant. Reservations are necessary. Under the same ownership, the equally popular **Paper Moon** ℂ (2) 895-1071, on Jupiter Street, has a friendly ambiance and serves classic antipasti and pasta dishes. Also in the Ayala Building is the chic **Giraffe Bar and Grill** ℂ (2) 815-3232. The food is good, though overpriced, and the raised bar is a fun spot for a pre-dinner drink. At N° 6750 Ayala Building is **L'Olivier** ℂ (2) 812-8596, a fashionable boutique restaurant with Mediterranean-based cuisine; there is live music for late diners every Tuesday. **Penguin Café** ℂ (2) 521-2088, on Remedios Circle, is popular with artists and young journalists and showcases the work of Filipino as well as foreign photographers. Also on Remedios Circle, **Guernicas** ℂ (2) 521-4417 has a Latin atmosphere and serves good Spanish food, with flowers for the women and mariachi

Music is an integral part of dining in many of the country's better restaurants.

performers eliciting singing requests with great persuasion. By midnight, the waiters and cooks (and you) are singing, too.

Cassarola ((2) 816-1935, at 102 Jupiter Street, Makati, is the best and perhaps only Portuguese restaurant in Manila. Also good for European specialities, **Europa Deli** ((2) 878310, at 150 Jupiter Street, has delicatessen dishes featuring imported produce, such as Angus beef, salmon, duckling and trout. For Tuscan-based cuisine, **La Vecchia Trattoria** ((2) 521-9431, at M.H. del Pilar Street, Ermita, is a good choice. At lunch, they serve great pizzas and have an appetizing buffet.

The five-star hotels offer some excellent dining. The Shangri-La Hotel Manila scores high for service and style: The **Cheval Blanc** ((2) 813-8888 is excellent for fine European food prepared in nouvelle cuisine style; it's open for breakfast, lunch and dinner, and reservations are required. Upstairs at the Shangri-La, **Conways** serves a lunch buffet of roast and selected dishes and becomes a music lounge in late afternoon. The Manila Hotel's **Sea Breeze** is perfect for a bayside meal overlooking the sea; chefs help you select and then grill your choice of meat or seafood. It is open Thursday through Saturday from 5 PM to 10 PM and closed during the rainy season. At the Mandarin Oriental, **Tin Hau** ((2) 816-3601 is an exceptional Chinese restaurant. **Spices** at the Peninsula Manila is especially good, with an array of sophisticated pan-Asian dishes.

For Asian food, **Mandarin Villa** ((2) 402935, at 789 Ongpin Street, is one of the better choices. Classic Thai cuisine can be found at **Sala Thai** ((2) 522-4694, located at 866 J. Nakpil Street, Malate. Also try **Baan Thai** ((2) 895-1666, on the second floor of the Villa Building, on Jupiter Street in Makati.

Another interesting experience in Manila is to wander through the clusters of stalls selling all sorts of dishes. You'll find food stalls in carinderias or working class cafés on the street or in the food halls located in the ground floor or basement of major shopping centers, such as the Shangri-La Plaza, Robinson's and Shoeman. You select *turo-turo*-style (*turo* which means "point" refers to the practice of pointing to make your selection) whatever looks appetizing. Dishes to sample include *sinigang* (a hot, sourish broth with meat, fish

or prawns), *arroz caldo* (chicken and rice soup topped with onions) *mami* dishes (noodles prepared with chicken or beef), *rellenong bangus* (milkfish, deboned and stuffed with chopped meat and vegetables then lightly grilled), fresh or fried *lumpia* (spring rolls) and *ihaw-ihaw* (chicken, pork or seafood grilled and served on a skewer). Other local delicacies include *banana-cue* and *camote-cue* (fried sugared plantain bananas skewered on a barbecue stick) and the ever popular *balut*, a partially cooked, fertilized duck's (not for the squeamish).

NIGHTLIFE

While in Manila you will be almost constantly exposed to the irrepressible Filipino

appetite for music, which pulses and buzzes in all directions all day and all night long. From Filipino taxi drivers insatiably addicted to their radio dials and checkout girls humming the latest Whitney Houston hit, infectious snatches of song are everywhere. Even the tiniest bars are enlivened by bands where you can hear talented renditions of pop tunes — you name it, they play it. There are Filipino bands who perform, note for note, gesture for gesture, pop classics just like the originals — The Supremes, Wilson Pickett, The Temptations, Smokey Robinson — to name a few; and they perform with all the passionate plaintiveness they can muster.

Like the Spanish, Manileños live for that hour when the sun goes down and the city wakes up. At sunset, cocktail shakers start competing with each other across Manila Bay. The **Manila Yacht Club** ((2) 521-4458 along Roxas Boulevard is a great place to welcome the dusk, although you may need to prove that you have some nautical affiliations to be admitted. Alternatively, there are sunset cruises most evenings around Manila Bay — check with the Department of Tourism Office.

Another place to idle over a sunset cocktail is the poolside bar at the Manila Hotel. Elsewhere in the hotel is the **Tap Room**, which performs old classic jazz favorites or the adjoining **Lobby Bar** where Philippine politicians and journalists get together

---

Cotton Club, Pasay City, Manila.

informally most Monday evenings. The more formal **Champagne Room** with its Imelda-esque decor is a place to drink some bubbly while being serenaded by the Champagne Strings band. A less formal, but no less elegant Manileño rendezvous for drinks is the **Conservatory** ((2) 812-3456, at the Peninsula Manila. The spacious room with its high ceiling overlooks a garden. Happy hour is from 6 PM to 8 PM and free appetizers are served.

In Ermita, traditionally the hyperactive center of Manila nightlife, a 1993 crackdown closed the raunchier strips along M.H. del Pilar and A. Mabini streets, which were famous for their bars. Most go-go establishments have now moved to Pasay and Makati. In Ermita you can enjoy a beer while watching the sun go down at the **Harbour View** ((2) 501532 at Rizal Park. Or check out **Hang's N** ((2) 597147 on L. Guerrero Street, just off the former Ermita strip. It's a friendly American-style bar popular with expatriates. Meanwhile, the Makati district has also been trying to rid itself of its image as a neighborhood for prostitutes (or commercial sex workers as they are known in police parlance). As any investigation of Manila nightlife will reveal, this "moral cleansing" has been only partially successful.

In Ermita, Jim Turner's **Hobbit House**, on A. Mabini Street, deserves its legendary status. From the moment you enter — to be welcomed by a series of dwarf waiters who cheerfully usher you to a table and bustle to attend to your order — you have arrived in a different world. The unpretentiousness and warmth that characterize the Hobbit House and the live singers who perform there, including the well-known Filipino folk singer Freddie Aguilar, make this one of Manila's most unusual and enjoyable bars.

Café society starts late — at around midnight or 1 AM. The best way to start is with a stroll around the Remedios Circle in Malate. The original bistro of Ermita, **Café Adriatico** ((2) 524059 opened in 1982, is still here. It is owned by journalist Larry Cruz whose empire has expanded to include **Café Adriatico 1900** ((2) 521-6682; **Bistro Remedios** ((2) 521-8097 for Pampangueno food (the cuisine from nearby Pampanga province); **Larry's Café Bar** ((2) 598762 for pasta, pizza and seafood;

and **Jazz Box** ((2) 505526 for a nightcap to the accompaniment of Louis Armstrong.

For Manila's upwardly mobile professionals, there are two clear favorites. The international chain of **Studebaker's** ((2) 883-1836 spans three levels of the Quad and is easy to find, located directly opposite the Shangri-La Hotel. The club is a mix of modernist and art deco styles, with the quieter **Fashion and Wine Bar** at its entrance. Upstairs there's a music lounge and brasserie-style restaurant, with a discotheque on the third level. **Zu** ((2) 813-8888, in the

basement of the Shangri-La Hotel, is considered the hottest nightspot in town. It combines karaoke, a sushi and oyster bar, live pop bands and an electrifying mix of styles.

SHOPPING

Authentic and inexpensive, Ermita's antique shops, concentrated along **Mabini Street** — their dank interiors crammed with Chinese chests, porcelain, carved Mindanao birds and lacquerware — are a good place to begin. Don't miss a visit to **Silahi's Arts and Artifacts**, Calle Real, Intramuros, with its wide selection of ethnic crafts and some fine antiques — probably the most extensive display of its kind in Manila.

Aside from the vibrant, bargain stocked bazaars and shops of Chinatown and Quiapo, the curio shops in Ermita and the fashionable boutiques in Makati, you will soon discover that Manila has developed the Asian mania for shopping malls and a stay here of a reasonable length of time is bound to mean encountering at least one or two of them. Shopping bargains at these malls are increasingly as good as those to be found in Hong Kong. The most unabashedly exclusive is the **Shangri-La Plaza**, the home of **Rustan's Department Store** (the Macy's or Marks and

Robinson's all have well-stocked Filipiniana departments.

Away from air-conditioned corridors, **Divisoria** is a good place to seek out bargains for local or imported fabrics, household ware, cheap jeans and discounted fashion industry castoffs. **Cubao** in Quezon City is good for bazaars and upmarket boutiques. The **Santa Cruz Mission** on A. Mabini Street, Ermita, specializes in T'boli and other ethnic crafts, along with **Pistang Pilipino**, a large complex of about 100 shops along M.H. del Pilar in Malate.

Spencer's of the Philippines) as well as a range of fine clothing shops and boutiques. On the other end of the scale, **Megamall** is a exactly that: two hangar-size buildings joined together to form an indoor consumerist megalopolis. It has an ice-skating rink in the basement level next to the enormous food court. **Harrison Plaza** in Ermita. The **Greenhills Mall** on Ortigas, **Robinsons Galleria** and **The Center** in Makati are all full of hundreds of shops and large department stores.

If you are looking for colorful, contemporary Filipino handicrafts, look for the reputable chain stores such as **Tesoro's** and **Susancrafts** as well as antique dealers such as **Jo-Liza** and **Via Antica** at the malls. **Rustan's**, **SM Shoemart**, **Landmark** and

The **Duty Free Philippines** complex is one of the largest of its kind in the world and worth a visit for shopaholics. Its main branch is at the **Fiesta Shopping Center**, by the Ninoy Aquino International Airport. It is a giant treasure trove of more than 85,000 different items, with everything from Christian Dior and Bally to children's toys, sporting equipment and high fashion from both Filipino and international designers. There is a smaller outlet in the airport complex. It has a good selection of high quality Philippine-made handicrafts and furniture in addition to the usual range of luxury items.

OPPOSITE: Shoes anyone? Itinerant vendor in Quiapo market. ABOVE: State-of-the-art shopping in Makati Commercial Center, Manila.

Luzon

HOWEVER FLIMSY THE ANALOGY, if Manila can be compared to a bar girl singing along to a Simon and Garfunkel song, then the island of Luzon is a teetotaling, provincial matron observant both of St. Jude and tribal spirits. Considered the nation's heartland, Luzon encompasses a vast swath of territory and offers many faces of the multifaceted Filipino personality.

The Luzon island group is the largest in the Philippines. It contains 37 provinces, including Metro Manila and the far-flung Palawan province (see PALAWAN, page 197). This cluster of disparate island provinces shares — like the rest of the nation — a perplexing welter of tribal cultures, languages and dialects. Its landscapes differ, too, ranging from the famous pea-green rice terraces of Banaue in northern Luzon, to the primeval black cliffs and dazzling pristine waters of remote Palawan — which is itself an archipelago of almost 2,000 islands — and sits as close to Borneo and Malaysia, as it does to Manila.

The largest single island in the Philippines, Luzon itself comprises more than 100,000 sq km (38,610 sq miles) and is home to half the archipelago's population of 68 million. Its central plain is dubbed the nation's "rice bowl". As you pass through its landscape, luminous tones of green rice paddies and spectacular layered terraces undulate toward the horizon. This is one of the country's richest agricultural regions, with plantations of tobacco, sugarcane, mangoes, coffee, and coconuts.

Luzon is often neglected as a destination. Perhaps that's because it can seem almost too dense, too much of an expedition, as opposed to a simple jaunt to a beach-resort-like Boracay or Cebu. Yet it has much to offer aficionados of tribal culture, remote beaches and Spanish baroque architecture.

Luzon is home to the Ilocanos people in the north and Tagalogs in the central plains; it is also the abode of many exotic ethnic groups whose lifestyles have changed little for centuries. Among these groups, tucked amidst the vertiginous Cordillera Central are the Ifugao tribespeople, architects of the best known of the spectacular sights in the province, Banaue's canyon-like stonewalled rice terraces.

Of Luzon's sights, it would also be a pity to miss the volcanic crater of **Lake Taal**; the burial caves of **Sagada**; the river rapids to **Pagsanjan Falls**; **Puerto Galera**, on the island of Mindoro, which is becoming almost as popular as Boracay; and the town of **Vigan**, with its well-restored sixteenth century mansions and churches.

Despite the relatively short distances covered to reach some of these places, they show a side of the Philippines that contrasts sharply with what you have already come to know, and perhaps chafe at, in Manila. As you leave

Manila and pass long stretches of outlying semi-slums and villages formerly claimed by other provinces (such as Tondo), you will see that not all is a rosy picture of rural bliss, despite an overall improvement in the region's economy. Scenes of Third World poverty never quite abate in Luzon, nevertheless, you should make this trip into the Filipino heartland.

Excursions throughout Luzon will offer you glimpses of the country's rugged splendor and of its people's soil-bound lifestyle. Certainly, the views from Tagaytay Ridge — from which you can see the breathtaking sight of the Taal volcano sitting within a crater lake of a larger volcano — instill a profound sense of the landscape's volatile beauty. After all, Mount Pinatubo's wrathful energies are close by. And as anyone who has witnessed the crucifixion rituals in Pampanga can attest, this region is renowned for the feverish intensity of its religious rituals.

OPPOSITE: The glowing and well-maintained façade of Baguio Cathedral. ABOVE: canoes for hire to take a closer and wetter look at Pagsanjan Falls.

ONE HUNDRED SIXTY KILOMETERS AROUND MANILA

If the length of your stay in the Philippines limits you to Manila, it is well worth taking advantage of the proximity of some of the most outstanding destinations nearby, which vary in distance from one to three hours driving from the city. From Manila, you can explore the province's fringes easily by car and return by evening, yet many of these destinations deserve at least a day or two. Getting there is made easier by well-paved highways and expressways. All the destinations in this section can be reached within three hours of driving. You may regard these destinations as stages en route while you travel onwards to further explore the island of Luzon. The Department of Tourism has information about guided tours of these nearby day trip destinations (see THE OPEN ROAD, page 38, for more on these suggested drives from Manila).

GENERAL INFORMATION

Manila car rental offices include:
    In Ermita: **Avis** ((2) 521-0062 or (2) 522-2082, 1322 Roxas Boulevard, corner of Padre Faura; **Budget** ((2) 522-2911, Manila Pavilion Hotel.
    In Makati: **Avis** ((2) 878497, Peninsula Manila; **Budget** ((2) 816-2211, Hotel Inter-Continental, Makati.

CORREGIDOR

You don't need to be an enthusiast of military lore to be fascinated by the battle-scarred island citadel of Corregidor, or the "Rock," as it is called by thousands of war veterans. It was the scene of some of the most grueling and bloody battles ever fought by combined American and Filipino troops against the Japanese. Reached by boat, this small, comma-shaped island fortress lies within a group of four other islands — Caballo, Carabao, El Fraille and La Monja — in the narrow entrance to Manila Bay.
    It was the last stronghold of the American and Filipino forces under General MacArthur during World War II and, along with

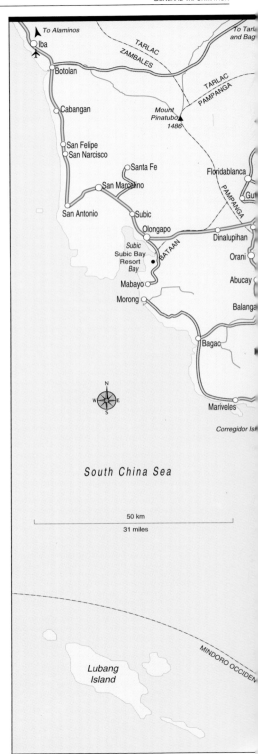

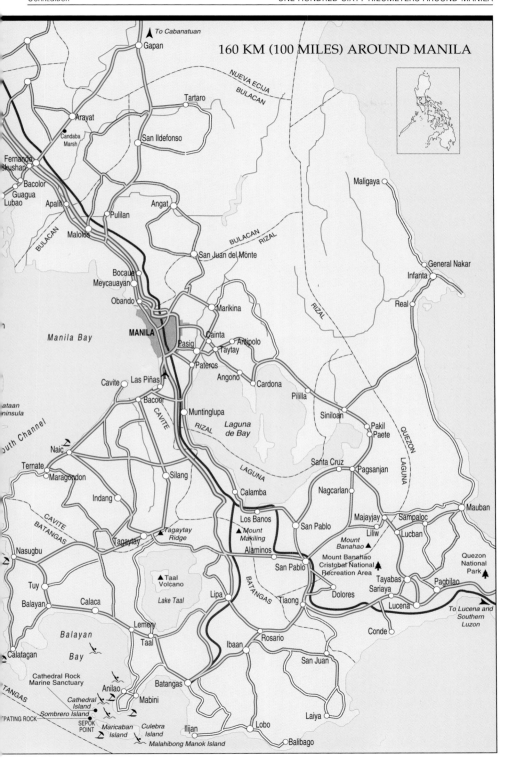

160 KM (100 MILES) AROUND MANILA

the Bataan Peninsula, witnessed intensive Japanese bombing and atrocities. The island, roughly the size of Manhattan, was where for more than three months the malaria-plagued troops defended their ever shrinking territory against the numerically superior Japanese invasion. Following their surprise attack on Pearl Harbor on December 7, 1941, the Japanese bombarded United States bombers and fighter planes stationed at Clark Air Force Base and from there invaded Luzon. Declaring Manila an "Open City" in order to protect its civilians and historic monuments from obliteration, MacArthur retreated to set up his headquarters at Corregidor, with the majority of his forces dispatched to the nearby Bataan Peninsula. He was accompanied by his family, Philippine President Manuel Quezon and United States High Commissioner Francis Sayle, along with a contingent of troops.

The decision to put up a defense from Corregidor was regarded by military strategists as one of MacArthur's bravest hedges, yet his position was ultimately hopeless. The island depended on daily barges from Bataan for water, food, medicines and ammunition. When the United States general-in-command at Bataan surrendered on April 9, 1942, President Roosevelt ordered MacArthur to Australia, inspiring his famous promise to return. The Japanese expected Corregidor to fall at the same time as Bataan. Yet incredibly, the 12,000-strong remnant of the army held out for a month before succumbing to heavy bombardment. Survivors were taken as prisoners of war on May 6, 1942. This date is known as Araw ng Kagitingan, or Day of Valor, and is a national holiday. This event officially marked the end of wartime hostilities in the Philippines and the period of the Japanese occupation until MacArthur recaptured the Rock on March 2, 1945.

A former haunt of an opportunistic Chinese corsair and bands of Moro pirates, Corregidor was partially fortified by the Spanish, who built a dockyard, a naval hospital, a lighthouse and positioned guns on its battlements. After the island was taken over by United States Admiral George Dewey in 1898, it was transformed under the Americans into an impregnable warren of bunkers, barracks, office quarters and storerooms, bristling with gun towers and coastal artillery.

Today, the island has been converted into a war memorial and you can walk throughout the ruined barracks, cannon and artillery emplacements, gaping batteries, tunnel mazes and the nineteenth-century Spanish lighthouse. Security personnel dressed in the 1930s uniform of the Philippine Constabulary add to the historical atmosphere. You can explore the various areas — known as **Topside**, **Middleside**, **Bottomside** and **The Tail** — either on foot or by tour bus. Topside is the island's highest point and the main center of the fort and now has a museum of war memorabilia housed in one of the reconstructed barracks. If you are walking, visiting all these locations and sights means covering a distance of about three kilometers (around two miles).

There is a sound and light show at **Malinta Tunnel**, a spooky warren of tunnels which began as an arsenal and an underground hospital and, during the siege of Manila, was used as the headquarters for the exiled Philippine government under Manuel Quezon before he escaped to the United States. **Suicide Cliff** has a Buddhist shrine to mark the place where many Japanese soldiers chose to jump to an honorable death rather than surrender. You can stay on the island at the **Corregidor Inn**, an authentic reconstruction of an old inn that was destroyed during the bombing raids. Its restaurant overlooks the two historic beaches. Otherwise, the **Beach Cottages** complex, located on the northern and southern shores of Bottomside, is pleasant. Contact the Department of Tourism in Manila for full information on making reservations.

How to Get There

The trip to Corregidor takes 45 minutes by boat from the PTA Cruise Terminal at the Cultural Center of the Philippines (beside the Folk Arts Theater) on Roxas Boulevard. **Sun Cruises (** (2) 831-8140 offers daily trips, departing early in the morning and returning in the late afternoon. From Corrigedor, **outrigger canoes** manned by local boatmen will take you to the fortress islands of Fort Drum, Caballo and La Monja.

Voyage to the Volcano's Rim

A drive from Manila to **Tagaytay Ridge** to see **Lake Taal and Volcano**, will carry you through the provinces of Rizal and Cavite. Just outside Manila you reach one of the oldest churches in the country. The **Las Piñas Church**, in **Las Piñas**, Rizal province, was built during the Spanish colonial period by Father Diego Cera, a Recollect Friar. Its unique bamboo organ, the only one of its kind, was built between 1816 and 1822,

If you wish to make a short detour to see one of Cavite's more interesting historic towns, then drive onwards to the early Spanish town of **Kawit**, 23 km (14 miles) from Manila, to see the **Aguinaldo Shrine**, which commemorates the life of General Emilio Aguinaldo. His house and its original furnishings have been turned into a museum, with an eclectic collection of Filipino and American national icons—American eagles mixed with Filipino flags. Aguinaldo's grave is here, too. On June 12, 1898, it was from his balcony that the First Philippine Republic

and its continued existence — it has survived earthquakes, typhoons and neglect — is a testament to the durability of the natural fiber which, assembled into this unique musical instrument, creates a distinctive range of sounds on its 174 pipes. A week-long **Bamboo Organ Festival** is held each February and attracts organists from around the world. Sometimes, usually in December, concerts are held in the Las Piñas Church grounds, under starlight from colorful lanterns, or *parols*. In Las Piñas, don't miss visiting the **Sarao Jeepney Factory** — home of the nation's famous jeepney. The factory here offers guided tours taking you through various stages of the jeepney's manufacture.

was proclaimed, and the new Filipino flag was raised. The Filipino hero led the resistance first against the Spanish and later against the Americans until he was overpowered at Biak-na-Bato in San Miguel. Both Aguinaldo's presidency and the First Philippine Republic were short-lived. In 1901, after his capture, Aguinaldo issued his final edict, ceding rule to the Americans and recommending that Filipinos make the best of the situation.

Thought to be the outer rim of an extinct volcano, shrub-covered **Tagaytay Ridge** is worth the 90-minute drive. It is a popular weekend retreat for Manileños and is dotted with country houses and hotels. You can

In Las Piñas, the country's famous jeepney factory.

stroll along the ridge walkways with its many picnic spots and it is also possible to go horseback riding or tour nearby flower and fruit farms. While in Tagaytay, you may want to sample dishes concocted from the unusual local mushrooms. They're sold at wayside stalls and apparently do *not* have hallucinogenic qualities.

From Tagaytay Ridge itself are many vantage points affording breathtaking views across the enclosed **Lake Taal and Volcano**. Despite its picturesque appearance and small size — the summit is only 406 m (1,332 ft) high — Taal Volcano has been one of the most active and devastating volcanoes in the archipelago. From the vantage point of Tagaytay Ridge, it is generally considered safe to witness the drama of its occasional fuming or even spewing of molten sparks. If the idea of exploring Taal Volcano up close interests you, take the winding and bumpy road down from the ridge to the lake's edge, where boatmen will ferry you across. Make sure you are happy with the agreed price at the outset. Lake Taal is also famous for its tiny fish — *pandaka pygmea* — the smallest of all known vertebrae, measuring only 1.3 cm (half an inch) at their most mature.

From Taal Volcano and Lake, you can easily continue on to the diving mecca of **Batangas**, which also popular with water sports enthusiasts and those needing some peaceful beachside relaxation.

Where to Stay

If you decide a day's visit is not enough, there are many hotels and hostels which have sprouted up because of the location's popularity and the summer festivals that take place here. The most exclusive and expensive is the **Taal Vista Hotel** ((19) 223226 and (19) 712-7525 FAX (19) 109225(MANILA (2) 817-2710 FAX (2) 818-8208, National Road, Kaybagal, Tagaytay City. This large hotel is set in gardens, with big sliding glass windows to take in the view, and it has good amenities. In the same range, the **Ridge Resort and Convention Center** has pleasant cottages, a swimming pool and a tennis court. Inexpensive to moderately priced accommodation can be found at the **Villa Adelaida** (MANUAL EXCHANGE 267 or (MANILA (2) 810-2016 to 19,

on Foggy Heights. Villa Adelaide has a modest swimming pool and a friendly restaurant.

Note that prices tend to go up at all hotels by about 20 percent at the weekends.

Formerly a tourist attraction in itself, the luxurious Palace in the Sky was built by the late President Ferdinand Marcos and his wife Imelda for a visit by President Ronald Reagan. The so-called palace, built at the highest point of a dramatic ridge overlooking the Lake Taal and Volcano, has been rechristened, **People's Park in the Sky** ((46) 413-1295 — and is being renovated under a program led by the current first lady, Amelita Ramos. Imelda used millions of dollars in public funds to build the structure during the early 1980s. But she dropped the project when the Reagans' abandoned their state visit amid growing protests over her husband's authoritarian rule.

BANYAN TREE

Close to Lake Taal and Volcanoe is the ultimate Philippine golf resort. The **Banyan Tree Nasugbu Evercrest Golf and Country Club** ((43) 473-4411 or (Manila (2) 712-9293 is a luxurious golf retreat tucked in mountain highlands. Here golfers can play on "The Masterpiece," an 18-hole championship course designed by Arnold Palmer. From the luxurious resort, you can take a climbing tour of the volcano or go out on horseback. There is a swimming pool, sauna, massage, Jacuzzi and a kid's club. Call the resort for information about special golf vacation packages.

THE CAVITE COAST AND RESORTS

On the Cavite coast are two of the most exclusive beach resorts located close to Manila. This is a pleasant area for a few days of relaxation and you can explore the surrounding sights of **Tagaytay**, **Cavite City** or even venture as far as **Pagsanjan** in Laguna. Close by is the small fishing village of **Naic**, where the triggerfish, called *papacol* or *baget*, around nearby Carabao and Fraile islands, draw keen game fishermen and anglers, especially between June and September. Past **Ternate**, nearby **Maragondon** is notable for its old church with ornate carved interior, where

Andres Bonifacio and his brother, leaders in the late-nineteenth century armed revolutionary brotherhood against the Spanish — the Katipunan — were detained and later executed by General Aguinaldo, on nearby Mount Buntis.

Whether you pass through it en route to the Batangas Peninsula, or as you return, the historic city of **Cavite** demands a brief stop, if only to see its old core of Spanish forts, dilapidated, formerly grand mansions and cobblestone alleys, with ruins of bastions on the headland used to repulse Moro pirates. Founded the same year as Manila (1571), Cavite was an important maritime and Jesuit center during the early colonial period. Here, giant galleons, constructed from the wood of molave trees, were destined to sail all the way to Mexico filled with exquisite goods from China. Cavite has a long tradition of maritime trade links dating back to the thirteenth century, when Chinese junks often moored here to barter for exotic goods. When the Philippines declared their independence from Spain, the first American naval expeditionary force arrived at Cavite as the new leader in the archipelago poised to take control. Because of its strategic port, Cavite was also a prime target for the Japanese when they invaded in 1941.

Puerto Azul Resort ((95) 574731 or **(** (95) 574036 FAX (95) 597074 **(** MANILA (2) 525-9246, beyond the coastal town of **Ternate**, is a five-star resort set within a private forested estate fringed by bays. With its health spa, swimming pool, championship golf course, tennis, squash and badminton courts and water sports equipment, this resort is clearly a destination for sports enthusiasts. Rooms are quite comfortable. Rates: expensive. The Puerto Azul also has luxurious and expensive suites.

Adjacent to Puerto Azul, amid the green hills surrounding a picturesque bay, is the **Caylabne Bay Resort (** (95) 732-1051 FAX (95) 818-4089. More upscale than the Puerto Azul, the Caylabne Bay has condominium style hotel rooms or suites with up to three bedrooms, a private marina and a helipad. It buzzes with activity on weekends, filling up with unwinding Manila executives, politicians and socialites. Rates: expensive.

BATANGAS PROVINCE

Easily reached in less than three hours from Manila and located south of Cavite, the province of Batangas has a pretty coastline, undulating with small bays and beaches and fringed by clusters of coral gardens. While its sands are not as spectacular as Boracay's and its waters are no longer as pristine as Palawan's, Batangas is nonetheless justifiably renowned as an easily accessible destination for serious divers, especially for its

famous **Cathedral Rock Marine Sanctuary**, off Balayan Bay, one of Asia's premier diving grounds.

Mabini, the main town of Batangas, is 124 km (77 miles) from Manila. Nearby **Balayan Bay** is regarded as Luzon's prime diving destination, also popular with windsurfers. The area's reputation has grown alongside the popularity of SCUBA in the Philippines and many of the conservation efforts now beginning to be put into practice elsewhere in the archipelago were initially pioneered here. Most of the diving and beach resorts in the region are found at **Anilao**, a *barangay,* or suburb, of Mabini located on sheltered **Janao Bay** off Balayan Bay, at the base of Calumpan Peninsula which rises to Mount Panay. Anilao is bursting with makeshift outdoor cafés, stalls, small traveler's hostels and offices renting out all manner of boats — from Hobiecats to yachts with full bar service — and every kind of water sports equipment, as well as serious diving outfits.

Cavite is a major port for fishing; here, the piers serving *bancas.*

Despite the long, bumpy road out to Anilao and the unimpressive beach, it is firmly on the international divers' map. Around the point of Balayan Bay and north to **Nasugbu** are dotted several more private resorts and additional, more pleasant beaches, also worth investigating for nearby dive sites.

What to See and Do

The small town of **Taal** is interesting; the former Spanish capital of Batangas has many colonial ancestral two-story houses and a lively market. Look for the local chocolate and peanut brittle candy (*balisongs*), fan knives and *piña*, the fabric woven from pineapple fiber and fashioned into the Filipino national dress, the barong tagalog. If you've been following the trail of the province's early revolutionary history — adjacent Cavite was a key player in the anti-Spain revolt — then all the more reason to visit the idiosyncratic **Agoncillo House**, the home of Marcela Agoncillo, the woman who sewed the first Philippine flag and who pawned her jewelry to donate the proceeds to the revolution. Close by, in **Lemery**, the baroque style **Taal Church** dates back to 1856. Although it is not particularly old, it has been twice rebuilt on the site of a much older church. The towns of **Batangas** and **Balayan** are particularly famous for their annual post-harvest thanksgiving parades featuring roast pigs, or *lechons*.

DIVING

Around Anilao are many compelling dive sites, including the spectacular **Cathedral Rock Marine Sanctuary**. This entirely man-made sanctuary features a coral garden in the form of a sunken amphitheater which was cultivated from seeded corals. It is also unusual in that its plentiful varieties of fish are attracted by the daily fish feeding.

Other diving spots include **Sombrero Island**, which has a wide hat-brim-like underwater rim perfect for shallow diving, while **Maricaban Island** is also good for snorkeling and has a resort (see below). The **Verde Island Passage** contains the two other marine sanctuaries in the region: **Culebra Island** and **Malahibong Manok Island**, both of which have many species of coral and reef fish in their narrow rock ledges, which are studied by marine biologists from a nearby base. **Verde Island** itself, a beautiful and idyllic place, is indented with alluring coral drop-offs and, on the south side of the island, it is possible to see the sunken remains of a Spanish galleon. Due to its proximity to the diving resort of **Puerto Galera** (easily accessible by ferry to and from Batangas across the strait in Mindoro Oriental), you may meet divers who have journeyed across for day diving excursions, or you may decide to make the opposite journey yourself (see PUERTO GALERA, page 156). When diving in most of these sites, it is advisable to have an experienced and licensed guide with you to ensure safe navigation through strong and sometimes unpredictable currents (see SAFETY in THE GREAT OUTDOORS, page 26).

Where to Stay

Most of the onshore dive camps and resorts offer inclusive packages that include inexpensive accommodation in cottages, tents or huts, simple meals and full SCUBA facilities. They also run courses so that beginner divers can gain PADI certification. Among the many resorts, the following are recommended: **Aquaaventure Reef Club** ((2) 816-7461 to 72 FAX (2) 813-1967, Bagalangit, Anilao, Mabini, **Dive South Marina Resort** ((2) 724-1129 or (2) 812-7073, Solo, Anilao, Mabini, MANILA Suite 2002, Cityland 10 Condominium, corner Ayala Avenue and H.V. dela Costa Street, Salcedo Village, Makati. Dive South has pleasant nipa and bamboo rooms, with a good restaurant and is located 30 minutes by boat from Anilao. On Maricaban Island (also known as Bonito Island) you can stay in splendid isolation at the **Bonito Resort** MOBILE ((912) 306-1696 FAX (2) 819-1157, at Pisa Tingloy.

If you prefer to laze on the sands, you'll want to head for the most pleasant beaches on the Batangas Peninsula; they're found on the more sheltered west coast. Both **Nasugbu** and **Matabungkay** are good western shore bases, with high quality resorts and possibilities for diving, snorkeling and fishing.

Nasugbu, idyllic and quiet, is dotted with several private beaches and resorts. Highly recommended is the well-located and tastefully landscaped **Maya Maya Reef Club** (MANILA (2) 810-6865 FAX (2) 815-9288, Balaytique, Nasugbu. Rates are moderate to expensive. Incidentally, Nasugbu is where 8,000 American troops came ashore in 1945 and advanced on Manila. It is easy to hire a pump boat from the town's port at Wawa and find your own private bay. The **Matabungkay Beach Club (** MANILA (2) 818-0054, at Matabungkay, Lian, is a well-organized, if holiday-camp-style resort. Facilities include a clubhouse style restaurant, tennis courts, swimming pools, water sports facilities — including catamaran sailing, fishing, windsurfing and snorkeling—a gymnasium with sauna and a massage parlor.

especially geared for enthusiasts of SCUBA diving. Rates: moderate.

LAGUNA PROVINCE

Just over an hour's drive south of Manila, Laguna province is regarded by many Manileños as the preferred place to live — within commuting distance — to escape the traffic clogged metropolis with its noxious polluted air. This means that the larger towns in the formerly unspoiled province — renowned for its beautiful freshwater lakes,

In the western corner of Batangas, **Calatagan** is the site of the picturesque, family-friendly resort of **Punta Baluartes (** (2) 894-1466 to 68 or (2) 894-5793 FAX (2) 893-4491, MANILA Suite 106, Le Métropole Condominium, 326 H.V. dela Costa Street, Salcedo Village, Makati. There are a variety of air-conditioned nipa cottages and suites, some tucked away like treehouses on the hillside, others framing the beach. Good water sports facilities (aqua-bikes, jet skis and even a glass-bottom boat), a swimming pool, golf course and tennis court as well as a horseback riding program and a playground for the children. These and other amenities make this a pleasant place to spend several days, although this is not a spot that is

rivers, waterfalls, mineral springs, coconut plantations and rain forests — are rapidly urbanizing, heralding the environmental blights of economic "development." Yet there is still much natural beauty to appreciate, especially around the Mount Makiling and Pagsanjan regions. Laguna's small towns have a decidedly Spanish feel and a gentle, tropical pace.

Laguna's lakeside communities came under Spanish control in 1571, led by Juan de Salcedo. Religious control was exerted by powerful Franciscan friars who dotted the province with missions and were feared and

In many parts of the Philippines, the faith is there, but the funds are not. Here a church in Kawit, Cavite.

plotted against by the native inhabitants. Along with Cavite, Laguna was one of the flashpoints for the revolutionary movement in the nineteenth century.

There are two ways to approach Laguna: either after exploring the Cavite and Batangas regions, or directly from Manila via Rizal province, winding through a string of communities ranged around the enormous, heart-shaped **Laguna de Bay**. Covering 922 sq km (356 sq miles), it is the largest freshwater lake in the country, encircled by the foothills of the Sierra Madre in the east, the

Calamba

If you are driving into Laguna via Cavite (perhaps after seeing Tagaytay and Lake Taal) you might find that a visit to Calamba, Los Baños and the Hidden Valley Springs, all located close to Mount Makiling, combine to make a good day excursion.

Perched over Laguna de Bay, the village of Calamba revels in its role as the birthplace of José Rizal, the physician and martyred nationalist leader, who with his execution became a saint-like figure for many Filipinos. A replica of Rizal's house — a two-story

plain of Metro Manila in the northwest and a phalanx of volcanic mountains in the south, including the reportedly supernatural Mount Banahaw, in nearby Quezon province.

Originally part of Manila Bay, Laguna de Bay was formed as the earth's crust tilted upwards. Although many small rivers flow into the lake, it only has one major tributary, the Pasig River, crawling along, becoming increasingly polluted as it flows 16 km (10 miles) through the capital to meet Manila Bay. This water highway allows easy passage for cargo boats and bancas laden with produce. Fertile waters and lakeside orchards have always been the raison d'être of Laguna de Bay, which supported thriving communities long before the arrival of the Spanish.

nineteenth century Spanish style building — has become the **Rizal Shrine**, exhibiting the revolutionary's original furniture, books, photographs and other family memorabilia.

Los Baños

Numerous hot mineral springs dot the Los Baños area, 39 km (24 miles) from Manila, which are fed by the thermal sulfur waters of dormant Mount Makiling. Thought to be curative, these waters inspired early Franciscans to build a hospital here in 1602 — the Hospital de Aguas Santas — which was later taken over and renamed Camp Eldridge by the Americans in 1903. During World War II, the Japanese turned Los Baños into a concentration camp. Fortunes were later reversed when General Yamashita was tried and executed as a war criminal at Camp Eldridge.

These days Los Baños is dominated by its many spa resorts, as well as by a variety of campuses — among others, the University of the Philippines has several agricultural research institutes located here, and the International Rice Research Institute set up by the Ford and Rockefeller Foundations — all attracted to the region by the exceptionally fertile volcanic soil found here. As for spas, you can't miss them as you drive along the highway from Calamba through Pansol

to Los Baños. If you wish to stop and test the waters, the **City of Springs Resort Hotel** ((94) 109-5731, 35 North Villegas Street, is a good choice. It has a decent restaurant and various swimming pools. The **Lakeview Health Resort** ((94) 50101, located at 1 Lopez Street, is another option. Both are inexpensive. You can stop for a few hours or stay overnight.

There is reason to stay longer: the beauty of **Mount Makiling**, which legend says is the home of the spirit Mariang Makiling. The upper slopes of the 1,000 m (3,283 ft)-high mountain are a national park full of forested pathways, some magnificent giant trees and alive with strange birds, flying lizards, beautiful butterflies and orchids.

Hidden Valley Springs Resort

The natural springs of Hidden Valley ((2) 840-4113 to 4114 or 818-4034 FAX (2) 812-1609, (postal address: Ground Floor, Cattleya Gardens, 111 Carlos Palanca Street, Legazpi Village, Makati, Manila) a peaceful, forested retreat, two hour's drive from Manila, are located in **Alaminos** on the southern side of Mount Makiling (known locally as Ilalim or "the place beneath," since the springs bubble up from a crater). Here, a series of spring baths, set amidst a green forest filled with wild orchids and tropical ferns, have been

turned into a resort — an oasis of cultivated tropical paradise. Paths wind through rain forest and open out to a series of cascading pools, where there are picnic huts and changing rooms. There are five pools of volcanically thermal yet clear mineral water, with temperatures between 29 to 31°C (84 to 88°F), fed directly from fissures in the rocks. The resort owner deliberately keeps the admission price high to ensure that this remains a sanctuary for tourists and wealthy Filipinos: the tour guide from the hotel where I stayed in Manila said although he had

---

OPPOSITE: A seven-kilometer (11-mile) river trip to the thundering Pagsanjan Falls. ABOVE: Tranquillity in the Hidden Valley Springs Resort, a popular spa hideaway.

driven visitors to the springs for years, he had never seen the interior of the resort because ordinary Filipinos cannot afford the entry fee. While it is possible to stay overnight, rooms are overpriced for what they offer, and most visitors come for the day. For all that, it is an exceedingly beautiful place and worth the visit.

Villa Escudero

About two hours drive from Manila is the lush coconut plantation hacienda style resort of Villa Escudero (MANILA (2) 521-1688, located in **Tiaong**, off the road at 10 km (six miles) south of San Pablo, Laguna's biggest city on the highway to Lucena, at the Laguna–Quezon provincial boundary. This is a pleasant place to stay overnight and offers a taste of the life led by Spanish plantation owners. The huge plantation is still a working enterprise, operated by some 300 families. The Villa's **museum** is an extraordinary repository of the Escudero family's heirlooms, including stuffed wildlife, Spanish and Mexican religious icons, antique Chinese porcelain, nineteenth century calesas, ethnic artifacts, clothing and World War II memorabilia. The late Don Arsenio Escudero was an avid collector, and this private museum is said to be one of the largest collections of Spanish, Filipino and Chinese treasures.

You can opt for a two-hour carabao cart tour of the museum, village and plantation, or you can stay at Villa Escudero's inexpensive cottages. There is a unique restaurant here where the tables are located ankle deep in a freshwater stream. As you dine, you can dip your feet into water — a pleasant and rustic sensation on hot tropical days.

LAGUNA EXCURSIONS

From San Pablo (either as you loop back to Manila or continue on to Quezon province or Pagsanjan) it is impressive to view the area's **seven crater lakes** by walking along the roads which wind around them. In addition, you can make breif stops in the villages of **Majayjay**, **Liliw** and **Nagcarlan**. Natives were forced by Franciscan missionaries, who were understandably reviled by the local population, to build the fortress-like Spanish baroque church in the village of Majayjay. The edifice has a most unusual design with three stories, triple perimeter walls that are six meters (20 ft) thick, and the entire construction is buttressed by massive stone. Liliw is a little artisan town, where you can inspect its distinctive locally-made shoes. The village of Nagcarlan has unusually narrow, colonial three-story houses, a pretty **baroque church** and a curious 400-year-old crypt, which was later used by anti-Spanish revolutionaries led by Andres Bonifacio to hold secret meetings with other Katipunan members.

Pagsanjan

A raft ride up the seven-kilometer (four-mile)-long, alternately serene and tumultuous Pagsanjan (pronounced Pug-sung-han) River and its rugged gorge to reach the 91 m (299-ft)-falls is one of the most invigorating and easily accomplished day trips from Manila, 102 km (63 miles) away. It is also somewhat adventurous, involving braving some not insignificant rapids and dodging boulders with energetic *banqueros* (boatmen) at the helm. Expect to be frequently soaked to the skin; bring plastic bags to protect your valuables, and bring a change of clothes. A sunscreen lotion is also essential.

Numerous boat operators make the trip, some of them well-intentioned and well-organized by locals. Yet complaints from tourists about being overcharged, robbed and harassed by banqueros are too numerous to ignore. Be aware that you should choose any freelance captains with caution. It is advisable to organize your boat trip to the Pagsanjan Falls while you are in Manila, working through a reputable travel agency or tour operator. You can arrange to go either as part of a group or on your own. If you haven't prearranged your trip in Manila, your hotel in Pagsanjan can offer recommendations.

The river journey takes about an hour each way and the boats depart and alight at the clearing opposite Pagsanjan's church. Initially, a row of bancas are towed up the river by a motorized boat to encounter the first set of rapids. Thatched nipa huts dot the riverbank, and you'll most probably see

Grandstand views of the 91-m (299-ft) Pagsanjan Falls from a raft platform.

villagers pausing to look up and wave. As you continue farther, the scenery becomes densely tropical, with forest furrowing the river edge and strange shrill calls of unseen birds. This part of the river was used as a location shot for Francis Ford Coppola's *Apocalypse Now*: it was here that the film's harrowing final sequence took place, in a replicated Khmer temple complex that proved to be the resting place of the anti-hero Kurtz. It is no coincidence that Oliver Stone took the cue to shoot his Hollywood movie *Platoon* in Laguna.

As you pass through the gorge, the riverbanks become dramatic cliff faces, as the tempo of the rapids increases. After being navigated through them by your trusty banqueros, it's time to disembark and clamber across the river stones to the Pagsanjan Falls, where you are given 20 minutes to explore nearby caves, admire the falls, swim or take photographs. The return journey negotiating the series of 14 rapids is the most adrenalin laden part of the trip, during which you will have to rely on the alacrity and experience of your banqueros. Rafting enthusiasts will prefer to tackle the rapids during the rainy season, especially from August through September, when the river is at its highest, with a challenging current. Otherwise, the river is frequently shallow and biddable.

WHERE TO STAY AND EAT

To enjoy the serenity of the river setting, it makes sense to stay overnight, so that you can make your river journey before the arrival of bused-in day trippers. Located in rustic surroundings, the most luxurious place to stay is the **Pagsanjan Rapids Hotel (** (92) 645-1258 or 645-1180 **(** MANILA (2) 834-0403 or 834-0404 FAX (2) 832-1212, located on General Taino Street, Pagsanjan, which has comfortable amenities and a good restaurant. Rates: moderate. The **Pagsanjan Village Hotel (** (92) 2116, on Garcia Street, is a comfortable, inexpensive place to stay, with air conditioning. The **Willy Flores Lodge**, also on Garcia Street, is popular, the management is friendly and it's extremely cheap.

Caliraya Lake

If river rafting doesn't appeal, but fishing and bird watching does, Caliraya Lake is a peaceful and enjoyable place and has the lure of a luxury resort. The large, tree-fringed manmade lake located in the vicinity of Pagsanjan, has many types of fish in its depths — bass, mullet, carp and catfish — and the angling season is between October and February. At the lakeshore, it is possible to hire a boat and fishing guide, either by the hour or the day. Windsurfing equipment, water skiing and horseback riding is available also. Filipino politicians and magnates retreat to the private **Lake Caliraya Country Club (** MANILA (2) 485151 to 59.

Visit the nearby lakeshore towns of **Paete** and **Pakil**, known for staging the colorful **Turumba Festival,** and also for their carvers who fashion intricate woodwork and filigree sculptures of doves, butterflies and trees.

RIZAL PROVINCE

Bounded by Metro Manila, many of Rizal's western suburbs have blurred into the capital's urban sprawl, among them the fishing port of **Navotos**, **Pateros** (which produces *balut*, the Filipino delicacy of fertilized duck's eggs) and **Las Piñas** with its remarkable bamboo organ. Named after the national hero of the Philippines, José Rizal, the province is mostly flat but becomes hilly and rugged as it joins the foothills of the Sierra Madre.

Whether you are driving out from Manila, or returning from Laguna or Quezon, there are several places to stop and see in Rizal, especially the towns of Angono and Antipolo, set amongst the foothills. **Angono** is an artist's commune and is the home of Carlos "Botong"

Francisco, one of the more well-known Filipino folk artists. It is a peaceful and bohemian community, with many ateliers and **workshops** to visit. **Antipolo** is otherwise uneventful aside from the religious celebrations that dominate the town every May, when devotees flock to the Shrine of the Virgin of Antipolo, feted for the image of the Madonna that was credited with miraculously saving galleons from stormy seas. Between 1641 and 1748 the Madonna was taken aboard eight return voyages. Believed to be the guardian of safe journeys, she has a large following.

Nearby, **Cainta**, **Pasig** and **Taytay** are notable as the towns captured by the British troops and Indian sepoys in 1762. The towns were handed back to the Spanish in 1763.

Another historical quirk, **Morong Church**, four kilometers (two and a half miles) beyond **Cardona**, is one of the finest churches in the region, with many oriental touches to its architecture left by the Chinese artisans who completed it in 1615.

QUEZON AND AURORA

East of Manila, the thin, boot-shaped province of Quezon has a long, exposed coastline which runs down to the Bondoc Peninsula. It was named for Manuel Quezon, president of the Philippine Commonwealth. Farther north, across the isolated reaches of the Sierra Madre, is Aurora, the province named for Quezon's wife. This province has a small following as a surfing destination. Somewhat off the beaten track, Aurora is chiefly a conduit for travelers who pass through it to Lucena on their way to catch the ferry to the islands of Marinduque and Romblon.

Quezon is justifiably famous for its **Pahuyas Festival**—a folkloric extravaganza and one that very young children enjoy participating in—celebrated in mid-May in the towns of **Lucban** and **Sariaya**. During the festival, housefronts are wreathed with brightly colored leaf-shaped rice wafers, called *kiping,* and garlands of fruits and vegetables to celebrate the year's harvest.

OPPOSITE: Rafting tourists right up to the Pagsanjan Falls before taking them back through a series of 14 rapids. RIGHT: The unique and justly famous organ in Las Piñas, Rizal Province, created entirely from bamboo stems.

MOUNT BANAHAW

Hardly ever active, but imposing nonetheless, this 2,177 m (7,142 ft) volcano sits on the boundary between Laguna and Quezon provinces and is the centerpiece of the surrounding national park. It is undeniably a spectacular hike, yet its reputation hovers firmly on the side of the supernatural: myths, superstitions and tales of strange happenings abound, attesting to the mountain's magical powers.

Long before the arrival of the Spanish, Mount Banahaw had become a cult icon to the natives who live around its flanks and worship a type of folk Christianity in Banahaw's springs and caves. Many believe the mountain exerts its own forceful electromagnetic and energy field. Several occult-like sects have highly apocalyptic viewpoints about the site. During Holy Week, worshipers ascend the mountain to bathe in its springs and hold ceremonies in the 30 m (98 ft)-high cathedral-like cave known as the *Kuweba ng Dios Ama* (Cave of God the Father).

Mount Banahaw historical lore also merges into myth. In 1841, the Spanish retaliated violently against the rebellious Cofradia de San José movement in Quezon

(then called Tayabas) and the survivors became *remontados*, or those who return to the mountains, living on the isolated slopes of Banahaw and nearby Mount Cristobel, in some ways behaving like the occult sect members who live on the mountain today.

Climbing Mount Banahaw involves at least four days. It is not advisable during the rainy season when leeches are everywhere and landslides are common. There are several routes up the mountain, from **Lucban** and **Dolores** in Quezon and various points from Laguna. The main trailhead

is in the village of **Kinabuhayan**. It is recommended to have a guide with you from the National Parks and Wildlife Station in the town of Santa Lucia, a 30-minute drive from San Pablo.

Even spending half a day on your own in Kinabuhayan and walking part of the way along the trail will give you a sense of the mysterious energy and beauty of Mount Banahaw.

NORTH OF MANILA: THE LUZON HEARTLAND

North of the capital city lies Luzon's vast central plain — a giant rice rich region that knits together the provinces of Bulacan, Pampanga, Tarlac, Nueva Ecija and the eastern flank of Pangasinan. Closest to Manila, the two provinces of Bulacan and Pampanga have much to offer, especially if you are traveling with children, who will appreciate the emphasis on colorful fiestas and prettily wrapped, homemade sweets. Children will especially enjoy visiting the only town in the world that celebrates Christmas every single day of the year. Both Bulacan and Pampanga mark Holy Week with passionate intensity, although these rituals, with flayings and crucifixions — with nails — are probably not suitable for children.

BULACAN PROVINCE

Bulacan is especially worth seeing if your visit coincides with the month of May or July, which is when festival fever overtakes the province. May's highlights are the three-day **Obando Fertility Rites** festival in the fishing town of Obando and the carabao fiesta in **Pulilan Carabao Festival** (see FESTIVE FLINGS, page 46). On the first Sunday in July, the river town of **Bocaue** overflows with pageantry and flotillas of kaleidoscopic hued outriggers for the **Pagoda Sa Wawa Festival**, celebrating the Holy Cross of Wawa (see FESTIVE FLINGS, page 48). The cross was miraculously found a century ago, floating on the river's surface, and it is the star of the procession, borne along on a own boat.

All these towns are easily reached by driving from Manila: Bulacan's capital, **Malolos**, is only 28 km (17 miles) away. It isn't the province's main attraction — but it is noteworthy for being the seat of government for Emilio Aguinaldo's first Philippine Republic. Throughout Bulacan, sweets are everywhere — sticky, sugary and swathed in intricate paper wrappings in bright colors. Ask for *puto* (rice cakes), *ensaimada* (sugared buns), and look for the bite-size cakes made of freshly grated coconut.

PAMPANGA PROVINCE

While Bulacan is noted for its sweets, Pampanga has a rival flair for its painstaking and ingenious folkloric artistry. This is amply demonstrated in the province's delightful **Giant Lantern Parade**, held in the provin-

cial capital of **San Fernando** on Christmas Eve. Enormous (five- to 10-m or five- to 11-yd-wide) *parols,* or paper lanterns, marvels of folk design and electronic wizardry, all lit up in moving colors are mounted on trucks for the night procession, which starts at about 11 PM and ends with an award for the best lantern in the town's main plaza after midnight. Villagers insist that the winning lantern is destroyed after Christmas Day, so that its design remains secret and not irreplicable.

A string of small towns close to San Fernando — especially **Apalit**, **Bacolor** and

Guagua — reflect the Spanish influence in Pampanga, with finely wrought churches and wooden houses. Bacolor's church, built in 1754, is a masterpiece of the province, along with **Betis Church** in Guagua, completed in 1670, with its ornately carved retable (raised ledge behind the altar), elaborately frescoed ceiling and ecclesiastical architecture.

On the outskirts of San Fernando, **Paskuhan Village** is obsessed with Christmas all year round. As artificial as a tree bauble, Paskuhan was constructed in 1980. The town is dedicated to endlessly re-enacting nativity scenes and to the production of Christmas decorations made from native materials. Just an hour from Manila by car (75 km or 47 miles), this village teems with shops, stalls and cafés that sell Christmas paraphernalia and delicacies, Filipino style. Paskuhan lies on the Olongapo–Gapan road, in the suburb of **San José**.

OPPOSITE LEFT: The Santacruzan Festival in Lucban Town, Quezon. OPPOSITE RIGHT: Ceiling fresco depicting the Goddess of Fertility, in a Bulacan church. ABOVE: Preparing to race water buffaloes at the annual Carabao Fiesta in Pulilan.

General Information

Inquiries about Paskuhan Village and surrounding areas can be directed to the **Department of Tourism (** (912) 961-2665, Paskuhan Village, San Fernando, or to the **Paskuhan Tourist Office (** (45) 602031 **(**/FAX (45) 613361.

Where to Stay

Although San Fernando otherwise is not a place to spend much time, if you have come to see either Good Friday's gory lashings and crucifixions or the more upbeat lantern festival, plan on staying overnight at the **Pampanga Lodge (** (45) 602033 or 615908, which has the overwhelming advantage of location; balconies overlook the main plaza and church courtyard. The lodge offers simple, rustic accommodation. It may be difficult to reserve ahead, so begin your planning early.

ANGELES

Up until quite recently, the main center in Pampanga province was the city of Angeles, which mushroomed into a raunchy "R & R" (rest and relaxation) satellite for nearby **Clark Air Force Base** during the Korean and Vietnam wars. It was rivaled only by Olongapo, which serviced Subic Bay Navy Base in neighboring Zambales.

Clark began in 1902 as Fort Stotsenburg, a United States Cavalry detachment. The base became the headquarters of the 13th United States Air Force, the largest American military facility outside of the United States, covering over 550 sq km (212 sq miles) and employing more than 9,000 Americans and 18,000 Filipinos.

In its heyday, Angeles, like Olongapo, was a watering hole and adult playground for the troops. With its thousands of bar girls, strip clubs, night clubs, restaurants and hotels, the promise of cheap sex and music lured a steady stream of male patrons. (Clark, incidentally, had the highest reenlistment rate of any American military base.) Since the Aquino government (as landlord) terminated the United States lease on the Clark Base in 1991 (as well as that of Subic), Angeles' malls, garish fast food outlets and rows of go-go bars have taken on a surreal, abandoned look. Accelerating the lease termination was the deadly eruption of Mount Pinatubo — the most devastating this century — which inflicted much misery and loss of life, as well as draping a pall of economic depression over the region.

In the aftermath of the disaster, Angeles looked like a moonscape, smothered in ash and debris. Because of the eruption, Clark Air Force Base was abandoned four months ahead of schedule and thoroughly looted. Local officials and foreign investors bade farewell to an era of freewheeling prosperity. Yet despite having seemingly landing in the obituary column, Angeles appears to be reinventing itself now. The city is showing signs of economic recovery, it is rebuilding and improving its infrastructure, offering Mount Pinatubo tours and resurrecting former bars, nightclubs and bordellos to reconjur its former attractions. Many Australians, who make up the bulk of the tourist traffic here, are finding it irresistible. Much of the activity that used to be associated with Ermita in Manila before it was cleaned up by Mayor Lim has moved here.

On a lighter note, the increasingly popular **International Hot Air Balloon Festival**, is held each January or February at the Clark Air Field.

General Information

If you wish to hire a car for the day to explore Mount Pinatubo's surroundings, contact **Avis** MOBILE **(** (45) 301-1885, Don Juico Avenue, Clarkview.

Where to Stay and Eat

Angeles has a profusion of hotels, bars and restaurants, either reconstructed from the damaged originals or brand new. The most luxurious place to stay is the **Holiday Inn Clark Field (** (45) 599-2246 FAX (45) 599-2248, Clark Field, a five-star hotel with excellent amenities and recreation facilities. Several hotels are favored by those in search of traveler's tales and the authentic Angeles experience, both inexpensive and under foreign management with pools. The **Sunset Garden Inn** MOBILE **(** (097) 378-1109 Malabanas Road, Clarkview, the **Swagman Narra Hotel (** (45) 30157, Orosa Street and **Derby Inn (** (45) 2074, Don Juico Avenue, Balabago.

Finding a decent meal is not difficult in Angeles. There is a profusion of bars, restaurants and cafés. The time-honored label of best restaurant in town is always conceded to the **Maranao Grill Restaurant** MOBILE ((45) 202-5847, in the Oasis Hotel at Clarkville Compound.

How to Get There

Now that **Clark International Airport** ((45) 599-2263 has opened, creating a new gateway for Luzon, Angeles is likely to become a more important travel hub, allowing easier access to Baguio, Banaue and La Union. Philippine Airlines flies to Clark International from Hong Kong, Bangkok, Jakarta, Singapore, Kuala Lumpur, Taipei, Tokyo, Brunei and Seoul. By automobile, Angeles lies 80 km (50 miles) away from the capital, a journey of about one and a half hours.

MOUNT PINATUBO

Tucked away in the Zambales Mountains — at the juncture of Zambales, Pampanga and Tarlac provinces — Mount Pinatubo had been peacefully dormant for some 600 years. It's eruption on June15, 1991 was a national catastrophe, which took vulcanologists by surprise. Volcanic activity continued in spurts until September the same year. The first rumblings began on June 9, but no one predicted the epic devastation that would follow: an explosion that vomited detritus 40 km (25 miles) high, accompanied by waves of violent earthquakes, typhoons and deadly avalanches of *lahar* (mud) and ash.

In what has been the worst volcanic explosion this century, some 900 people died — including the Ayta tribespeople living on the volcano's slopes—and 250,000 were left homeless, as more than a hundred villages were engulfed, many completely buried under mud and lava flows, especially in Pampanga. Since the eruption, millions of tons of ash sit on the volcano's slopes, sliding inevitably downwards, continuing the saga of destruction of villages within its radius. Many of the villages have constructed dikes to hold off mud flows. Temporary shacks still house many of those left home-less. Vulcanologists predict that the 1,700 m (5,577 ft)-high Mount Pinatubo is by no means dormant and that it may not be until the year 2010 that the volcano once again resumes its deep sleep.

Making the best of the situation, hotels and tour operators in Angeles offer jeep tours to Mount Pinatubo, west of the city. It is a riveting experience to survey the extraordinary geological carnage that took place during the eruption as you walk along the crater's ravines, with huge swells of hardened lava and ash, eerie formations and half-submerged villages to be seen in the surrounding area. If you remain curious and fearless and want to swoop into the volcano's still active crater, aerial tours are also available.

THE BATAAN PENINSULA

Although parts of the Bataan Peninsula have been rapidly industrialized, the Bataan Peninsula, along with the Zambales coastline, will have a special allure for war buffs and those in search of deserted beaches with fine sunsets over the South China Sea. Fiercely contested during World War II, the strategically-located Bataan Peninsula lies at the entrance to Manila Bay, ringed by impressive and formidable volcanic mountains, amongst them Mount Pinatubo. Until November 1992, the peninsula was also home to the other major United States military base — the **Subic Bay Navy Base**.

In the words of General MacArthur, "No soil on earth is more deeply consecrated to the cause of human liberty than the island of Corregidor and the adjacent Bataan Peninsula." In Bataan, after holding out for three months, the outnumbered Filipino and American troops surrendered to the Japanese on April 9, 1942. Of the 64,000 Filipinos and 12,000 Americans, at least a tenth died in the months to come, some of starvation and disease and some by brutal torture at the hands of their Japanese captors. Many perished on the horrific forced 112-km (69-mile) trek that became known as the "Death March." Throughout the province, historical markers commemorate sites of battles and bombings, the route of the Death March and wartime encampments.

What to See and Do

Many of the interesting places to visit in the province recall the Battle of Bataan. Near the border with Pampanga, the town of **Hermosa** has the First Line of Defense marker, while **Pilar** was the scene of intensive fighting. Hermosa is also notable for the **Roosevelt Game Reserve**, located nearby. On **Mount Samat**, the Dambana ng Kagitingan (Altar of Valor) is a dramatic giant cross, made of concrete and steel, 95 m (312 ft) high and clearly illuminated at night. It honors the war dead. On clear nights, it can be seen from as far away as Manila. The viewing gallery offers vertiginous vistas for kilometers across land and sea. Wreath laying ceremonies are held each year commemorating the Fall of Bataan and Corregidor. The provincial capital, **Balanga**, is where General Edward King of the United States Armed Forces officially surrendered to the Japanese.

Where to Stay

Montemar Beach Club (MANILA (2) 815-8306 to 08 FAX (2) 818-8544, Barangay Pasinay, Bataan, is the most pleasant place to stay in Bataan. This secluded resort has a wide and private beach tucked into the shore within a headland. Water sports, bird watching and fishing are available, as well as swimming pools, tennis courts, a playground and a nine-hole golf course. Rates: moderate.

How to Get There

As well as driving or taking regular buses for the three hour-long trip from Manila to Bataan's capital Balanga, it is possible to get to Bataan by boat from Manila. **Sun Cruises (** (2) 831-8140 FAX (2) 834-1523, PTA Cruise Terminal, Cultural Center of the Philippines, Roxas Boulevard, Manila, makes regular stops at the beach resort between Balanga and Mariveles.

THE ZAMBALES COAST AND OLONGAPO

One hundred twenty eight kilometers (79 miles) from Manila, Zambales offers an authentic slice of coastal life. Its thin coastline has spawned a string of small fishing villages that also subsist by making *bagoong* (fermented fish sauce), harvesting salt and by their cottage industries. Craggy moun-

tains range behind the coastline, making a natural barrier for the province. Most of the indigenous tribes — the Zambals and the Ayta — melted away into Luzon's interior with the arrival of the more dominant Tagalog and Ilocano settlers.

In Zambales, **Olongapo** — a three-hour drive from Manila — has always been closely tied to **Subic Bay** 19 km (12 miles) away, former home of the United States Seventh Fleet. This was the biggest overseas base and supply depot for the United States Navy until November 1992, when it finally closed. Many freely admit this has meant economic disaster for nearby Olongapo, like Angeles, where almost everyone — from bar girl to office worker — depended on the Americans for their income.

Since then, the base has been turned into a free port, attracting a great deal of Taiwanese investment and mushrooming new resorts, factories and duty free malls. The **Subic Bay Freeport Zone**, mobilized energetically by Chairman and Olongapo Mayor Richard J. Gordon, has been provided with hefty grants and a loan package from the World Bank and the Asian Development Bank. As a result, the former military airport in Cubi Point — Subic International Airport — is now the country's most modern airport, while the Barrio Tipo Highway has greatly improved road links to Manila. The city has been known for its active night life — centered around **Magsaysay Drive**, a strip full of raunchy go-go bars, once nicknamed "Sin City" — but also a performance mecca for legions of talented Filipino musicians.

Now that the Americans have departed, their place is being taken by vacationing Japanese, Taiwanese and Australians. With all its infrastructure in place, the base is now a Special Economic Zone awaiting investment and promoting its future as a convention center.

Not far from the former base is a large stretch of tropical jungle, where tribes known as Negritos live in the style of their ancestors and where United States troops used to do their survival training. It's possible to arrange overnight jungle tours. Don't expect decent beaches around Subic Bay — you will need to head north to San Miguel (near San Antonio) and farther afield up the Zambales coast. Aside from Olongapo and Subic Bay, as you travel up the coast, small fishing villages and beaches become gradually less populated, and exposure to local life here is a compelling draw. The provincial capital of **Iba**, 83 km (51 miles) from Olongapo, only really comes alive during the **Kalighawan Festival**, celebrated every March with agricultural and beauty contests — the beauties and the beasts. You can give Iba a miss as a place to stay.

General Information

The Tourism Department offers some interesting tours, such as "ecotrips" into the jungle and visits to the Calapan Negrito settlements, as well as cruises on reconstructed Spanish galleons and guided tours of the former Subic Bay base. The **Visitors Center** ((46) 384-3776 will assist.

Where to Stay

The most luxurious and comfortable hotel is the **Subic International Hotel** ((45) 888-2288 FAX (45) 894-5579, Santa Rita Road, Subic Bay Freeport Zone, which caters primarily to business travelers. Travelers congregate at the moderately priced **White Rock Hotel** ((45) 5555 and (45) 2398, with its well-kept rooms, a good swimming pool and a restaurant. In Barrio Barretto, which has clusters of bars and restaurants relatively close to the sea, there are also several private resorts. Try the inexpensively priced **Marmont Hotel** ((45) 5571, which has a restaurant, nightclub, swimming pool and gymnasium. In Olongapo, many cheap hotels line Magsaysay Drive and Rizal Avenue. The best of the bunch are probably the Plaza Hotel and the Diamond Lodge, both inexpensive and located on Rizal Avenue.

How to Get There

Subic Bay has the Subic Bay International Airport. Otherwise, air-conditioned Victory Liner buses ply the route from Manila, 128 km (79 miles) away, throughout the day; it's a three-hour journey. There are also regular bus connections to and from Angeles, San Fernando and Baguio. Jeepneys shuttle continuously between the former base area of Subic Bay and Olongapo.

PANGASINAN PROVINCE

The oddly-shaped Pangasinan province has a slow tempo and is known for its salt production, oysters and fish farms. Its main attraction is for divers keen to explore the **Hundred Islands**, which are composed of about 400 coralline islands strewn along the coastline in the Lingayen Gulf; many of them are still unexplored. The most popular of the islands — for clear waters, snorkeling and diving — are **Quezon Island**, **Cathedral Island**, **Devil's Island**, so named for its mysterious waters and **Shell Island**, with its fine white shell-strewn sands. The jumping-off point is the wharf town of **Lucap** and the village of **Alaminos**, where fishermen hire themselves and their bancas out to ferry tourists and divers out to the island of their choice. It is possible to camp on some of the larger islands, an experience which will be more atmospheric than staying in either of these towns. Divers should contact the **Philippine Commission on Sports SCUBA Diving (PCSSD)** ((2) 503735, Department of Tourism Building, T.M. Kalaw Street, Rizal Park, in Manila.

LA UNION PROVINCE

This thinly sliced coastal province has become a popular beach destination and a jumping-off point for SCUBA divers keen to explore the Lingayen Gulf. Non-divers will enjoy it too — its towns have a tropical sleepiness, lush with bougainvillea and flame trees. But don't expect the sublime beaches and pristine ambiance found elsewhere in the Philippines. The popular beaches are centered around **Bauang**, which is a convenient stop en route to Baguio. But the main highway is located along the coastal strip. You could base yourself for a day or two in Bauang, enjoying the beach strip before heading up to the mountains. **San Fernando**, the provincial capital, and **Agoo** aren't recommended as places to stay.

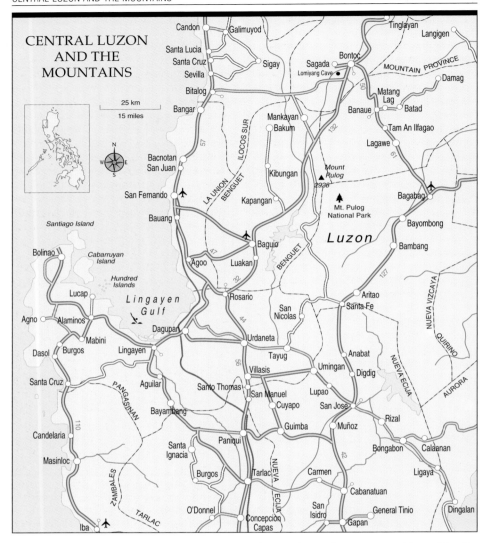

Where to Stay

In Bauang, the **Villa Estrella Beach Resort** ((72) 413794 FAX (72) 413793, at Paringao is well-maintained, with a modern Spanish colonial feel and a decent restaurant. Another recommendation is the **Bali Hai Resort** ((72) 412504 FAX (72) 414496, also at Paringao, which has air-conditioned rooms and pleasant duplex cottages, as well as a restaurant and swimming pool. Both are inexpensive.

How to Get There

Philippine Airlines flies irregularly to San Fernando, but sometimes cancels flights during the typhoon season. From Manila, by car or bus, the drive to Bauang takes five or more hours. From San Fernando, jeepneys make the trip to Bauang in 30 minutes.

THE CORDILLERA CENTRAL

North Luzon's mountain region is dominated by the Cordillera Central massif mountains, which separate the Cagayan Valley from the Ilocos coast. This is the home of many highland tribes, notably the Bontocs, Ifugaos, Igorots, Kalingas, Isnegs, Kankanays and Tingguians, some of which were formerly headhunters.

BAGUIO

Resting on a summit of the Cordillera Central, the summer resort of Baguio lies 250 km (155 miles) north of Manila, a six- to seven-hour drive through increasingly dramatic scenery.

Beloved by Filipinos as a holiday retreat, Baguio was developed as a vacation resort at the turn of the century by homesick colonial Americans. It retains traces of American influence in its architecture and also in the strange American twang discernible in the dialect of the indigenous Igorot, whose grandparents were under the tutelage of American missionary teachers.

At an altitude of 1,500 m (4,920 ft), Baguio is a sylvan realm of year-round cool breezes, pine forests, panoramic views, lovely Spanish houses and flower-strewn parks — the perfect summer retreat, it is, indeed, regarded by Manileños as their summer capital. It also has a following for its faith-healing practitioners who declare to "open" the skin of their patients and "operate" with their bare hands. This region — which also includes the nearby destinations of **Sagada**, **Bontoc** and **Banaue**, as well as many small villages of great interest — can easily keep you amused for at least five days, and it is a good place to be relax and slow your pace.

General Information

The **Tourist Information Center** ((74) 6708 and (74) 7014 is at the Department of Tourism Complex, Government Park Road, Baguio. They can provide free maps and tell you about workshop tours and visits to surrounding Igorot tribal villages. It is easy to get around the hilly city by foot, if you have strong calf muscles, or by jeepney or taxi.

To rent a car, contact **Avis** ((74) 4018, located in the Padilla Building, Harrison Road.

What to See and Do

Baguio — which is spread across almost 50 km (31 miles) — is still recovering from a fatal 1990 earthquake, which inflicted much damage, devastating the tourist spot's main hotels, parks and golf course. Nevertheless, it is rebuilding itself, and its key attractions have not changed. Most of the interesting streetlife, cafés and shops are located downtown. In the city, you can explore relics of faded Americana and militaristic parks — and poke around the vibrant **Baguio City Market** which, as well as selling mountain produce and brassware, has stocks of ethnic fabrics, woven items, silver, jewelry, Igorot woodcarvings and Ifugao baskets and craftware. It is also crammed with carinderias serving inexpensive Filipino food. At Christmas time, this market becomes the focus for celebrations when hundreds of Filipinos arrive to celebrate the holiday.

Both **Burnham Park** and the **Cathedral** are worth seeing. The park is named for the American architect who created Baguio's layout and has a pretty orchidarium and terrace restaurant. The Cathedral is notable as an icon of endurance during World War II — 5,000 citizens sheltered here while the city was under siege, and the church grounds are full of war dead. The **Baguio Botanical Gardens**, previously known as the Imelda Park, offers beautiful panoramic views, and close by, **Wright Park** is known for its horseback riding trails — horses and guides are available for hire.

Baguio, the country's premier hill station. Here, boats for rent in Burnham Park. The comprehensive orchidarium in the park is also worth a visit.

The **Baguio Mountain Province Museum**, which is next door to the Tourist Information Center on Government Park Road, will give you a clear impression of the history and cultural traditions of the region's minority ethnic tribes. It also has exhibits from other tribal groups within the archipelago.

The **Good Shepherd Convent**, run by Belgian nuns who provide a home for unwed mothers, sells various souvenirs along with fruit preserves. In the nearby garden-farming suburb of **La Trinidad**, a visit to **Narda's**, run by weaver Narda Capuyan, is

Camp John Hay has a important history: it was here that World War II started and ended in the Philippines. This was where the first Japanese bomb was dropped and where General Yamashita moved his headquarters, along with the puppet government under José Laurel. Yamashita spent the last weeks of the war in Baguio in an underground warren, before being overpowered by United States and Filipino forces and finally returning to Camp John Hay to sign the Japanese surrender at the United States ambassador's headquarters on September 3, 1945.

a chance to see her designs based on a blend of ethnic themes and patterns, with unusual clothes and other items for sale. You can see Igorot cloth being woven on traditional backstrap looms at the **Easter Weaving School**.

Baguio City encompasses both the **Philippine Military Academy** (the West Point of the Philippines) and **Camp John Hay**, formerly the rest and recreation station of United States military troops. Since being turned over to the Philippines in 1991, it has become a government-run tourist resort complex, with restaurants, playing fields and sports facilities. Both the **Baguio Country Club** and **Camp John Hay** have excellent 18-hole golf courses.

For the best view of Baguio and its surrounding mountains, climb up **Dominican Hill** to the **Diplomat Hotel**, which used to be a Dominican seminary. Many stories are told about the building — it was previously owned by one of the country's most famous faith healers, the late Tony Agpaoa, who practiced his faith "surgery" here. En route, you'll pass rows of antique shops, perhaps worth a browse, while the nearby **Lourdes Grotto**, located 225 steps up the hill, becomes a frenzied pilgrimage site during Holy Week.

Where to Stay and Eat

Baguio has scores of inexpensive hotels and guest houses catering to seasonal swarms of Filipino tourists and just as many restaurants and cafés, as well as many nightspots. The two most comfortable, well-located hotels are the **Vacation Hotel Baguio** ((74) 442-4545 FAX (74) 442-3108, 45 Leonard Wood Street and the **Woods Place Inn** ((74) 442-4642, 38 Military Cut-Off Road on the corner of Wagner Road, both moderately priced, with biggish, pleasantly furnished rooms, television and baths. Also good moderately priced choices are **Baguio Hotel Ambassador** ((74) 442-2746, 25 Albano Street and the **Baguio Midtown Hotel** ((74) 442-7164, Magsaysay Avenue. Probably the most popular with

miles) from downtown Baguio. If you hire a car, or come by bus, the 246 km (153 mile) long journey — which becomes increasingly scenic — takes up to seven hours. It's not a good idea to try to travel by road during the rainy season, when landslides become a problem along the high mountain roads. Several bus companies, including Victory Lines and Philippine Rabbit, run day and night services. Baguio is a good starting point for exploring Sagada and Banaue — which have the cachet of being the former realm of headhunters — which are a day's excursion

budget-conscious travelers is the **Swagman Attic Inn** ((74) 442-5139, 90 Abanao Street, which is managed by Australians. The **Burnham Hotel** ((74) 442-2331 or (74) 442-5117, 21 Calderon Street has a peaceful feel, agreeably furnished with a good Chinese restaurant and offers very good value.

Traditional Cordillera cuisine and mountain brews are served at **Café By The Ruins**, opposite the city town hall — it is worth visiting to sample its seasonal specialities, *tapuy* (rice wine) and *basi* or *salabat* (ginger tea).

How to Get There

Philippine Airlines flies from Manila to Baguio daily; the flight takes 50 minutes and the airport is at **Loakan**, about 12 km (seven

away, farther north. Jeepneys and buses connect the main towns and travel across the provincial borders to Cagayan Valley, Ilocos Sur, Ilocos Norte and Abra.

BANAUE RICE TERRACES

Banaue is known for its spectacular rice terraces, meticulously carved by hand into a canyon of stairways and a testament to the determination of the Ifugao tribespeople, the most ancient mountain tribe in the area. The Ifugao (literally, "eaters of rice") have

Baguio — A newspaper vendor OPPOSITE LEFT touts the latest headlines; Camp John Hay OPPOSITE RIGHT and ABOVE is one of the most popular golf links in the country.

lovingly maintained these terraces, with their water-retaining dikes, for hundreds, perhaps thousands, of years. The staple grain they reap is said to have been a gift from their deity, Kabunyan, and in return the Ifugao built the rice terraces, both a source of their survival and a magnificent stairway to their god's heaven.

What to See and Do

Clearly, the main attractions are the rice terraces themselves. If measured from end to end, the terraces would stretch a total length

While in the region see **Batad Village** for its beautiful tiered and contoured rice terraces and large cascading waterfall, 20 minutes walk from the village. About a two-hour walk from Batad is **Cambulo**, an Ilfugao village nestled amidst the rice terraces which remains relatively untouched. The first 12 km (seven miles) from Banaue can be covered by vehicle, but you have to walk the remaining four kilometers (three miles). The tough hike is rewarded when you finally reach the breathtaking views across the terraces and the village with its thatched huts. It can be

of 22,400 km (13,888 miles). They rise up to over 1,500 m (4,900 ft). The best time to visit is from March to May, when the terraces are green with rice shoots and the scenery is superbly lush. Trekking tours are the best way to experience the terraces, although the **Banaue View Point** has panoramic views for those just passing through. Tourism has flooded this formerly hermitic tribal region, and it is feared that the Ifugaos may soon find catering to tourists more interesting than tending to the fields. The tribespeople, who you will encounter here and in their villages, seem to have accepted that their colorful attire and patterned headdress make them natural targets for picture-snapping tourists — and they expect some pesos in return.

accomplished as a day trip, or you can stay overnight in Batad.

Tam-An Village is a recreation of a typical Ifugao village, where beads and woodcarvings are fashioned and sold, located behind the Banaue Hotel. The original Tam-An is located several meters away, and many of the dwellings here have ancestral skeletons visible beneath their raised floors. A well-marked trail from Banaue takes you on a two- to three-hour circular walk through the rice terraces to the Ifugao villages of **Bocos** and **Matang Lag**. The Ifugao are remarkably talented artisans, and it is fascinating to watch

OPPOSITE: The fabulous 2,000 year-old Banaue rice terraces. ABOVE: Freeing the spirits — the cliffside burial site of the Igorot tribespeople at Sagada.

a variety of crafts being made in village workshops. At Tam-An and Matang Lag villages you can see handicrafts, copper, silver jewelry, fabrics — including handwoven blankets — being created. Finally, **Guihon Natural Pool** is wonderful in summer for a swim and a picnic.

Where to Stay

The best place to stay in the area is the **Banaue Hotel** ((73) 386-4087 to 88 FAX (73) 386-4048, Banaue, Ifugao, or (MANILA (2) 812-1984 FAX (2) 812-1164, Ground Floor, Maripola

you can reach Banaue from Baguio by car or bus, via Bontoc. Banaue is 348 km (216 miles) from Manila, via Cabanatuan City and Lagawe roads. Another way to get there is to take a Philippine Airlines flight to Baguio City and then make a six hour journey by bus or car onwards to Banaue. The drive takes you on a beautifully scenic trip through the Cordillera Central. The last — winding — stretch of the drive between Bontoc to Banaue, a 50-km (31-mile), two-hour journey across the Mount Polis range, is one of the country's most spectacular experiences, with vertigo-

Building, 109 Perea Street, Legazpi Village, Makati, Metro Manila. This is a tastefully furnished 90-room establishment, with private balconies overlooking the rice terraces. It has a restaurant, swimming pool and sun terrace and rooms range from moderately priced to expensive. You can use the facilities — notably the swimming pool — if you are staying at the inexpensive **Banaue Youth Hostel**, which is under the same management. Book the hostel at the same contact numbers and addresses as the Banaue Hotel.

How to Get There

From October to May, annually, Aerolift flies from Manila to **Bagabag**, the nearest airfield to Banaue, two hour's drive away. Otherwise,

inducing and awe inspiring views across the emerald canyons. This drive is equally as impressive as the destination itself.

SAGADA

Tucked amongst mountains some 1,530 m (5,025 ft) above sea level, Sagada is in a lush region of waterfalls, underground pools, mysterious caves, tribal burial sites and "hanging coffins." Don't miss visiting this popular traveler's hangout.

What to See and Do

The lure of cave exploring attracts not a few spelunkers to Sagada, though some people may not relish the thought of wading through icy underground rivers. Most of the burial caves do not demand such exertions and are located within half an hour's walk of the small town.

For centuries, according to Igorot tribal custom, the dead have been buried above ground or attached to pegs halfway down a cliff in the belief that this would allow their spirits to roam free. Probably the most dramatic cave open to tourists is the beautiful **Matangkib Cave**, which contains numerous sealed coffins from 20 to 600 years old; the older coffins are much smaller, since the

coffins, some of which lie open, revealing decayed bones and clothing fragments. Another place to see is the **Hanging Coffins View Point** — where coffins can be seen hanging like bats against a sheltered section of limestone rock.

Where to Stay

Sagada is the most appealing place to stay in Central Luzon — rather than Baguio or Banaue — because of its spectacular views of the mountains, rice terraces, hiking trails and for the calm pace of village life there.

bodies were laid to rest in a fetal position. Sadly, many of the coffin lids have been pried off and the skulls removed — apparently the work of decades of tourists wanting to claim souvenirs. Located in a gorge, Matangkib is set above an underground river, and the sounds of rushing water can be heard echoing below it.

Latipan Cave, also known as the "Big", or "Marcos" cave, is the largest, and is considered the most exciting for adventure spelunking — a dizzying maze of winding paths, water pools, narrow passages and huge limestone formations.

Lomiyang Cave is the most visited cave, for rather macabre reasons: placed at the cave's wide entrance are numerous piles of

There are a good number of guest houses that cater especially to foreigners — as opposed to vacationing Filipinos — and café food can be good. Accommodation tends to be cheap and fairly basic. Try the **Olahbinan Resthouse** or the **Green House**. The **Masfrerre Restaurant and Lodging** has a loyal backpacker following.

Travelers congregate at the **Rock Cave** near the Underground River, which has a cozy, pub-like feel, with a fire place. The **Cabine** is the pick of the restaurants.

OPPOSITE: Igorot tribal chief in front of his home in Sagada Town. ABOVE LEFT: Typical Ifugao stilted house in Kiangan. ABOVE RIGHT: Vegetables for sale in Bontoc market, en route to Banaue.

How to Get There

Sagada is 139 km (86 miles) north of Baguio and seven kilometers (four miles) south of Bontoc. It is best reached from Bontoc by bus (a one-hour ride) or on foot.

ILOCOS REGION

Consisting mostly of La Union, Ilocos Sur, Abra and Ilocos Norte provinces, the region of Ilocos sprawls across northwestern Luzon. There is a strong Spanish influence in the architecture, called "earthquake baroque",

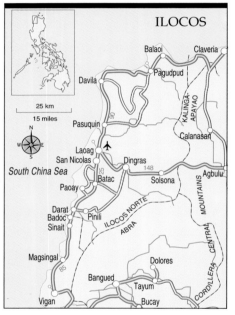

which evolved to withstand all too frequent violent typhoons and tremors. This stoical style can be seen in the grander homes and churches. This is a region of stately, if faded, cobblestone towns founded in the sixteenth century, balustraded Castillian style houses with porticoes and courtyards, grand Augustinian churches and tobacco, garlic and rice plantations — dry and arid in the summer and waterlogged during the rainy season.

VIGAN

If you are going to choose one destination in Ilocos, make it Vigan, the capital of Ilocos Sur and the third oldest city in the Philippines. Here, the Spanish influence is at its

most visually appealing. This well-preserved colonial town has cobbled streets, spacious plazas and beautiful colonial Spanish houses, many built by Chinese mestizos, with narra wood floors, high ceilings, intricate grillwork, *azotea* (tiled patios) and *capiz* (shell) windows. It began as the religious and political capital of Northern Luzon towards the end of the sixteenth century, founded by the 22-year-old conquistador, Juan de Salcedo, the grandson of Miguel Lopez de Legazpi, the former governor-general and founder of Manila.

What to See and Do

Vigan is easily explored on foot, though horse-drawn calesas still serve the city's residents. Start with **Vigan Cathedral**, also known as St. Paul's Cathedral. Built in 1574 and rebuilt in 1800 — in current earthquake, baroque style — the façade features carvings depicting Chinese Fu dogs, reflecting Vigan's Chinese heritage, and its main altar is lined with beaten silver panels. The cathedral's bell tower stands apart in Plaza Burgos, on the south side. Adjacent to the cathedral is the **Archbishop's Palace**, an eighteenth-century building with capiz windows and fretted carvings. It was used by Filipino revolutionaries in 1896 and taken over by American troops three years later.

Nearby, the **Ayala Museum** has a remarkable display of antiques, artifacts from the local Tingguian tribe and the Ilocanos and was also the birthplace of the martyr-priest Father José Burgos. **Salcedo Plaza**, which faces Vigan Cathedral, is a park surrounding an obelisk commemorating the young conquistador founder.

On Quirino Avenue, **Syquia Mansion** is the most exceptional example of Vigan colonial architecture, built in 1830 for a Chinese merchant. It later became the residence of Elpidio Quirino, who was the president of

How to Get There

By car or bus, Vigan is a seven-hour drive from Manila. Various buses make the journey, including the Philippine Rabbit. An alternative is to fly to Laoag in Ilocos Norte, then make the two-hour trip by road to Vigan.

LAOAG AND ILOCOS NORTE

The attractions of typhoon and earthquake-prone Ilocos Norte can be summarized in one word: **Paoay**. This small town, which lies 20 km (12 miles) south of the provincial capi-

the Philippines from 1948 to 1953. You will see many beautiful houses, not open to public view, as you stroll around town — Vigan is frequently used as a film set. **Mena Crisologo Street** is especially pretty. Also see rotund *burnays*, traditional pottery urns, being made in small workshops along Rizal Street.

Where to Stay

The most pleasant place to stay in Vigan is the **Cordillera Inn (** (77) 2526 FAX (77) 2840, 29 Mena Crisologo Street, a renovated and restored colonial home, with a good restaurant. Otherwise try the **Ancieto Mansion** off Plaza Burgos, which has a pretty outdoor garden and simple arrangements.

tal, **Laoag**, is a beautiful place to see, reflecting the taste and ambitions of the Augustinians who founded it in 1593. Its centerpiece is **Paoay Church**, the finest example of earthquake baroque style, with its massive lateral buttresses, exterior staircases and façade designed to withstand the wrath of the elements. It also has unusual oriental crenellations and niches reminiscent of Indonesian temples. The secret of the church's strength is its unusual construction: Its thick coral rubble walls are sealed with a mixture of sugar cane juice and lime mortar. The belltower is imposing — it was used by the Katipuneros and later by local guerrillas in

An old-fashioned *calesa* trots down a street in Vigan.

World War II as a hideout and lookout tower. The **Paoay National Park** with its large lake provides another incentive to visit the area.

Traveling to Paoay from Laoag, you will pass through **Batac**, the boyhood home of former president Ferdinand Marcos. The colonial style Marcos family home has been turned into the museum–shrine **Balay Ti Ili** and displays Marcos memorabilia.

Once he had scaled the presidential heights, Marcos returned to Batac to build his **Malacañang del Norte**, a giant palace which is now also a museum.

It was, however, at **Sarrat**, near Laoag, that Marcos was born—a typical provincial town with its main claim to historicity being the large Augustinian **Sarrat Church**. The town was transformed in a frenzy of construction when it was used as the venue for the wedding of Marcos' daughter, Irene in 1983. Imelda demanded that the entire town—and an additional 3,000 workers — toil day and night for two months to turn what had been a scruffy, sleepy village into a splendid, "aristocratic" town lined with Spanish mansions. In addition, an international airport was built at Laoag as well as the five-star Fort Ilocandia Resort Hotel with its lavish casino. A few days after the wedding a violent earthquake collapsed many of the buildings and the church.

Laoag

Because of its airport, the capital of Ilocos Norte, Laoag, is a hub for getting to the far reaches of Luzon. It has some interesting Spanish colonial buildings and churches, including the **City Hall**, the **Tobacco Monopoly Monument** and the Renaissance inspired design of the **Cathedral of Saint William**, built between 1650 and 1700. Laoag is a good place to browse through antique shops. It's an especially good spot for pottery, santos, figurines and Ilocano woven cloth.

GENERAL INFORMATION
The **Department of Tourism** ((77) 220-467, Ilocano, Heroes Hall.

WHERE TO STAY
The premier hotel in the province is **Fort Ilocandia Resort Hotel** ((77) 221166 to 70 FAX (77) 422356. Located along Suba Beach, the region's main beach destination, this somewhat kitsch hotel is a self-contained complex with a golf course, swimming pool, restaurants, disco, beach buggies and casino.

ABOVE LEFT: Church in Paoay — once a colonial splendor, now neglected. ABOVE RIGHT: A band precedes a funeral procession in Vigan. RIGHT: Four simple walls and a roof constitute the average rural home, such as this in Paoay.

The Marcos clan adored it. It is expensive and located 10 minutes out of town. Inexpensive, unexciting accommodation can be found within Laoag itself at the **Modern Hotel** ((77) 2348, Nolasco Street or the **Texicano Hotel** ((77) 2499 on Rizal Street.

If you prefer more rustic accommodations, go to **Pagudpud**, 60 km (37 miles) north of Laoag, which has one of the most pleasant beaches in northern Luzon, Saud White Beach. Simple nipa cottages on the beach — such as the **Villa del Mar** and the **Ivory Beach Resort** are peaceful and have basic amenities but no telephone for advance booking.

HOW TO GET THERE

Laoag has an international airport catering to tourists from Taiwan who are promised the delights of the Ilocos beaches and the casino at the region's premier resort, the Fort Ilocandia. From Manila, the Philippine Airlines flight takes an hour. Driving, by car or bus, from Manila takes 10 hours. Philippine Rabbit and Times Transit are the most reliable bus companies.

SOUTHERN LUZON REGION

By far the most popular destination within southern Luzon is Puerto Galera, a beach resort on the island province of Mindoro. Somewhat more off the beaten track is beautiful, untouristed Marinduque Island, and destinations for adventurous island hopping, which offer ample opportunity to live out Robinson Crusoe fantasies.

MINDORO

Composed of two provinces — Mindoro Occidental and Mindoro Oriental — this island faces, to the north, the Verde Island passage and Luzon's diving resort of Batangas and, to the south, the islands of the Visayas. Away from its coastal villages, the dense jungle interior is home to Mangyan tribes.

There are several reserve areas in Mindoro Occidental for the endangered *tamaraw*, a fierce buffalo species found nowhere else in the world. The best known of these reserves is near Mount Iglit, close to the settlement of Puy-Puy; another, also near Mount Iglit, is

in Sablayan; and, within the reserve of **Mount Calavite**, in the island's northwest point is a third.

Puerto Galera

A pretty, former sea port, Puerto Galera has become increasingly "discovered" and now vies alongside Boracay as one of the most popular beach and dive resorts in the archipelago. Located on the north shore of Mindoro Oriental, Puerto Galera town is knitted together by a string of coastal villages and has a lovely natural port.

In the sixteenth century, the Spanish regarded Puerto Galera as an ideal cove for protecting their fleet of great ships from tropical storms, which is why it became

known as "port of the galleons". It has become a diving and beach playground, where you can also go treasure hunting and take cruises in restored Spanish galleons. Tourism has quickly transformed the otherwise sleepy settlement, bringing with it a slew of new hotels, beach cafés and business ventures; one hopes this will not destroy the ambiance that initially made the place so attractive.

GENERAL INFORMATION

At Puerto Galera pier, the **APP International Travel Corporation** and **Swagman Travel** can offer advice and handle booking information. You can also make international calls from here.

WHAT TO SEE AND DO

Diving is the main attraction and dive shops and activities abound. Nearly all of them have good facilities and equipment as well as their own dive boat. Experienced divers are usually keen to explore the most popular, though somewhat distant, internationally renowned sites: **Apo Reef National Marine Park** to the west of Mindoro and Busuanga in the Calamian island group. For beginners, however, Puerto Galera is an excellent place to learn. Beach exploring is a natural here, and you can take your pick. The busiest beaches are **White Beach** and **Sabang Beach**, both of which have many

Fort Ilocandia Resort, along Suba Beach, near Laoag.

restaurants, discos and bars and are lively at night. Both the **Big La Laguna Beach** and **Small La Laguna Beach** are enticing, either for swimming or snorkeling over coral reefs. You do your beach exploring either by jeepney from Puerto Galera to Sabang, or by hiring a banca.

WHERE TO STAY

Because it is becoming so popular, Puerto Galera's hotels and restaurants are undergoing a state of flux. Simple nipa cottages with basic facilities abound, but increasingly more elaborate resorts are sprouting up. Prices vary, depending on how successful the season is. Of the many choices, two resorts stand out: **Coco Beach Resort(** MOBILE (912) 304-7017 FAX (912) 305-0476 is the largest and most luxurious, with its bamboo cottages, swimming pool and landscaped terraces that descend to a private beach and coral reef drop-off. This resort has attracted many European tourists since it received approving newspaper reports. It offers exceptional value and its inexpensive rates include buffet breakfast and transport from Manila on the Coco Beach Express, a bus/ferry transfer which runs daily. **La Laguna Beach Club and Dive Center** MOBILE **(** (912) 304-7017 FAX (912) 306-5622 or (2) 521-2371 to 75, is also recommended. It has lovely landscaped gardens, the rooms are luxurious and air conditioned, and there is a swimming pool. The restaurant offers international and local cuisine. The PADI–IDC-rated five-star diving center offers courses in several languages. There are 20 dive sites within a 15-minute banca ride and a 60-ft live-aboard banca is available for charter.

HOW TO GET THERE

Philippine Airlines flies daily to **San José** and **Mamburao** and Pacific Airways flies to **Calapan**, closest to Puerto Galera. By boat, the best way to reach Puerto Galera is from Batangas and from there a ferry boat — the MV *Batangas Express* or the MV *Princess* — to Puerto Galera, a two-hour journey. There are banca connections between Puerto Galera and **Abra de Ilog** in Mindoro Occidental throughout the day, every day, a two-and-a-half-hour trip. Like the rest of the Philippines, strong winds and typhoons are common

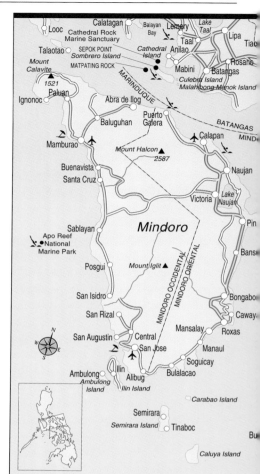

during August to October. During this time, trips usually made by road are accomplished by circling the island in a banca. A new boat and bus service from Manila is being established — a five-hour, relatively comfortable journey — and the Department of Tourism will have the latest details.

MARINDUQUE

The delightful outlying island of Marinduque is rarely visited by tourists, outside of its festival season. This in part lends to its unpretentious and rustic charm. It is an ideal choice for an island hopping excursion from Mindoro, and it offers a taste of life in the busy island backwaters.

The towns of **Boac**, **Gasan** and **Mogpog** on this heartshaped island come alive for the

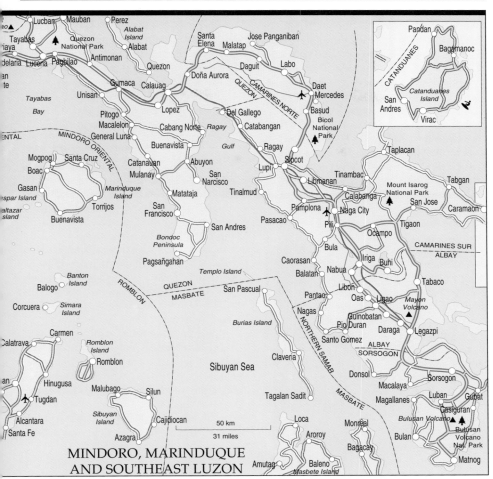

MINDORO, MARINDUQUE AND SOUTHEAST LUZON

Moriones Festival at Easter, when traditional masks, helmets and outlandish costumes imitating Roman centurions are paraded (and sold to tourists) with abandon as the colorful re-enactment of the crucifixion takes place. Although most of the island's towns perform passion plays, the largest and most outstanding is held at Boac from Easter Thursday to Easter Sunday. Aside from its festivities, Marinduque's **village markets** are great for buying carved birds, ornaments and baskets.

What to See and Do

Boac, Marinduque's provincial capital, is situated on the west coast. It is a sleepy settlement, dominated by a large church building, and dotted with wooden houses which seem to be staving off encroaching tropical foliage. Transport by horse-drawn rickshaws are commonplace, and village life — which may seem dull at first — soon reveals a seething bed of intrigue the longer you stay and the more you pay attention to the local, clannish gossip. Much activity centers around **The Lady of Biglang Awa** (Sudden Mercy), a shrine credited with miraculous powers. For at least a day during your stay, visit the **Tres Reyes** (Three Kings) **Islands**, which lie off the coast of **Gasan**, 13 km (eight miles) south of Boac. Of these islands, **Gaspar Island**, **Melchor Island** and **Baltazar** Island are 30 minutes away by hired outrigger banca and are perfect for swimming, fishing and snorkeling. Only experienced divers with local guides should attempt to explore the complex network of underwater caves that lie beneath these islands.

On the northern coast, the town of **Santa Cruz** is worth visiting for its church, built in 1714, but mostly for passing through en route to **Bathala Caves**, 10 km (six miles) away and **White Beach** at Poctoy near Torrijos, although jeepneys can be scarce for transport. South of Marinduque on **Elefante Island** Japanese investors created a private club, complete with golf course, named the **Fantasy Elephant Club** ((2) 817-5702. You can visit via boat from **Lipata**. The luxury resort has been so popular that another version is being constructed on Marinduque Island.

Where to Stay and Eat

The island's main cluster of guesthouses and eating places are found in Boac, but don't expect great luxury on Marinduque. In Boac, the **Susanna Inn** (VIA OPERATOR 1997, has comfortable rooms with air conditioning and bath; there's also a restaurant. The **Aussie-Pom Guest House** (no telephone), in **Caganhao** between Boac and **Cawit,** offers basic, spacious rooms and snorkeling equipment for the nearby (pebbly) beach.

The best place to stay on the island is the **Sunset Garden Resort** (MANILA (2) 801-6369, Pangi, about two kilometers (one and a quarter miles) outside Gasan. It has cottages with bath and fans and the island's best restaurant.

How to Get There

You can fly to Boac from Manila with Philippine Airlines, a daily 30-minute flight. Otherwise, from Mindoro Island, there is a daily boat service from Pinamalayan for Gasan, leaving at 8:30 AM, a journey of three and a half hours. It is also possible to make the longer boat journey from Lucena in Quezon to Balancan, in northwest Marinduque.

SOUTHEAST LUZON

It is left to intrepid souls to venture along the undeveloped, seahorse-shaped, southeastern peninsula on the main island of Luzon, which extends through the provinces of Camarines Norte, Camarines Sur, Albay, Sorsogon and Catanduanes Island. This is a fertile, volcanic region known for its lakes, beaches, hot springs — and hot, spicy cuisine — but not generally popular with tourists. The island of **Masbate** lies to the south, a stepping stone to the Visayas group.

At the region's center, in Albay province, **Mount Mayon** is the area's dominant volcano which has a track record of being frequently active and has exerted a sometimes fatal allure for vulcanologists and climbers. Mayon is distinctive for its perfectly symmetrical cone. The 2,450-m (8,040-ft)-high volcano has erupted four times since 1968, most recently in February 1993.

Legazpi, Albay's provincial capital, is accessible by air. It has a modest reputation as a crafts center, specializing in woven abaca mats and baskets. Within the area, the **Tiwi Hot Springs**, the ruins of the Spanish Church of **Cagsawa**—built in 1578 then buried under volcanic lava — and the **Hoyop-Hoyopan Caves** are the main attractions.

Not to be missed, the annual Moriones Festival on the island of Marinduque. LEFT: A reveler in Mogpog sports his colorful Roman centurion garb. OPPOSITE: During Holy Week, a Passion Play is presented with great realism. Here, a young Marinduque resident reenacts Christ's last steps.

Cebu
and the
Visayas

LOCATED IN THE HEART of the Philippines, between Luzon and Mindanao, the Visayas entice you to go island hopping, explore the history of colonial towns with their ornate Spanish churches and ancestral homes and experience some of the more spectacular undersea landscapes that the country has to offer. Alternatively, you may prefer to stay put and simply laze about in any one of the Visayas group's many beach resorts. Most are designed to resemble villages of *nipa* huts — a palm thatch and bamboo version of a hotel cabana.

The Visayas comprise six of the major 11 islands in the Philippines, as well as many smaller islands, and are divided up into 14 provinces. The main islands within the Visayas are Cebu, Negros, Panay, Bohol, Leyte and Samar. The reliable and efficient boat services which operate around the islands, as well as the short connections, make it practical to move around from island to island, unlike the large distances necessary to cover in some other more far-flung parts of the archipelago.

CEBU AND MACTAN

Lying within the middle of the Visayas island group, Cebu itself comprises 167 islands, many of which are startlingly beautiful and well known to divers. The historic city of Cebu is considered the regional center for the Visayas island group and over the past few years has undergone an economic transformation Cebuanos refer to as "Ceboom." Despite its rapid development and increasingly industrial skyline, Cebu has a relaxed ambiance and is well-endowed with fine architecture from its rich Malay and Hispanic past, reflecting too the ancestral wealth associated with surrounding sugar cane, mango, tobacco and hemp plantations.

In the thirteenth century, "Zubo" or "Sugbo" as it was then known, was a pre-colonial port town visited by Asian and Arabic traders. In 1521, Portuguese navigator Ferdinand Magellan made it his base on his explorations and incursions throughout the archipelago. He was welcomed by King Humblon and Queen Juana, who were converted to Christianity. By 1565, Cebu was made the Spanish headquarters, led by

Miguel Lopez de Legazpi, and for six years it was the capital of the Philippines.

When the Americans took over, they met with fierce resistance in the Cebu region, leading to the Toledo Bay skirmish in 1900. Cebu's strategic position in the central of Philippines also made it a prime target for the Japanese, who first bombarded it and then made it a base. Some of World War II's bloodiest battles here occurred in the Antuanga and Babag hills before the Japanese surrendered.

As well as being the oldest colonial city in the Philippines, Cebu is also one of the

nation's high profile seaside resorts, blossoming with tropical flowers and fringed by clustered coral reefs. On nearby Mactan Island, connected by bridge to Cebu, are several luxury resorts, dozens of small, locally-owned beach resorts and some well-patronized SCUBA diving centers. Also, Cebu has major international air links with international destinations, including Hong Kong and Sydney. From Cebu, there are many interisland flights daily to key provincial destinations throughout the archipelago.

Don't expect the city of Cebu to be a peaceful backwater without some of the development problems and social ills associated with Manila. It is doing its best to put up as many new hotels, shopping complexes and sky-scrapers as it can, while the nearby reclaimed Mactan Export Processing Zone is bristling with new factories, industrial estates, and an international container port is planned. Still,

OPPOSITE: In the heart of Cebu City, Fort San Pedro was originally built by the Spanish to protect themselves from Muslim invasions. ABOVE: Children returning home from a Bohol church.

the city retains much charm and piquant beauty and its historical buildings, façades and sites are preserved with care.

GENERAL INFORMATION

It is a 30-minute drive from Mactan International Airport to downtown Cebu, and jeepneys ply the route frequently. There is a convenient **Department of Tourism** office ((32) 254-2811 FAX (62-32) 254-2711, directly opposite Fort San Pedro. They can tell you about the range of tours on offer. The best way of getting around Cebu is by taxi — they're clean, air conditioned, metered and, for the most part, the drivers are honest. The Spanish colonial style *tartanilla*, or horse-drawn carriage, is still used in some parts of the city. Although you might want to take one, it can be distressing to observe how skinny and overworked the horses are. You can negotiate your fare with the ubiquitous jeepney and tricycle drivers. The local dialect is Cebuano or Bisaya, although English and Tagalog are widely spoken.

WHAT TO SEE AND DO

Most of Cebu's sights can easily be seen in a half-day on foot or by taxi, or a whole day if you wish to take your time. Meanwhile Mactan Island, a 20-minute drive away, is a world unto itself of beaches, resorts and diving attractions. In Cebu City **Fort San Pedro** is a good place to begin. Originally built as a fortress by the Spanish as their stronghold against Muslim raiders, it has been used subsequently as a barracks for Filipino revolutionaries, the American army and a Japanese internment camp for prisoners of war. The museum displays part of the treasure recovered from the Spanish galleon, *San Diego*.

Several blocks away, the **Basilica Minore del Santo Niño** houses the gem-festooned statue of the child Jesus, given by Magellan to Queen Juana. It is said to be the oldest religious relic in the country. Nearby, a shrine opposite City Hall contains the remnants of **Magellan's Cross**, originally planted there by Magellan to mark the spot where King Humblon and Queen Juana and 400 of their entourage became the first Filipinos to be baptized in 1521. During the

eighteenth century, this cross was pillaged by devout Catholics who believed that even tiny wooden chips from it had miraculous powers. Ceiling murals inside the shrine depict the first Catholic mass held in the Philippines.

Cebu has a number of small, but worthwhile museums which house collections of art and antiques. The **Cebu City Museum**, on Osmena Boulevard, has the most extensive and regionally representative display, with many collections donated by Cebu's old families. **Casa Gorordo**, on Lopez Jaena

Street, was the former residence of Cebu's first Filipino bishop and recreates the style of a Cebuano household in the nineteenth century. The **Sala Piano Museum** at 415 Gorordo Avenue, has pianos of all sizes and styles. The **Osmena Residence**, on Osmena Boulevard is also the former home of former president, Sergio Osmena and displays his memorabilia and antique collection. Included here are some historically interesting effects that belonged to General MacArthur. **Jumalon's Museum**,

OPPOSITE: Magellan's cross in Cebu marking the spot where he converted King Humblon to Christianity. ABOVE: Basilica Minore del Santo Niño, Cebu City, houses the oldest relic in the country — a gem-studded statue of the child Jesus.

located at 20 Macopa Street, Pardo, is remarkable for its collection of mosaics made from butterfly wings, bound to intrigue lepidopterists. They are the work of Professor Julian Jumalon, who collected together damaged butterfly wings from all over the world to create his artworks.

You may wish to take a taxi to visit the impressive **Taoist Temple**, atop 99 steps, with its views across the city from the affluent suburb somewhat self-consciously named Beverley Hills. On the way, you'll pass the **Cebu Capitol**, the domed legislative seat of the provincial government. Another place of interest is the **University of San Carlos**, established in 1565 by the Jesuits and the oldest school in the country. Within its museum and grounds, it sports a wide collection of archaeological, ethnic, botanical and zoological exhibits.

From here, via the city's main boulevard of Colon Street, the **Carbon Market** is worth seeking out for its warren of bazaars which can turn up some interesting bargains. It is also fun to browse in the section of the market which sells fresh fruits, flowers and sweets. Sample some of the region's mangoes, fresh or dried, *otap*, a crunchy sugar coated biscuit and *turrones*, a rolled wafer filled with peanut or cashew candy.

Bear in mind during your visit, that fashion accessories and rattan furniture are top exports from the Philippines and consequently Cebu has become a major port of call for international business people who buy direct from factories in the Mactan export zone. Standards of quality and workmanship are high. In particular, look for ethnic handicrafts such as basketwork, modern rattan and antique furniture, ceramics, *capiz* (shell), coral and fossil stone jewelry and shell inlaid guitars. Bear in mind, however, that in some parts of the world, the import of coral and shells is forbidden and it might be prudent to choose a souvenir which is more ecologically sound. You will find lists of manufacturers and exporters at the Department of Tourism office, and you can call ahead to arrange a visit.

Beaches, Islands and Churches

The eastern coast of Cebu, where you'll find Mactan Island, has many beautiful sandy bays. The more luxurious resorts either on Mactan itself, or dotted along the coast, have well-equipped dive centers and qualified instructors. There are equally plenty of facilities available for riding Hobiecats, jet skiing, or windsurfing at most resorts. Because the island has so many beaches, dive sites and some picturesque towns, hiring a car to explore is a good idea. Cebu Island is 300 km (186 miles) long and 40 km (25 miles) wide and has reasonable coastal roads.

You do not have to be an experienced diver to appreciate the beauty of many of the island's most spectacular and accessible dive sites. **Mactan** is a diving mecca, and its sites are good for beginners. **Olango Island** is accessible by boat from Mactan and gets high ratings from experienced divers for its underwater life. It is also rich in bird life. On the northwestern side of Cebu, **Moalboal** attracts serious divers with its amazing variety of sites, with coral gardens, caves, wide variety and shoals of fish and sea snakes. From Moalboal you can gain access to sites on **Pescador** and **Badian islands**, with their rich and colorful coral formations. **Sogod**, a one-and-a-half-hour drive north from Cebu, has dramatic cliff scenery, caves and beautiful secluded bays as well as some pleasant places to stay.

If you hire a car or decide to take a tour southwards to the resort area of **Argao**, make sure you stop at **Carcar**, south of Cebu City, a little town which has a beautiful **Spanish baroque church** dating back to 1876, facing a plaza lined with Spanish **colonial mansions**. The countryside, too, is attractive in this more rural part of the island. Also on the way, **Naga** is worth a stop to see its main church made out of coral and limestone and festooned with carved angels and gargoyles.

WHERE TO STAY

Cebu City is likely to experience a hotel boom in the next decade or two. Four new large resorts are being built along the Mactan

ABOVE: Plantation Bay Hotel, on Mactan, Cebu. BELOW: Borrowing ideas from traditional Philiippine handicrafts, this luxury hotel at Alegre, north of Cebu City, combines simplicity with luxury.

coast and others are on the drawing board. There are plenty of accommodation options. The nearby beach resort area of Mactan is where most visitors choose to stay, which, although its tropical setting and sandy bays are appealing, is rapidly becoming over-developed.

Luxury

Many regard the **Shangri-La Mactan Island Resort (** (32) 310288 FAX (32) 311688, Punta Engano Road, Mactan Island, as the finest the Philippines has to offer. It has five-star accommodation and facilities, a range of plush restaurants and bars, an excellent health club, interesting shops, all the conceivable amenities for business travelers and beautifully-landscaped gardens leading down to a white sand beach. It is the newest, biggest and most luxurious of all the Mactan resort hotels and usually the hotel chosen by those who have come to do business in the nearby export zone. It caters for families with its "Mactan Gang" all-day child care program. Overlooking the city from the Nivel Hills, **Cebu Plaza Hotel (** (32) 311231 FAX (32) 312069, Nivel Hills, Lahug, Cebu City, is regarded as Cebu City's premier business address. It is located at about a 10- to 20-minute drive from Cebu's central downtown area. Although it has great views, there is no beach in sight. In terms of accommodation, amenities, landscaped gardens and price, it falls somewhat short of what the Shangri-La Mactan can offer. The hotel is now undergoing a US$6 million facelift. **Plantation Bay (** (32) 340-5900 FAX (32) 340-5988, Marigondon, Mactan Island, is the newest entrant, billing itself as the "penultimate tropical lagoon resort." It has a wide expanse of private land overlooking an undisturbed powdery sand beach, with 38 elegant native-style bungalow suites nestled around a lagoon. Each of its 188 rooms are furnished with four-poster beds, embroidered linen and indigenously crafted Filipino furniture, with spacious private balconies. As well as all water sports, the resort offers evening cruises on its 18-m (60-ft)-long twin deck boat. There is a luxurious freshwater pool with built-in whirlpools, as well as tennis courts, a miniature golf and a health spa.

Expensive to Moderate

Moderately priced alternatives abound, with four-star hotels in both Cebu City and along the Mactan beach strip. In Mactan, **Cebu Beach Club (** MOBILE / FAX (32) 912-501-2610, Buyong, Mactan Island, is one of the most pleasant options, with its curved network of air-conditioned guest rooms, lagoon-style swimming pool (with Jacuzzi) and pleasant restaurant and beach bar. **Mar y Cielo Beach Resort (** (32) 253-2232 FAX (32) 253-4134, Barrio Angasil, Mactan, is an elegant, comfortably mid-size resort with a tranquil setting, pleasant views and native-style air-conditioned bungalows furnished Maranaw or Cebu style. Its central pavilion has three restaurants which serve seafood, European and Japanese cuisine. **Maribago Bluewater Beach Resort (** (32) 211260 or 217617 FAX (32) 912-510-0663, Maribago, Mactan, has 40 grass-thatched bungalows set around a white beach with a lagoon-shaped pool, with a small and personal atmosphere. **Costabella Tropical Beach Resort (** (32) 210828 or 210838 FAX (32) 314415, Buyong, Mactan, is a comfortable, relaxed resort with a pleasant beach setting. Also recommended is the **Coral Reef Hotel (** (32) 211-1191 or 211-1193 to 4 FAX (32) 211-1192, Agus, Mactan.

In Cebu City, both **Cebu Midtown Hotel (** (32) 253-9711 FAX (32) 254-6363, Fuente Osmena and **Park Place Hotel (** (32) 253-1131 FAX (32) 211131 or (32) 210018, Fuente Osmena, are typical high-rise hotels with good facilities and convenient location. Beyond the Cebu Plaza Hotel, in the Busay Hills, 35 minute's drive from Cebu, **Swiss Chalet (** EXTEL CELLPHONE (097) 323-0086 has a deliberately Swiss ambiance and pristine, mountain location. Owner Roland Wero and his wife Remy, a Filipina, also serve excellent Swiss dishes, including (of course) fondue specialties. Bring warm clothes as the mountain air can be bracing.

Inexpensive

In Mactan, the 75-room **Tambuli Beach Club (** (32) 211534 or (32) 211544, Buyong, Mactan Island, is probably too large for anyone looking for seclusion, but it might appeal to families. It has good facilities, landscaped gardens, child-friendly swimming pools and buffet-style dining. In Cebu City, the best choice is the **Montebello Villa Hotel** ((32) 313681 FAX (32) 314455, Banilad, Cebu City. Although located in suburban surroundings, it has large gardens that are a pleasant respite from the city. **Centrepoint International Cebu** ((32) 254-7111 FAX (32) 253-0695, Plaridel Street corner of Osmena Boulevard, is a good choice for staying in the city's historic downtown area. **Hotel de Victoria** ((32) 254-1331, 174 Manalili Street, offers unexceptional but economically priced rooms.

Remote Resorts on Cebu Island

If you are looking for peaceful luxury or simply peace, there are several resorts a few hours' drive from Cebu City and Mactan. The most exclusive and attractive of these is located in **Culumboyan** near **Sogod**: The **Alegre Beach Resort** ((32) 311231 FAX (32) 214345, is an upmarket resort run by the same group that runs the Cebu Plaza, located a 90-minute drive north from Cebu. It is perched on a dramatic cliff overlooking two white sandy beaches, with luxurious cabanas set amidst well-landscaped gardens. It has good tennis courts and a pleasant swimming pool for those wary of swimming in the sea. Rates: Luxury. Also in the Sogod area, is the inexpensive, **Cebu Club Pacific** ((32) 79147 FAX (32) 231-4621, a good base for exploring the surrounding beaches.

In **Dalaguete**, a two-hour drive south of Cebu, the **Argao Beach Resort** ((32) 72620 (MANILA (2) 522-2301, set on landscaped rolling grounds overlooking Cebu Strait, is a good base for water sports fans. It has a good diving center and instruction for would-be divers and windsurfers, as well as Hobiecats and paddle boats for hire. The resort has a 15-m (49-ft) glass-bottom boat that allows you to see Camay Reef. Boats trips for diving and island hopping are regularly scheduled.

On the west coast, at a distance of 100 km (62 miles) south of Cebu, with accommodation in the three- to four-star range, are two options. **Badian Island Beach Club** ((32) 253-6364 or (32) 253-6452 FAX (32) 263-3385, Badian, Cebu, is an upmarket and well-run, beautifully-landscaped resort

perfect for a peaceful island getaway. From Cebu, it is reached after two and a half hours by road and 10 minutes by boat. On the main island, **Cebu Green Island Club** ((32) 95-935 FAX (32) 231-1269, Lambug, Badian, Cebu, is a moderately priced resort that also has a golf course within its grounds. A few kilometers before the town of **Badian** is the **Moalboal** area, which has become well-known among serious SCUBA divers. The small, bungalows you can find close to the sea here are popular with budget travelers.

WHERE TO EAT

If you are staying in Cebu City, **Alavar's Seafood House** ((32) 96120, Gorordo Avenue, is one of the better restaurants, with excellent seafood and convivial atmosphere. The **Crab House** (231-5165, located along Archbishop Reyes, serves a delicious selection of crab dishes, each weighing no less than 600 g (1.6 lb). Along a similar culinary theme, but with a barn-like atmosphere, is **Seafood City** ((32) 213795, J.Y. Square, Lahug. **Café Adriatico** ((32) 217366, Ramos Street, is where Cebu's yuppies gather to see and be seen and snack on Westernized Filipino food. **Ginza** ((32) 281419, Second Floor, Belvic Complex, General Mailom Avenue, is where to go for the best Japanese food in Cebu. **Lumpia House**, in the Gaisano Country Mall, offers a range of appetizing Chinese and Filipino dishes. **Govinda's**, in Don Ramon Aboitiz Street, has interesting vegetarian food.

Lechon, roast suckling pig, waiting for hungry takers in a market stall, Cebu.

Up in the hills of **Busay**, are two recommended restaurants, both with lovely views. **Chateau de Busay** offers standard European fare offset by a pleasant setting. Also the hotel, **Swiss Chalet** serves excellent fondues.

If you check in to one of Cebu's resorts in **Mactan**, you may find yourself somewhat entrenched. Sampling the restaurants and bars of resorts other than the one you're staying in can be made difficult by obstacles along the beach as security guards, rock clusters and fences. With the exception of the Shangri-La Mactan, most of the restaurant food and

entertainment begins to wear thin after a day or two. In Mactan, it can be fun to take a taxi ride to the seafood market cafés which surround the monument in Punta Engano where Magellan was slain by local chieftain Lapu Lapu in 1521. **Anton's**, located on a pier beside the airport road junction, is also good.

NIGHTLIFE

Nightlife in Cebu, as in Manila, caters to all persuasions. Like the capital city, there are after-dinner diversions galore, and the only difference is that in Cebu the prices are lower. Bars and lounges at the main hotels are popular meeting places, especially **Pards** at the Cebu Plaza Hotel.

The following places, tucked here and there throughout Cebu City, offer something for everyone. **Cebu Casino** is the city's premier night spot. Located in the Cebu Plaza Hotel, it attracts both tourists and local high rollers. **Music Concourse Outback Lounge**, on D. Jakosalem Street, is a lively venue for some of Cebu's best bands, while **Frankfurter Hof (** (32) 54192, on Osmena Boulevard, is for country and western music devotees. **Caruso Music Bar**, at the corner of Escario Street and Kamagong streets, has an unpredictable ambiance. **Our Plaza**, at the corner of Pelaez and Sanciangco streets, is an expatriate hangout. **St. Moritz** is considered the most sophisticated of the city's go-go bars, while those seeking more titillation can move on to **Thunderdrome** or **Bigwig** on F. Ramos Street. With droves of Japanese, Korean and Taiwanese tourists flocking to Cebu City, karaoke and videoke bars have become quite popular here, and you will see them just about everywhere. Your taxi driver will know where to find the latest karaoke spots.

Cebu's fashionable dance floors are **Bai**, at the Cebu Plaza Hotel, **Balls** on General Maxilom Avenue and **Motions** at the Centrepoint. Note: These are not just discos; they also offer sessions of ballroom waltzes, tango, fox trot and salsa.

HOW TO GET THERE

The Mactan-Cebu International Airport is located at Lapu Lapu. Internationally, Cebu is on the scheduled route networks of Asiana, Cathay Pacific, Japan Airlines and SilkAir, as well as Philippine Airlines. There are direct flights from Sydney, Japan, Hong Kong, Malaysia, Guam, Singapore and Taiwan. Both Grand Air and Cebu Pacific Air intend to start international flights to Cebu from the main Asian cities. The new terminal is in its final stages of completion and will include an airport hotel and casino complex. The airport charges an extra P25 terminal fee, in addition to the (at the time of writing) normal P3 tax to help pay for the new amenities.

Cebu's domestic airport is not impressive. Philippine Airlines has daily flights to 22 domestic destinations within the Philippines, including Manila, an hour's flight.

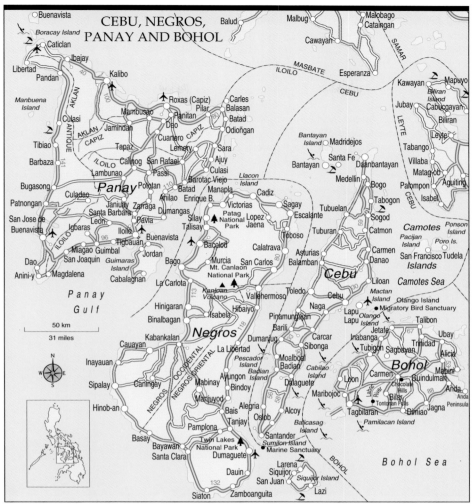

Grand International Airways has twice daily Airbus flights between Manila and Cebu and also to Davao. Cebu Pacific Air, controlled by the super-rich Gokonwei clan, has been given the government's go ahead to launch a Manila–Cebu service and has ambitious plans for five daily flights (on Boeing 737s) to Cebu with routes to Davao and other southern cities to follow. There is also a small domestic airport tax but it doesn't seem to be improving the standard of facilities. Not a place to linger if you can help it.

Cebu's port is the gateway to the southern Philippines. Manila is 22 hours away via most of the standard ferries. **WG&A Superferry** (see TRAVELERS' TIPS, page 252) has an excellent new, brisk service linking Manila with Cebu and a number of other destinations within the Visayas.

BOHOL ISLAND

Southeast of Cebu across the Tanon Strait, the rounded island of Bohol is notable for its strange geological formations and its lush, tropical forests rich in exotic flora and fauna.

Bohol is also a pleasant place to stay for a day or two, to enjoy the atmosphere of its small coastal towns, Antillan mansions and colonial churches. Like Cebu, Bohol has a variety of resorts, most notably the Bohol Beach Club and many surrounding dive

OPPOSITE: Roadside foodstall, in the heart of Cebu.

spots, of which the best known is Panglao Island. You can also use the island as a base for visiting the spectacular marine sanctuaries and coral reefs around the smattering of beautiful outlying islands which dot the Cebu Strait, the Bohol Sea and the Camotes Sea. Whales and dolphins are frequently sighted in these waters, while in the deeps are large mantas and hammerhead sharks. The island is also the home of the rare tarsier monkey, reputedly the world's smallest primate, which can fit into the palm of a human hand.

GENERAL INFORMATION

Contact the **Punta Cruz Diving Club** (/FAX (32) 54114, at **Maribojoc,** for information about diving.

WHAT TO SEE AND DO

Bohol is most famous for its **Chocolate Hills** — exactly 1,268 perfectly shaped haycock mounds (one wonders who bothered to count them all) which undulate throughout the townships of **Carmen**, **Batuan** and **Sagbayan** — roughly in the center of the island. These hills, which range in height from 40 m (131 ft) to 120 m (394 ft), derive their name from the effect each summer, when the

sun burnishes the tussock grasses of the hills a dark brown. They are at their most chocolaty between February and May and are green after July, when the monsoons keep them lushly carpeted. There are all sorts of local legends about the phenomenon. One story tells of two giants having a fight here, throwing huge boulders at each other. Another claims that the boulders are tears shed by a giant when he fell in unrequited love for a mortal Filipina girl; the tears hardened into stone. Scientific speculation has it that the hills are formed by buckling limestone cav-

erns beneath the earth's surface, or that as a massive volcano self-destructed, it spat huge balls of stone, which were then covered in limestone and lifted up from the ocean bed to assume their present abode. Whatever their origin, the Chocolate Hills of Bohol are one of the region's great wonders. You can either get there by guided tour from Tagbilaran or hire a car. The island's highlights are easily seen in a day or two.

Bohol's sleepy capital, **Tagbilaran**, has both an Hispanic and a Moorish air with its Jesuit churches and colonial stone and tiled-roof mansions. Tagbilaran's **city market** is interesting for its variety of woven mats, winnowing baskets, buri hats and handicrafts made from capiz and coconut shells. The market is also a good place to find exotic shells themselves. The **Bohol Provincial Museum** has a dusty grandeur. Once the mansion of Carlos P. Garcia, a former president of the Philippines, it has been turned into a showcase for ethnic relics, papers and political memorabilia.

In **Bool Barrio**, a couple of kilometers south of the city center, you can see the commemorative marker which designates the famous "blood compact" which took place here. It was here that Spanish conquistador Miguel Lopez de Legazpi and the island's

seum with some Spanish icons, native religious art and ecclesiastical garments, as well as librettos of church music printed in Latin on animal skin. You'll need to rouse the priest to get permission to enter. The town of Baclayon itself is interesting, too, for its taste of rural island life.

You may wish to stop at **Bilar** to see the man-made forest there with its exotic plants and the chance to glimpse the remarkable tarsier monkey, a shy nocturnal creature which does not often survive in captivity. Sadly, most of those captured by poachers

chief, Sikatuna, drew their own blood, mixed it with wine and drank it, sealing a pact of peace between their people. Each June, this place becomes the scene of a colorful re-enactment of the blood compact ceremony during the Sandugo, or "One Blood," Festival.

As you take the main road out to the Chocolate Hills along the southeast coast, make sure you stop at **Baclayon Church**, six kilometers (three and three quarters miles) away from the city center. Built in 1595, it is the oldest stone church in the Philippines. You can see faint remnants of the gold leaf paint work on the carving adorning the central and side altars, housing antique santos. The original ivory faces were stolen in the 1970s. An adjacent convent has a small mu-

in the pet trade die, as pitiful stuffed tarsiers seem to be a popular commodity. Bohol is also home to flying lemurs the size of large house cats, although their numbers have been decreasing at a worrying rate because of the destruction of their natural habitat with the development of villages and tourist complexes on the island. As well, they face being hunted down for native hotpots. Butterflies are at their most exuberant in Bohol from November to May, which is when scores of enthusiastic Japanese butterfly hunters have been known to descend on the island.

OPPOSITE: A traditional village house in laid-back Bohol. ABOVE: Living up to their name, the ever-changing brown hues of the Chocolate Hills.

When you return to Tagbilaran, it's a short detour to the nearby town of **Maribojoc**. The **Punta Cruz Watchtower** with its adjacent cross stills stands guard over the bay, just as when it was used by the Spanish to watch out for Muslim pirates.

An idyllic way to spend a sunny afternoon in Bohol is to float down the winding **Laboc River** to **Busay Falls**, watching the scenery drift by, hearing the sounds and breathing in the scent of the jungle. The Bohol Beach Club (see WHERE TO STAY AND EAT, below) organizes these river safaris.

government tourism plans. On the island, **Hinagdanan Cave** has a mysterious atmosphere, with its underground springs lit by natural skylights. Although quite old, the look of **Dauis Church** is unremarkable, yet it has certain following within the Philippines for the supposedly restorative powers of its natural spring which bubbles up from under the main altar.

The surrounding islands of **Balicasag** and **Pamilacan** — as well as **Cabilao** and **Pangangan** farther south — are justifiably sought-after destinations by divers, although

Along the eastern coast of Bohol, the region around the **Anda Peninsula** is unspoiled and has some breathtaking coves to explore. This area remains almost entirely undeveloped. Archaeological finds around in this region date the earliest human remains found here to around 10,000 BC, and many dugout molave wood coffins have been found, some decorated with reptile heads or flattened skulls in accordance with ancient burial practices.

Panglao Island
The largest island near Bohol, located off its southwestern tip near Tagbilaran, Panglao Island has been recently singled out for special priority in newly conservation-minded

simply enjoying their natural beauty is wonderful also.

WHERE TO STAY AND EAT

Moderate
Situated in Panglao Island, **Bohol Beach Club** ((32) 211091 or (32) 211543 or (32) 211544 FAX (32) 211545, or (MANILA (2) 522-2301 FAX (2) 522-2304, Suite 1401, Victoria Building, United Nations Avenue, Ermita, Manila, is a sister property of the Tambuli Beach Club in Cebu and is accessible by 20-minute transfer from Tagbilaran. It has the advantage of being far more private, with pleasantly furnished, native style bungalows with fans and private verandahs. A pool, Jacuzzi, spa and saunas,

a tennis court and a range of water sports facilities make up the resort complex. The island itself is pretty, with a three-kilometer (two-mile) ring of sand.

Inexpensive

Crystal Coast Villas ((32) 3179 **(** MANILA (2) 828-0441, 234 El Grand Avenue, B.F. Homes, Las Piñas, Manila, is also on Panglao Island, at Tawala. It's is a small, comfortable, less expensive resort and is conveniently-located. **Balicasag Island Dive Resort (** MANILA (2) 812-1984 or 810-3655 FAX (2) 812-1164,

Ground Floor, Maripola Building, 109 Perea Street, Legazpi Village, Makati or **(** BOHOL (32) 3369, Governor's Mansion, CPG North Avenue, Tagbilaran City, Bohol, located 45 minutes from Panglao Island by boat, has basic bungalows and simple fare. This resort is more rustic than Crystal Coast, but it offers good value for serious divers, for whom it is geared.

HOW TO GET THERE

PAL has a daily direct flight from Manila to Tagbilaran City. This flight takes one hour and 55 minutes. Daily direct flights are also available from Cebu and take 25 minutes. Fast ferry services are avail-

able between Cebu and Bohol and take about 90 minutes.

NEGROS

Across the Guimaras Strait from Cebu is the lushly beautiful island of Negros, with its cloud-wreathed purple mountains, fertile forests and volcanoes, hot springs and paradisiacal beaches. Yet more than any other island, Negros symbolizes the feudal and economic rifts and struggles that have plagued the Philippines. The fourth largest island in the archipelago (some 215 km or 133 miles in length) most of the sugar plantations in the Philippines are concentrated on Negros. Once one of the richest islands in the archipelago until the 1980s collapse of world sugar prices, it has now become one of the poorest. The plummeting price of sugar plunged the future of some two million migrant workers on the island into turmoil. It has been calculated that five million Filipinos were affected adversely, albeit sometimes indirectly, by the crash. Worst hit were the 300,000 sugar workers and their families. Their existence was perilous at the best of times, but they were suddenly exposed to destitution and starvation on such a miserable scale so as to put Negros on the world poverty map and send economic shockwaves throughout the Philippines.

Until the nineteenth century, Negros was almost uninhabited, but by 1893, it had become an ant-like hive of industry devoted almost entirely to sugar production with 274 steam operated sugar mills surrounded by hundreds of thousands of hectares of sugar cane fields to supply them and an enormous migrant worker population, most of whom had swarmed from outlying islands in search of wages. Related to the island's economic suffering, Negros has also witnessed a communist insurgency, in a way that has been described both on Negros and throughout parts of the Philippines as *ningas cogon* ("sudden brush fire"). Turbulence is traditional here.

OPPOSITE: Sunlight filters through the canopy of trees in a Bohol rainforest. ABOVE: In Baclayon harbor, in front of the Philippines' oldest stone church, a small flotilla of bright *bancas*.

In the resplendent sumptuous *haciendas* — airy ranch houses on stately plantation estates — built by wealthy Negros landowners, pious churches, tropical expanses of cane and violently beautiful sunsets, there are strong echoes of the American antebellum South. In some settings, you half expect to see a Filipina version of Scarlett O'Hara calling out for her maid from a polished, antique-filled mansion. The Spanish called the island after its predominantly Negrito population.

Steam and smoke still belch out from the chimneys of the Victorias Milling Company, one of the largest sugar refineries in the world. Antique steam engines still ply the tracks along with their modern brethren with their endless loads of sugar cane from the fields to the mills. Yet now Negros both hopes and actively anticipates that its future may improve with the increase of another and new industry — tourism, as the many recently constructed hotels and facilities attest. With its location between Cebu and Panay, the island of Negros — both Occidental and Oriental — makes a perfect stopover if you have time to spend in the region.

BACOLOD

Surrounded by plantations, Bacolod — capital of Negros Occidental — exudes all the peculiarities of a formerly feudal society. A relatively modern city, it has its share of wealthy landowner's mansions and churches. It is interesting to pass through Bacolod, perhaps at the time of the **Masskara Festival** in October, but rather than stay in Bacolod overnight, opt for the island's beach resorts. In recent years Bacolod has been striving to become the convention capital of the Philippines.

General Information

The **Department of Tourism** office ((34) 29021 is located at the Bacolod Seawall.

What to See and Do

Start your explorations in the **Plaza**, which draws multitudes each Sunday and on fiesta days. It is flanked by the **San Sebastian Cathedral**, built in 1882. Aside from some fine regional government buildings and city

mansions, try to see some of Bacolod's antique collections, often private museums that are family run. The **Torres Antique Collection**, near the Airport Subdivision, with its Ming dynasty porcelain and Hispanic and native santos is worth seeing, as is the **Vega Antique Collection** at Nº4 19th Street with its fine collection of wooden and ivory votive statues, Indochinese furniture and pottery and the **Buglas Collection** on Lizares Avenue. In **Santa Clara**, near Bangao Wharf, is a little chapel with an extraordinary mosaic mural fashioned from thousands upon thousands of shells. You may need to book your visit in advance.

In Bacolod's **markets**, look for the sugar-laden delicacies Negros is famous for: dulce

gatas, sweetened carabao milk, *pinsasugbo* (sticky, sugarcoated banana) and *pi-aya* (a flaky, sugar-filled pancake).

Bacolod is known throughout the Philippines for its fine ceramics and handpainted porcelain, but you'll also see curious creations of colorful artificial flowers made out of wood shavings. Places to shop include **Philippine Antiques and Artwares** on Mandalagan Street, **Goldenfield Commercial Complex** and **Recuerdos de Bacoclod** on Rizal Street near the Plaza and **Samodal Woodshave Shop** on Second Street, Banahaw, in Villamonte.

It is possible to visit the **Victorias Milling Company** and be given a guided tour of its operations, throughout the day. You can take the Rainbow minibus from Bacolod which makes the 34-km (21-mile) trip out to the town of **Victorias**, then catch a jeepney to the mill compound, which functions as a mini-township. Like exploring the shipyards of Poland, there is a certain political frisson to visiting the mills in Negros. The **St Joseph the Worker Chapel**, built in 1948, has on display a remarkable mosaic made of broken beer and soft drink bottles by the American artist Ade de Bethune which featured in a *Life* magazine report. It depicts Christ as a brown-skinned Filipino in native dress, and for this the chapel is more commonly known as the "Chapel of the Angry Christ."

Thatched village home on Panglao Beach, Bohol.

As you drive out to Victorias, stop by at **Silay**, which lies 18 km (11 miles) north of Bacolod. It is a pretty coastal city of languid Spanish-era mansions and plantation estates, quietly moldering away like that of Dickens' Miss Haversham. Make sure you stop to see **Hofilena Art Collection**, 5 de Noviembre Street, which has an eclectic and serious collection of painting. It also houses the country's oldest printmaking workshop.

Patag, 25 km (16 miles) inland from Silay, is notable as the last Japanese stronghold in World War II and has a memorial marker.

Where to Stay and Eat
MODERATE
Bacolod Convention Plaza Hotel ((34) 83551 to 9 FAX (34) 83392, Magsaysay Avenue, is the best hotel in Negros, designed to soothe away the cares of weary conference goers. It has most amenities including a fine swimming pool and the best restaurant in town. **L'Fisher Hotel** ((34) 82731 to 39 FAX (34) 819-2502, corner 14th and Lacson streets, is secluded, located in the northern part of town, with attractively furnished, comfortable rooms that have most modern conveniences. **Goldenfield Garden Hotel** ((32) 83541, Goldenfield Complex, located near the airport, this hotel is noted by locals for its good swimming pool and lively discotheque.

INEXPENSIVE
Bascon Hotel ((34) 23141, Gingaga Street, is a good choice for its friendly management and clean, air-conditioned rooms. **Jara Beach Resort** ((34) 22054 FAX (34) 25446, lies 16 km (10 miles) south from Bacolod, at **Calumangan**.

EXCURSIONS FROM BACOLOD

Endowed with bubbling sulfur springs, **Mambucal** is a popular Negros beauty spot, yet it remains a tranquil place to visit, an hour's drive from Bacolod. The **Mambucal Mountain Resort** is a base for exploring the area's hot springs and mountain trails. Within the region, there are some dramatic climbing and walking trails in and around **Canlaon Volcano**, with challenging climbs that encounter a white sand bank called

Marghaha Valley, its twin craters rising 2,465 m (8,087 ft) above sea level. The bridge between the two craters of Balinsayao and Danao draws speculating vulcanologists who monitor the volcano's geological pulse.

ILOCOON ISLAND

At the northern tip of Negros, shaped like a gibbous moon, Ilocoon Island is a haven for snorkeling and diving, rich in marine life, coral reefs and strewn with exotic shells on its sands. Villagers will only know it by its colloquial name of "Lakawon", so be sure to ask about it using this name. It is a lovely place to visit, and it's interesting as well to see the villages en route.

DUMAGUETE

The provincial capital of Negros Oriental, **Dumaguete** draws divers for the multitude of magnificent dive sites in its surrounding clear blue waters. The main destinations to seek out from here, rather than spending much time in the town, are **Apo Island**, **Sumilon Marine Park** and **Siquijor Island**.

General Information
There are two useful local companies which can advise on diving trips: **JMC International Travel and Tours** ((2) 873109 FAX (2) 817-5556, Santa Monica Beach Resort, Banilad, Dumaguete, and **Magnum Marine Corporation** ((2) 813-1696 FAX (2) 818-5043, c/o South Sea Hotel, Bantayan.

What to See and Do
In Dumaguete, both **Silliman University** and the university's **Anthropological Museum** are worth a stroll through, especially the latter for its painstaking collection gathered from throughout the province and beyond in archaeological digs, with such oddities as well-preserved human bones and relics, limestone burial jars, witchcraft accoutrements and ancient Chinese pottery shards. Silliman University was the first private American Protestant university in the Philippines and was built in 1901. It is known for its conservation-minded, marine and ornithological research and programs.

Within its extensive grounds is also a bird sanctuary.

APO ISLAND

Declared a marine sanctuary in order to protect its rare and unusual coral formations and fish, Apo Island is used as an offshore study center by the Silliman University. Despite some troublesome currents, the profusion of fish makes it a remarkable diving and snorkeling spot.

SUMILON ISLAND

Developed as a marine sanctuary, largely through the efforts of Silliman University, Sumilon Island later became the source of much disputation between the region's provinces, local fishermen unwilling to give up their usual practices and some unscrupulous dive operators. Despite local tensions, the **Sumilon Island Marine Sanctuary** has lovely beaches, snorkeling and diving and should be visited. Offshore, dolphins and whales are frequently sighted. With its magnificent marine life, the island is a valuable laboratory base and scientific observation post for Philippine and visiting marine biologists.

Where to Stay
INEXPENSIVE
The small **Santa Monica Beach Resort(** (34) 3441, Banilad, four kilometers (three miles) south of Dumaguete, is popular with divers.

How to Get There
Both Bacolod and Dumaguete are linked by daily Philippine Airlines flights from Manila (about one hour) and Cebu (about 30 minutes). By boat, Negros has regular links with Manila and the main ports of all the neighboring islands — Cebu, Bohol, Panay, Guimaras, Mindanao and Siquijor. The super quick and luxurious *St. Michael* ferry plies between Iloilo and Bacolod twice each day, except Sunday. There are also direct Cebu–Bacolod buses that traverse the route in one day, a rather gruelling experience. Apo Island is 10 km (six miles) south of Dumaguete and Sumilon Island Marine Sanctuary, about 12 km (eight miles) northeast of Dumaguete. Both are reached by hired banca.

SIQUIJOR ISLAND

Mystery permeates Siquijor Island, renowned as a destination for those in search of supernatural assistance. Filipinos will warn you of strange curses, wanton witches, macabre practices and unexplained mystic events that occur on this island.

The Spaniards called it "Isla del Fuego" or "Fire Island," although quite why they named it so is not established; some speculate that the name derived from the fiery specks of glow worms are sometimes sighted from sea. Approximately 75,000 people live on the island, most eking out a rustic existence that is deeply entwined with voodoo-like rituals. The donning of *anting-anting*, or amulets supposedly invested with specified powers, enjoys a special significance here.

It is a fascinating island to visit, although you may sometimes feel you are following in the exhaust of all the anthropologists and travel writers who have been here before you. The worldly-wise Siquijorians have witnessed much. During Easter, for example, the Holy Week rituals here are particularly excessive. The native *mangkukulam*, or island healers and witches, have earned a reputation that is difficult to ignore — they are believed to cure illnesses, cast out evil spirits and apply or reverse curses. The process usually involves eye-to-eye contact between the mangkukulam and his or her client. There are also *bolobolo* men, or bubble men, who spirit away ills from people's bodies in a ceremony involving a bamboo straw and a glass of water.

What to See and Do
The main towns of Siquijor are **Larena**, the sleepy port where ferries dock, the capital **Siquijor**, the mountainous hamlet of **San Antonio** and **Lazi**, a rustic wharfside settlement where the main entertainment is cock fighting. San Antonio is the epicenter of the archipelago's faith-healing community, which comes to life during Holy Week, when alleys are strewn with dried herbs, strange wafts of noxious-smelling brews permeate the air and healing rites are conducted behind closed doors. The special herbs and

plants they use are found in the mountains surrounding San Antonio. On the southwestern side of the island, **Paliton Beach**, near **San Juan**, is one of the most attractive beaches, with a resort conveniently located on it.

Where to Stay and Eat

Don't expect fine accommodation or good cuisine here, nor the atmosphere of Siquijor to be particularly welcoming. (Some inhabitants feel that tourists should stick to other islands instead of coming here.) At Paliton Beach, the **Coco Grove Beach Resort** has inexpensive rooms with air conditioning and bath, as well as an unexceptional restaurant. It is a good base from which to hire transport — either a jeepney or a banca.

Larena offers some opportunities for shelter and sustenance, with small guest houses and eating houses that open their doors when the ferries dock. The **Paradise Beach** at **Sandugan**, which is run by an Englishman and his Filipina wife, has a good restaurant, while the **Hidden Paradise** at **Bitaog** is run by an irrepressible hotelier who is also a tricycle driver and can escort you around the island for a reasonable fee. Booking is pot luck since — as like many of the remoter islands in the Philippines — telephones are scarce on Siquijor. **Bitaog** is nine kilometers (six miles) northeast of Larena, just before the town of **Enrique Villanueva**, about 300 m (328 yds) off the ring road, while Sandugan is closer to Larena, at the island's northern point, called Sandugan Point.

How to Get There

Siquijor may soon be added to the Philippine Airlines service to Cebu. In the meantime, the island is reached via public ferry, which runs twice daily from Dumaguete's main pier, or by enlisting a willing boatman to take you across the strait.

PANAY

The triangular, mellow island of Panay is framed by lush vegetation, rural scenes, pretty Spanish stone churches and some glorious beaches, encompassing the resort of Boracay Island. Panay has four provinces: Iloilo, Aklan, Antique and Capiz.

ILOILO

One of the loveliest Spanish colonial settlements, Iloilo is a charming place, with its white stone carved, sixteenth century churches, aristocratic ancestral mansions, plentiful gardens, unspoiled beaches and bustling markets. If you choose a more elaborate route through the Visayas and want to see some its sleepy backwaters, this is a good place to start. From here, you can explore the rest of Panay, visit the offshore islands of

Guimaras and Sicogon, idle away time at the nearby resort of Isla Naburot and travel to Caticlan bound for Boracay. From Iloilo, flights can take you to regional islands.

What to See and Do

The **Miag-ao Church**, declared a World Heritage Site by UNESCO, is the centerpiece of Iloilo's architectural tradition. Built in 1786, the Spanish colonial church has an unusual façade that bursts with botanical motifs in carved naive-style motifs that bear a likeness to Aztec designs. Its unconventional shape and pillared columns give it a playful, unique charm. The fascinating **Museo Iloilo** should not be missed. It is a well-presented repository of prehistoric artifacts dug up from

Panay burial grounds and offers a detailed impression of the early lives of the island's tribes. Among its exhibits are gold-leaf death masks, antique seashell jewelry and other decorative ornaments worn by Panay islanders. The museum also displays some of the recovered treasure from a nineteenth century British cargo ship that was wrecked off Guimaras Island, a scarcely damaged array of Victorian china, port wine and Glasgow beer.

There are a number of rather unusual churches in Iloilo, musty and quietly redolent of an impassioned Catholicism left behind by the departing Spaniards. The Gothic-Renaissance-style **Molo Church**, which dates from the 1800s, was built on solid coral, the **Jaro Church** is an impressive Gothic-style cathedral and the red-stone Renaissance-style **Pavia Church** has unusual window frames made of coral rock. The **San Joaquin Church**, built in 1869, has a bas-relief that depicts the historic faraway Tetuan battle fought between the Spanish Christians and the Moors of Morocco. The **Cabatuan Cemetery**, its entrance flanked by Gothic-style gates and chapel, is filled with elaborate ancestral tombs and graves dating from 1875. Six kilometers (three and three quarters miles) west of the town, **Arevalo** has some fine nineteenth century mansions.

In the main **markets**, look for the unique fabrics from this region, *piña* and *jusi*, made from pineapple and banana fibers and then hand-embroidered and fashioned into Filipino clothes, such as the barong tagalog. It's interesting to browse for handicrafts, nata de coco or native-made soap and baskets.

GUIMARAS ISLAND

Located 15 minutes from Iloilo, this pretty island is a good place to come for a morning or a day, with its many beaches, water-

falls, springs and rich marine life. On the island, you might notice the curious summer house known as the **Roca Encantada**, perched on a promontory overlooking the Guimaras Strait, built by the distinguished Lopez clan. You may need directions to find the **Catilaran Cave**; ask a local. On Good Friday, hundreds of devotees clamber through its half-kilometer (one-third-mile)-long cave tunnel, reciting Latin prayers, hopeful that this will ensure protection from evil spirits. Priceless Ming jars have been unearthed here.

OPPOSITE and ABOVE: Party time during the annual Ati-Atihan Festival held each January in Kalibo, Aklan Province, on Panay Island.

Within the Guimaras Island, the **Tiniguiban Puland Payasan Beach** will appeal to divers, with its quantities of rare red shrimps that breed in a nearby lake and emerge at high tide.

ISLA NAGARAO

This is a charming island to visit, for a day or longer, if you want to stay at the simple bungalow resort here, which has peaceful vistas. Its various bays can be reached by a 45 minute boat ride from Fort San Pedro in Iloilo.

Where to Stay
MODERATE
Run by the Saldena family, this simple, secluded and gloriously situated **Isla Naburot Resort** ((33) 76616 or (33) 75867, Sinapsapan, Jordan, Guimaras, is a special place to stay, despite its lack of electricity. Surrounded by such natural beauty, candlelight only adds to the ambiance. The resort is simply, but attractively designed, with thatched bungalows set amongst palm trees, some built for two people, others for as many as eight, all under airy lofts and full of unusual features such as carved wooden doors. The coral island itself is rimmed with soft white sand and blue waters, with a lush interior of prolific vegetation. With its peaceful coves, this is a perfect place to come for a few days of snorkeling and relaxing by the beach. With spacious, attractively decorated bungalows and good facilities, The **Costa Aguada Island Resort** ((33) 831-2261 FAX (33) 833-0357, Inampulugan Island, Guimaras, is well recommended, although it lacks the fabulous scenery offered at Isla Naburot. **Nagarao Island Resort** ((33) 78613, Nagarao Island, Jordan, Guimaras, is another getaway beach resort, with a restaurant and swimming pool overlooking the bay.

INEXPENSIVE
While not as lovely as other island options, **Sarabia Manor Hotel** ((34) 72731 to 35 FAX (33) 79127, 101 General Luna Street, Iloilo, is equipped with all the basic amenities. In addition, it provides a pleasant option for those who wish to stay in the town.

How to Get There
Iloilo is connected by daily one-hour Philippine Airline flights from Manila and from Cebu, Zamboanga and some destinations within Panay. Ferry services ply between Iloilo and Bacolod. Contact WG&A SuperFerry (see TRAVELERS' TIPS, page 252) to check their schedule from Manila to link with Visayan destinations. Within Panay, a range of jeepneys, buses and bus coaches make connections daily between Caticlan and San José de Buenavista in Antique province and Roxas in Capiz province, but be prepared for a long and bumpy trip.

FARTHER AFIELD

Located on the eastern side of Panay, **Marbuena Island Resort** (MANILA (2) 77777 is worth going out of your way to find. Its owners run this moderately priced hideaway along environment-friendly lines and it sits within its own forested coral island, home to wild parrots and fruit bats. Its pretty beaches feel secluded and the trail that runs across the island was created so that guests can experience the stillness and beauty of its exotic vegetation. Nipa-walled rooms are simple but comfortable and there are facilities for snorkeling, canoeing and SCUBA diving. To reach the resort hire a taxi from Iloilo to **Culasi**, where a 15-minute pump boat ride will take you to Marbuena.

KALIBO

Kalibo, the provincial capital of Aklan, is most famous for its raucously festive and exuberant **Ati-Atihan Festival**, held on the third week of January (see FESTIVE FLINGS, page 42). Otherwise, it is merely a place to pass through en route to the island of Boracay.

BORACAY

Washed by the South China and Sulu seas and rimmed with legendary sugar-textured white sands, Boracay is one of the Philippines' best known and loved islands. This butterfly-shaped island lies north of Panay, south of the island of Romblon and southeast of Mindoro. The superlatives uttered about its silky sands and clear blue water remain accurate, yet this delicate little island is suffering from the onslaught of careless development and too many visitors.

Boracay was considered a well-kept secret by cognoscenti travelers when it was first discovered as an idyllic haven in the early 1970s. Back then, visitors to the island stayed with villagers, or in tiny, makeshift huts, temporarily experiencing the lifestyle of a remote, clannish island, which depended almost entirely on subsistence fishing and agriculture. Local Boracayans are a mixture of races, primarily of Negrito descent.

Today, however, life in Boracay is almost entirely dedicated to accommodating and entertaining droves of tourists. Some of these visitors are hardy travelers making their way through the region, while others have flown in from Hong Kong or Australia for an uncomplicated beach holiday in blissful surroundings. The tiny island — 1,000 hectares (2,500 acres) — hums with beachfront hotels, cafés, restaurants and shops. Village boys rove the beaches in search of customers to take around the island on their outrigger banca canoes; groups of middle-aged women — usually mothers well-versed in the art of massage — offer to rub tired shoulders and limbs under a tree; children sell shells on the sandy pathway that passes as Boracay's main street on White Beach.

There is concern that the impact of tourism is not only disturbing the island's ecological balance but also causing social rifts within the lives of the native Boracayans, who have had to adjust sharply to keep pace with the mushrooming tourist-based economy. Yet, the islanders are proud of their idyllic home and old traditions and are eager to preserve them. Tourists, who outnumber residents, are considered "guests" and should take care to respect the mores of the locals who look askance upon public nudity, brawling and displays of loud, bad manners.

Since the pre-electricity days of the 1970s, when the nearby airfield in neighboring Caticlan, Panay, was merely a tin shack and a grass strip, the island has been transformed. Neon lights and disco strobes have replaced flickering kerosene lamps in the tourist havens, and the new airstrip has been slightly upgraded. The main mode of getting to the island is still by banca outrigger.

Dotted with hotels, the main attraction is White Beach which, despite the large numbers of visitors to the island, remains lovely. The beach is only slightly marred from time to time by the fairly recent seasonal algae phenomenon which was caused by unprocessed waste being washed back on shore. Environmental groups on the island and in Manila are concerned that the island ecosystem may be placed under greater strain if permission is granted to an estate conglomerate to create a golf course along with a massive 600-room resort. Already, the

island's ground water has been so contaminated by waste and sewage that it is only possible to drink bottled water.

As you walk along the beach, especially away from White Beach, you will see the pretty puka shells that are part of Boracay's charm. They used to be exported from here, but islanders now worry that they will all disappear.

GENERAL INFORMATION

The usual (and more effective) way to make reservations and get information for Boracay resorts and hotels is to contact their Manila representative office, rather than calling them on the island directly, which can be difficult. If you do want to call direct to Boracay, note that local telephone numbers given below do not include the area code, since you will probably have to place the call through an operator.

Good winds have earned Boracay a reputation as a windsurfing and sailing center. ABOVE: A *banca* competing in a Boracay Regatta.

Prices indicated below apply to the peak season from November to May. During the off season, rates can drop as much as 30 percent. On White Beach, close to Angol Beach, the **Boracay Tourist Center** offers a reasonably efficient service for dealing with most arbitrary business needs such as making telephone calls, sending mail and faxes and changing currency. It has a travel desk where you can arrange onward ticketing and make bookings. It's also the place to get up-to-date information. Next door is a well-stocked shop. There is a doctor's clinic and pharmacy near Angol along White Beach. The *Boracay Dateline*, the island's newspaper and the *Boracay Sand Paper*, the weekly tourist broadsheet, are the local reads.

WHAT TO SEE AND DO

Boracay has three main villages: **Balabag**, **Manoc-Manoc** and **Yapak**, each of which bustle with stalls, little shops and impromptu outdoor cafés. White Beach, facing the Sulu Sea, is lined with shops, cafés and hotels. Near its south end, the *talipapa,* or **flea market,** is a good place to shop for beach clothes, hats, cotton bags and cheap jewelry. Tie-dyed shirts and sarongs are especially popular, along with perishable flour sack clothing.

The widest, longest and most sheltered beach on the island is **White Beach**, which stretches from **Diniwid Beach** at its tip to **Angol Beach** and has relatively safe (currentless) swimming as far as 50 m (55 yds) out. At the northern tip, **Yapak** and **Puka beaches** are both beautiful, with sheltered sandy coves and inviting water with a deep ocean floor, good for SCUBA and snorkeling close to shore.

When you tire of lazing ashore, hire a banca and cruise around the island, either for snorkeling, SCUBA diving, or to choose a secluded bay in which to swim. This is the Philippine version of renting a gondolier and rates are negotiable, usually by the hour. Ask around and at your hotel for the going price. The Boracayan sailors who offer their services know their island's currents and swells — they and their ancestors have been plying these waters for centuries in similar boats. A popular place to stop and have lunch while you are cruising around is the **Puka Beach Café** which prepares excellent

grilled fish, squid and serves fresh coconut juice and beer.

There are several relatively serious-looking SCUBA outfits along White Beach where you can enroll yourself in diving lessons at your own discretion. They offer daily expeditions to surrounding dive sites, including nearby **Laurel Island**.

The more expensive resorts, such as Friday's and Lorenzo's have various water sports facilities, and you can browse for windsurf board rentals along White Beach. Boardsailing (as windsurfing is known here)

is an entrenched fad in Boracay, which hosts the **Boracay International Funboard Cup** — touted as Asia's best boardsailing event — each January. The untamed eastern side of the island facing the Sibuyan Sea is popular with windsurfers.

As well as walking trails across the island, there is a horseback riding stable at the end of White Beach, near Friday's Resort. You can cross the rocky routes either from north or south of Balabag and head for the caves in Yapak from which bats fly out regularly in search of fruit.

Bicycle and motorbike hire is easily found throughout the island. There are tennis courts and equipment available for rent, north and south of White Beach.

With good reason, sunset watching is regarded as a sacred activity along White Beach. Whether you are strolling along the sands, watching from a bar tucked away in a forested hillside, or have made the expedition out to the Kon-Tiki floating bar, it is an event. On a full moon, gazing at the heavens is equally awe inspiring.

The island's pace is somewhat quickened with the advent of the **Fiesta Sa Bora-Boracay-Cay** festival, held variably between November and December, with parades, regattas, food, art contests and sporting events.

WHERE TO STAY

There are about 200 establishments to choose from, a wide range of accommodation — from full-service resorts to simple cottages which are clustered around White Beach. Thus, you can choose to stay on the island with the luxury of most modern conveniences, including CNN on the television, or rough it by candlelight or kerosene lamp. The most pleasant cottages are made with native materials, palms and grasses and slatted with bamboo poles, a variation on the theme of the typical Boracayan cottages. The resorts that have deliberately chosen to go concrete aren't nearly as pleasant to stay in. At the opposite end of the island, on the northwest, the more private

coves of Diniwid, Balinghai and Punta Bunga offer secluded and simple accommodations. Telephone numbers starting with (2) are Manila contact numbers.

Expensive

Located at the peaceful, western end of White Beach, **Friday's (** (2) 892-7443 FAX (2) 819-0281, was one of the first resorts on the island and is still the best, with an intimate, comfortable and relaxed atmosphere. Its style is understated, with polished bamboo and thatched cottages, air conditioning and good

facilities. Despite being a four-star resort, it has five-star prices. Make sure you reserve in advance and request a room or villa near the beachfront, rather than the rear villas where water pressure can be weak. The alfresco, sand-floor restaurant and bar is a pleasant place to linger throughout the day, and it serves great breakfasts, with a range of fresh seafood barbecues for lunch and dinner. They also have the island's best wine list. Relocated farther north from White Beach, in a wide but secluded cove on the Punta Bunga Beach, **Club Panoly Resort (** (2) 536-0682 FAX (2) 58-6928, is has been some-

Dresses OPPOSITE and sunhats ABOVE LEFT make a colorful display at Boracay. ABOVE RIGHT: Vacation cottages on Punta Bungo Beach.

what modernized, a little isolated now perhaps, but with all the amenities you could want, including a pleasant beachside pool and Jacuzzi. **Lorenzo South (** (2) 990-719, 926-3958 FAX (2) 961726, is situated right at the southern tip of the island, in Angol Beach. This is a smallish, well-designed resort with good facilities, private balconies and a secluded beach that is also just a few minutes walk from the main bustle of White Beach. Around the headland, the **Lorenzo Grand Villa**, run by the same company, is more ambitious in scale but less aesthetic — an architectural carbuncle which destroys the appearance of the otherwise beautiful forest. One hopes this is not an indication of Boracay's future.

Moderate

Lorenzo Main (VIA OPERATOR 3808 or 3204 (or book through Lorenzo South, above), is a basic, well-positioned bungalow-style hotel that offers good value. Rooms are simple but comfortable and are not air conditioned; food is good and service is friendly. You may want to avoid the nightly folk show entertainment and head off for nearby bars and cafés. **Sandcastles (** (2) 500906 FAX (2) 504967, is an Australian-managed resort. The location is good, and the ambiance is comfortable and relaxed. There are bungalow-style rooms or villa suites, with fan or air conditioning, all furnished with native materials, with large modern bathrooms. Food served here is of a fairly high quality, with good Thai fare available at the Thai Castle restaurant. **Nigi Nigi Nu Noos (** (36) 288-3101 FAX (2) 922-9750, is less expensive than the two options above. This resort is recommended for its well-maintained, thatched pagoda-style, non-air-conditioned cottages furnished with traditional native materials, woven palm leafs, rattan grasses and tropical hardwoods and set in a jungle-like garden. This resort seems especially popular with Australians and has a good restaurant and bar area. **Pink Patio (** (2) 812-9551 FAX (2) 810-8282, is a modern apartment-style hotel with a clean, efficient feel. Air-conditioned rooms are cozy; some bathrooms even have a tub as well as shower — a rarity in Boracay — and some have a private garden. The Patio Café serves good breakfasts with excellent cof-

fee. Managed by an Austrian family, **Mona Lisa White Sands (** (36) 288-3205 FAX (2) 924-7052, is a pleasant, small bungalow complex. Small and private, **Palm Beach Resort and Lanai (** VIA OPERATOR 3408, is a good, less expensive moderately priced option, with a choice of air-conditioned or fan-cooled bungalows, each with a private verandah and garden.

Inexpensive

La Isla Bonita Resort ((2) 261940 FAX (2) 827-7470, is is good value, with landscaped native bungalows, simply furnished, but comfortable with verandahs and hammocks. There are air-conditioned deluxe cottages which have more elaborate bathrooms for

twice the price of the regular bungalows. **Coco-Mangas Hotel Beach Resort (** (2) 521-9443 FAX (2) 817-9978 is a justifiably popular travelers haunt and has one of the liveliest bar scenes at night. **Jony's Jony's Place (** VIA OPERATOR 3119 has simple, native-style, rattan furnished bungalows with the basic amenities, including mosquito nets. Both **Paradise Lodge Beach Resort (** (2) 833-7908 FAX (2) 833-7908 and **Laguna de Boracay (** VIA OPERATOR 3603 are reasonably priced and comfortable options. **Galaxy Beach Resort** is pleasant and well-run. **Family Cottages** caters for Japanese travelers with its futon beds, but will appeal to any nationality, with its quiet and relaxing lawn, located a two-minute walk from White Beach.

Cebu and the Visayas

Diniwid Beach is an idyllic secluded part of Boracay and is in many ways the loveliest and most private part of the island. A number of foreigners have bought land here and some of the dwellings can be seen tucked into the hillside and above the rocks. You can stay here in simplistic seclusion at **Mika's Place**, which has 12 bungalow rooms for extremely reasonable prices, starting from about US$15, with clean shower and bathroom facilities. There is a non-fussy family-style café, serving fresh grilled fish and simple, appetizing dishes. You can have dinner here and the owner will help make arrangements to get you back to your resort

Named for its dazzling sand, White Beach, Boracay.

by boat if the tide is in. It is a magnificent place to enjoy the sunset.

If you want to come here directly from Caticlan, just tell the boatman you want to go to Diniwid Beach, rather than White Beach. There may be a nominal surcharge. You can also reach Diniwid by tricycle. Or walk to the end of the White Beach, past Friday's at low tide. An alternative route (by foot, bicycle, tricycle, motorbike or horse) is to follow the main road until you reach the Diniwid road and then follow it to the beach.

WHERE TO EAT

White Beach is full of beachfront bars and restaurants, run by all nationalities and with such fresh fish and fruit in abundance you might think it easy for island chefs to prepare wonderful meals. Yet you need to choose your restaurant carefully here, since it is unfortunately all too easy to end up being served a mediocre meal in many of the restaurants which see a high turnover of tourists. Here are some carefully selected recommendations:

Severo de Boracay, at Angol, close to Lorenzo's, is run by Larry Mariano Tasa. There is something special about Severo, unlike any of the other restaurants on the beach strip. Perhaps its almost secluded, eastern end of the beach locale contributes to its ambiance. Whatever its secret, it is magical to dine at one of their eight tables

It is worth investigating some of the open-air cafés patronized by locals. The barrio market will give you an indication of what is on offer, with its fresh fruits served on sticks, dried squid and on special occasions, *lechon de leche,* or roasted piglet. Don't miss trying *buko,* the healthy coconut juice, served fresh in the coconut shell and a drink mixed with *calamansi,* the tart citrus fruit unique to the Philippines, or if you are more adventurous, *lambanog,* a native palm liquor.

Other local dishes to look for on menus include squid with mango sauce, *rellenong bangus,* milkfish stuffed with raisins and pork, and *tapa,* or salted beef.

NIGHTLIFE

Aside from moon watching and drinking long into the night, there are a number of bars and beach discos to suit hyperactive tastes. Probably the best known and patronized is **Moonshiners Bar**, in front of the Coco-Mangas complex, which sometimes becomes an impromptu disco. The floating **Kon-Tiki** bar, some meters off White Beach and reached by boat, is worth sampling day or night and a good place to watch the sun go down. The most quirky bar is the **Music Garden**, tucked into the hillside at Angol Beach, with its murals of rock stars of bygone years and repertoire of old rock-and-roll classics.

HOW TO GET THERE

Philippine Airlines flies twice daily from Manila to Kalibo City in Aklan province on Panay Island, southeast of Boracay. The onward journey from Kalibo takes about two hours by bus or jeepney overland to the coastal town of Caticlan — a pleasant ride flanked by winding paddy fields.

From Manila to Caticlan, Aerolift has two direct daily flights and Pacific Airways has several daily flights. Connecting motorized outriggers then ply between the Caticlan point across the Tablon Strait to Boracay, 15 minutes away. Be prepared for both yourself (and your luggage) to get wet on this journey, and possibly to wade thigh deep to board or disembark.

on the powdery beach and hear the sough-ing of surf as you sip your wine. The service is friendly and the food very good. The restaurant and bar at **Friday's** is worth visiting. They serve the best breakfasts on the island and have a good menu, with daily specialities and a decent (for the island) wine list. Back on White Beach, **La Reserve**, serves French cuisine. Aside from everything else, including a good wine list, they have cigars from Havana. Finally, make sure you sample at least one fruit shake at **Avenhja's Fruit-shakes**. They serve shake variations of sweet mango, tart green mango, cantaloupe, coco-banana, choco-peanut, with or with-out the addition of the infamous Philippine rum.

OPPOSITE: one of Boracay's rustic beachfront night spots.

It is also possible to reach Boracay from Manila via the once-weekly **Aboitiz Super Ferry** during the summer season. Bear in mind that transportation from Kalibo to Caticlan can be prearranged with your chosen resort or hotel. Boracay can also be reached from Tablas in Romblon by boat.

LEYTE

A densely forested, fertile island, Leyte was where General Douglas MacArthur fulfilled his pledge and returned to the Philippines, landing on the island with four American invasion divisions at midnight on October 19, 1944. As Stanley Karnow wrote in *In Our Image*, his book about the American empire in the Philippines: "Leyte, a grim tropical battlefield, presaged Vietnam." It was to be the largest naval engagement in history, with four months of "bitter, exhausting, rugged fighting, physically the most terrible we were ever to know", as a United States Army historian has described it.

In the events leading up to the battle of Leyte, some 28,000 American men had been lost in the Pacific and MacArthur had to convince Roosevelt and his joint chiefs to pledge more lives, promising quick, dramatic results in the stepped-up battle against Japan. Some 7,000 American craft—from warships to transports—bearing 200,000 troops were sent streaming to Leyte. General Yamashita then had 200,000 troops to defend the entire archipelago, most of which were concentrated on defending Luzon at the expense of the other islands. He ordered only 20,000 men to Leyte, giving them instructions to bedevil potential United States invaders from their mountain roosts, rather than along the shores. But this miscalculation proved to be the Japanese general's undoing. It was not until 11 months after MacArthur landed on Leyte that the Japanese finally capitulated, brought down by the bombing of Hiroshima.

The eve before the Leyte landing, MacArthur wrote in his diary: "Men lined the rails or paced the decks, peering into darkness and wondering what stood out there beyond the night. There is a universal sameness in the emotion of men, whether they be admiral or sailor, general or private, at such a time as this." Before the American

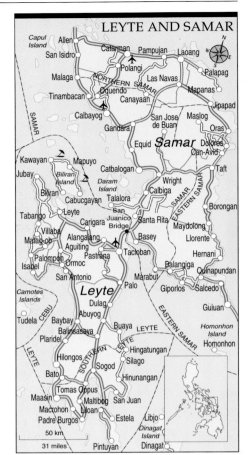

fleet opened fire on Leyte at dawn, MacArthur spoke through a radio transmitter, stoking the emotions of the pious Filipinos whose support he was counting on: "People of the Philippines, I have returned. Rally to me! The guidance of divine God points the way. Follow in His name to the Holy Grail of righteous victory!"

The months that followed saw fearsome casualties and battles, with the Japanese unleashing scores of kamikaze pilots and both sides repeatedly strafed and bombed. Yet by December, as Karnow writes: "Despite his initial opposition to the venture, Yamashita had by Christmas squandered 60,000 troops, nearly his total force, on Leyte. He now elected to abandon the island, knowing that the bloodbath had already sapped his strength to defend Luzon, his main priority. The Japanese soldiers left behind to fend for themselves suffered agonies of betrayal.

"Thus the Americans were able to advance in the Philippines and edge closer to Japan. The critical United States victory at sea, however, hinged as much on luck as it did on skill and courage."

A veteran, Shohei Ooko, recounted his experience in his remarkable novel, *Fires on the Plain*, which vividly describes the horrific scale of the carnage — as land battles, often hand-to-hand, commenced across the island's coastal towns, steamy jungles, craggy cliffsides and mountain caves—and of the realization that his starving fugitive comrades were turning to cannibalism as they roamed the island. Though he was starving himself, he managed to survive on insects, before being captured by Filipino guerrillas who turned him over to the United States Army. About 60,000 Japanese died on Leyte. The United States Army lost 4,000 men there, with 15,000 wounded.

Anyone whose life has been touched by the experience at Leyte will need no exhorting to realize the dramatic resonance this island has, and both Americans and Japanese have returned to visit, remember and grieve. In preparation for your visit to Leyte, you may find it interesting to watch the film *MacArthur* in which Gregory Peck plays the general, characteristic pipe cocked in mouth and face set in a scowl of determination.

TACLOBAN

Capital of Leyte, this is the main township of the province, with a bustling port set around a deep water harbor. Two personalities have thrown larger-than-life shadows across Tacloban, albeit in entirely different ways, yet their lives briefly collided: MacArthur and Imelda Marcos. Imelda's origins as a beautiful, yet impoverished scion of one of the province's old but not powerful aristocratic families — the Romualdez family — mean that much of her life and identity has been filtered through her powerful need to expunge the memories of her early years as the "Rose of Tacloban."

When MacArthur and his troops landed in Leyte, "Meldy" was a budding beauty of 16 and she stepped into an early spotlight of stardom when she sang for the battle-weary American GIs (although she came from the

nearby town of Tolosa). Barely a town fiesta, civic parade or fundraising benefit would pass by without her being asked to sing a few songs. Today, Imelda Avenue and numerous buildings, including her reconstructed ancestral mansion, bear her name.

General Information

The **Department of Tourism** office ((53) 325-5279 is found at the Children's Park, Tacloban. They have published a tour map of Tacloban, which includes visits to village relief projects, memorial sites and religious icons, as well as battle sites.

What to See and Do

Clearly, for veterans, the entire island of Leyte has a significance that could be lost on mere tourists, its beautiful forests and coasts laced with memories of massacres.

It's possible to see most of Tacloban's historic sites within a day's visit. Palo's **Red Beach** is the best known tourist site, 12 km (seven miles) away from Tacloban and the scene of MacArthur's landing. At the **MacArthur Landing Memorial**, larger than life statues commemorate the event, depicting the general striding through the waves, flanked by Sergio Osmena (who became president of the Philippine commonwealth) and General Carlos Romulo. Each October 20, "Liberation Day" is held at Red Beach. In Palo town, the imposing **Neo-Gothic cathedral**, built in 1596 and with an additional seventeenth century gold altar, served as a sanctuary for local people during the Leyte battle and later as an evacuation hospital for wounded American soldiers. In the vicinity, **Guinhangdan Hill**, or Hill 522 in military parlance, was a notorious battlefield and is now covered with commemorative white crosses. You can walk to the summit and survey the hillside views out to sea and view the bunkers and foxholes used by the Japanese. Another infamous battlefield, **Breakneck Ridge**, lies 72 km (45 miles) west of Tacloban, near Limon.

In Tacloban, on Plaza Rizal, see the **Santo Niño Church** which contains the ivory image of the child Jesus, patron saint of Tacloban and Leyte. Referred to as the "Capitan", the image was once lost on a sea voyage in 1889, only to mysteriously resurface some months later. A sudden outbreak of cholera that allegedly ceased as soon as the statue reappeared increased its miraculous powers in the eyes of the town. This event is celebrated with great color and gusto during the annual city fiesta (worth timing your visit to witness) on June 30. At Easter, a similar frenzy of devotion surrounds Palo, when hooded flagellants make bloody parades re-enacting the Passion of Christ. Notice the grand house nearby that was built as a guest residence for the Marcos family, personally supervised by Imelda. Both the **Heritage Museum** and the **People's Center and Library** are interesting to visit, the latter for its dioramas on ethnic tribes. The **Madonna of Japan Shrine**, set in a small park along Magsaysay Boulevard, was presented by the people of Japan as a peace symbol.

From Plaza Rizal, the **Price Mansion** is two blocks away, notable for its role during World War II. Now the Governor's Guesthouse, it was used as a Japanese officer's club during the occupation and later as MacArthur's headquarters in Leyte. Close by, the **Divine Word University** has a quirky museum that provides insights into the ancient history of the region, with 6,000-year-old Stone Age relics unearthed around the Sohoton Caves, antique Chinese ceramics and tribal burial jars.

Tacloban is also the jumping off point for a visit to the Sohoton Natural Bridge National Park, nearby in Samar Island (see SAMAR, below).

Where to Stay and Eat
INEXPENSIVE

A modern, functional hotel, with an enormous swimming pool, **Leyte Park Hotel** ((53) 321-3304, Magsaysay Boulevard, Tacloban City, is a comfortable and serene place to stay. Nestled into spacious grounds, along the historic Red Beach, **MacArthur Park Beach Resort** ((53) 323-3015, Government Center, Candahug, is located on the site of perhaps the most dramatic World War II naval battles in the Pacific. Small and friendly, situated on an island just offshore from Tacloban, **Dio Island Resort** ((53) 321-2811, San José, Tacloban City, has good facilities and is the least expensive option.

How to Get There
Philippine Airlines flies to Tacloban from Manila twice a day, with a flight time of one hour and 10 minutes. From Cebu, there are four flights a week, taking 30 minutes. Several shipping lines operate regular services to Tacloban, linking the town with Manila, Cebu and Samar. The best service is the WG&A SuperFerry (see TRAVELER'S TIPS, page 252), which offers a luxurious and efficient service between Manila and Tacloban. As Leyte is linked by road to Samar, across the San Juanico Bridge, it is possible to make the journey from Manila by bus or car, with a break for the car ferry service from Luzon to Samar.

SAMAR

The second largest island in the Visayas, Samar is considered rather off the typical tourist track in the Philippines, even though the island is peppered with alluring offshore islands and has much natural beauty. The people of Samar are of Visayan extraction and speak Waray-Waray, the local dialect. Periodically, central and eastern Samar townships become the datelines for tales of new incidents in the NPA insurgency, which means that if you are determined to travel throughout the island you should inquire about the political status quo before you set off.

If you drive to Samar, which is connected by bridge to Leyte, you will be crossing **San Juanico Bridge**, the longest in Southeast Asia, more than two kilometers (one and a half miles) long and quite a remarkable feat of construction.

Within Samar Island, there are some rewarding destinations to seek out.

One of the most dramatic stretches of scenery lies along the coastal road from **Allen**, the small port town at the island's northern tip and **Calbayog**, a journey of about an hour and a half each way. The most beautiful scenery is concentrated en route before reaching **Viriata**, as the road skims mountains and steep cliff faces and looks out across offshore islands and curving bays. The town itself is pretty enough, with a large waterfall and walks through surrounding forest, but the drive rather than the destination is the real highlight of this trip. From Calbayog, the main highway south passes through the provincial capital, **Catbalogan**, before continuing on down to **Basey**, the jumping-off point for the **Sohoton National Park**.

The eight-square-kilometer (three-square-mile) park is the province's main attraction with its beautiful native forests, marbled caves and birds, monkeys and butterflies. It is best reached from Tacloban in Leyte.

SOHOTON CAVES

Reached by water, the **Sohoton Natural Bridge National Park** is an awe inspiring place. Rich in archaeological finds, it has a steamy, almost fearful beauty and its primeval landscape can be explored for hours.

Although the park is located in Samar Island, it is more convenient to reach it from Tacloban, Leyte. Whether you get there from within Samar Island, or from Tacloban, you enter the park by banca via **Basey**, on Samar. The boat journey upriver from Basey takes about 90 minutes and is in many ways as spectacular as the destination. The only time it is possible to visit the park — with its **underground cave chambers** and **waterfalls** — is between March and July, when the river level is relatively low. The caves deserve a two-day trip, although it is possible to visit in a day. Check with the Department of Tourism office and the Community Environment and Natural Resources Office in Basey, which can also help you with transport and a guided tour of the park, including equipping you with such all-important items as kerosene lamps to see the wondrous cave interiors.

The journey to Basey from Tacloban, 27 km (17 miles) — either by jeepney or by hired car — takes about an hour.

Offshore on the northeastern tip of Samar **Biri Island** is favored by divers for its untouched beauty and coral reefs, exotic scenery scattered with large boulders.

Off the northwest coast, **Capul Island**'s history is interwoven with the early Spanish galleon trade, hence the name Capul, a corruption of Acapulco. This legacy is evidenced by the town's seventeenth century church and tower. A network of caves are found on the other side of the island, of

which **Bito Cave** is the best known, some 20 m (66 ft) deep.

WHERE TO STAY

In **Calbayog** the best place to stay is at the **Seaside Drive Inn (** (57-41) 234, located in the outlying suburb of Rawis, while in **Catbalogan**, the best option is the **Fortune Lodging House (** (57-41) 680, on Del Rosario Street. Both are inexpensive. Neither destination justifies a stay beyond recuperating from the drive.

HOW TO GET THERE

Philippine Airlines runs flights from Manila to Calbayog five times each week, while a weekly ferry runs connects Manila with Catbalogan. Overland travel from Manila is by the Pan Philippine Highway (renamed the Maharlika Highway by ex-president Marcos) which links Samar and Leyte with the southern tip of Luzon's Bicol province.

A large monitor lizard making an appearance out of the thick forest. These mostly harmless reptiles are fairly common in most forested parts of the Philippines.

Palawan

REGARDLESS OF how well-traveled you are, or how many spectacular visions of nature you have encountered, you cannot fail to be awed by the scale and beauty of Palawan. Majestic black limestone and marble caves with deep secretive forests arouse wonder, while marvelous seascapes beneath the waves have been described by the late diving guru Jacques Cousteau as the most beautiful he had ever seen.

The least developed of all the large Philippine islands, Palawan defies superlatives. Here, more than any other part of the archipelago, nature appears at peace with itself and man merely a temporary witness. In some of the island's remotest reaches, it is easy to imagine, as your boat slides past giant crags rimmed with white sand and emerald sea, how early explorers felt when they saw this vision of undisturbed nature for the first time. Ashore, there are birds, animals and plants seen nowhere else in the Philippines. These include the rare parrots, peacock pheasant, Palawan mongoose, mouse deer, king cobra and the iron tree. Palawan has wondrous butterflies — over 600 species — including the country's largest, the black and green papilo trojano.

The 400-km (248-mile)-long, 40-km (25-mile)-wide ribbon-shaped island is the largest province in the Philippines, making up some five percent of the country's total land area. It has islands scattered around both its tips, with the best known island groups being the Calamian islands in the north, the Balabac-Bugsuk group in the southeast and the Cuyo islands in the northwest. There are 1,768 islands within its perimeters, the best known being Busuanga, Culion, Coron, Cuyo, Dumaran, Balabac and Bugsuk.

Inland, gigantic mountain crags make much of central Palawan almost impossible to explore, and traveling to different parts of the island can be difficult. In some cases, the journey by coast hugging boat proves to be less time consuming. Travelers have been known to arrive in Puerto Princesa, the island's capital in central Palawan, and then — after being so impressed by the natural beauty of that area — decide to explore the remote north — and to do this, they have returned to Manila to pick up the charter flight back to El Nido, the airstrip in the north.

Palawan hit the world's headlines in 1978 when anthropologists discovered a small kinship-based community of cave dwellers — the Tau't Batu, or "People of the Rock" in Singnapan Basin, close to Ransang, in the Quezon area of the island — thought to have lived this way for many thousands of years, without outside contact. The Tau't Batu live in labyrinthine limestone ledges, some linked by wooden catwalks and survive by hunting bats, frogs and birds with huge swats (made out of bamboo and woven palm fronds, laced with rattan thorns) and by

gathering fruit, insects and crabs. When a creature has died or is killed they place a wood or stone representation, apparently in compensation to nature. Their caves have been decorated with charcoal drawings of many kinds of anthropomorphic figures, thought to be representations of animals, birds and ghosts. This entire region is off limits to visitors and, traveler beware, this ruling should be respected.

Elsewhere, Palawan is sparsely populated, with some of its dwellers originating from the Visayas. Among the indigenous tribal communities are the Batuk and Pala'wan, who are quite shy and (perhaps understandably) wary of foreigners. Nomadic Negrito tribes, who survive by hunting in the jungle, have resisted most attempts to coerce them to attend schools or to use more modern agricultural techniques. In Palawan's northern tip, the Tagbanua live in settled coastal villages. They fascinate

OPPOSITE: El Nido; despite the luxury of the resorts, simple boats are *de rigeur*. ABOVE: Fun at the Puerto Princesa Foundation Day Festival.

anthropologists, such as the Hanunoo of Mindoro, with their syllabic writing system.

Palawan's natural wonders include the Tubbataha Reefs, which lie 150 km (93 miles) east of the island in the Sulu Sea, where you'll find one of the most spectacular marine reserve areas in the world. In southern Palawan, St. Paul's Subterranean National Park contains the world's longest underground river, eight kilometers (five miles) long, about half of which is navigable by boat. The experience of witnessing these glowing stalactites and stalagmites, deep under the earth, is impossible to convey. All who visit come away in amazement at the glorious complexity of nature. In the north, El Nido and its surrounding limestone caves offer magnificent scenery both above and below the sea and two well-run resorts which are perfect as diving or snorkeling bases.

The central and northern islands of Palawan are home to some of the finest resorts in the Philippines. Amanpulo, on Pamalican Island in the Cuyo Group, the El Nido resorts on the islands of Miniloc and Pangulasian and Club Paradise on Dimarya Island in the Calamian group, are all havens of comfort, providing a very high standard —in Amanpulo's case, exceptional standard — of comfort and relaxation.

Palawan's southernmost point reaches out towards Malaysia and is bounded to the west by the Kalayaan Islands, within the South China Sea, a cluster of 53 tiny coral islands, islets, reefs, shoals and cays called the Kalayaan group, better known as the Spratleys. Scattered over a vast area of sea, these islands, said to be rich in oil and other mineral deposits, are hotly contested by China, Vietnam, Taiwan, Malaysia, Brunei and the Philippines. The Philippines today occupies a handful of these isles.

The future for Palawan is uncertain. Will the Philippine government be able to preserve this spellbinding sanctuary from the many environmental depredations that have proved so devastating elsewhere in the archipelago? Since oil was discovered off Palawan's northwestern coast, the imminent development of this industry looks almost certain. Widespread logging has already devastated much of Palawan's precious forest — at least 20,000 sq km (7,700 sq miles)

so far — and with their habitat gone, many endemic species have been lost. The environmental effects of any more industrial development may spell disaster for this fragile island paradise.

"The tragedy of the oceanic islands lies in their uniqueness, their irreplaceability of the species they have developed by the slow process of the ages. In a reasonable world, men would have treated these islands as precious possessions, as natural museums filled with beautiful and curious works of creation beyond price because nowhere in the world are they duplicated." When the prescient Rachel Carson wrote this 30 years ago, she could well have been writing about Palawan.

Yet, many Philippine environmentalists and the Palawanese themselves are determined not to see their home altered for the worse and there is a high level of awareness of these issues even in remote villages.

PUERTO PRINCESA

Palawan's provincial capital is the most convenient destination from which to start your

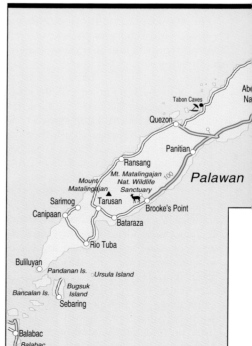

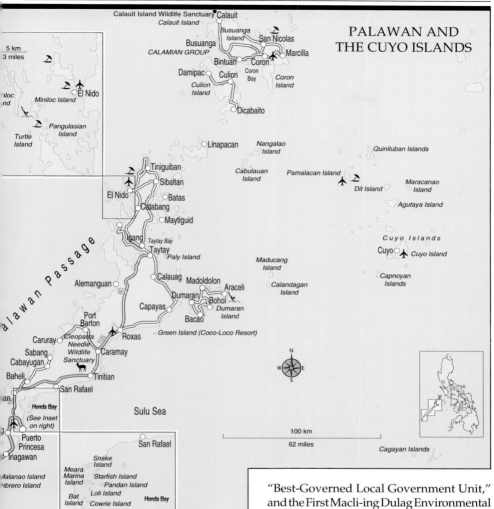

PALAWAN AND
THE CUYO ISLANDS

"Best-Governed Local Government Unit," and the First Macli-ing Dulag Environmental Achievement Award and was cited as the "Cleanest and Greenest City in the Philippines." Recently the city captured the Development Award, the first time that a local government was elevated to the elite circle of management award winners.

Much of this acclaim is owing to the efforts of, among others, Mayor Edward S. Hagedorn and Governor Socrates P. Socrates, who have headed a drive to protect their island, by keeping out polluting industries, developing "green" tourism and replanting forests. They initially launched the Bantay Puerto Program, a campaign against forest environmental degradation. One of its offshoots was the Pista Y Ang Kageban, or "Feast of the Forest," initiatives

trip to other parts of central Palawan. If, however, you plan to visit the more remote parts of the archipelago then it is much more practical to charter an aircraft from Manila.

There is ample reason for civic pride in Puerto Princesa. This relatively modern city of 100,000 residents has won much praise. In 1993, Puerto Princesa won the Earth Day Award for "World Wildlife and Protected Area Management". In 1994, it was given the National Distinction Award for being the that mobilized thousands of Palawanese to plant some 700,000 trees throughout the island. Another was the establishment of a sort of guardian angels volunteer network on the sea, the Bantay Dagat, whose efforts led to the arrest of more than 7,100 vessels for violation of fishing laws such as illegal dynamiting and cyanide poisoning. In addition, local officials are seeking alternatives for islanders who endanger the forests through slash-and-burn farming — and to encourage Palawan farmers to grow seaweed instead.

It is impossible not to be impressed by these efforts. Yet smokers beware! Puerto Princesa is positively Singaporean in its non-tolerance of those amongst you who attempt to throw away your cigarette butt in the street — you will incur a stiff and immediate fine if you do this.

Puerto Princesa was founded by the Spanish in 1872 and named after the Queen of Spain's daughter, Asunción. After her early death, the town's name was changed to Puerto de la Princesa, then shortened.

Most visitors come to Puerto Princesa with the intention of seeing **St Paul Subterranean National Park** as ecotourists. While in the capital, however, there are a few intriguing places to visit, not to mention some amusing signs along the main Rizal Avenue: the "Infant Jesus Learning Center," and "Tecson's Derm Center (We Take Care of Your Skin)" to start with. The twin-spired **Puerto Princesa Cathedral** looms over the center, which includes a number of modest Spanish colonial buildings, including the Governor's General's Residence and the Holy Trinity College. The **Palawan State College Museum** might be interesting to visit if you have time to spare. It has some ethnological treasures culled from prehistoric dig sites, including fossils and crude implements.

Located near the airport, the **Vietnamese Refugee Center** seems an unlikely subject to mention in a guide book, yet visitors may otherwise be baffled by the large population of Vietnamese in Puerto Princesa. Nicknamed "Little Saigon" it was opened in 1979. The camp, staffed by foreign aid workers, is essentially an orientation camp for refugees who have been admitted into

the Philippines for resettlement, and its inhabitants are freely allowed to visit the city. It is worth sampling Vietnamese snacks and soups at the cafés just outside the camp.

GENERAL INFORMATION

The information counter at the airport may be able to help you with immediate queries. The **City Tourist Office**, on Rizal Avenue near the Roxas Street corner, is helpful. The **Provincial Tourist Office**, in the Provincial Capitol Building on Rizal Avenue, is useful to visit if you need more regional information. Both of these organizations are independent of the government tourist office you may have encountered on other Philippine islands. Visiting in person is

advised. You should clear your travel plans to protected or remote areas with the **Conservation and Resources Management Foundation** ((4821) 705-5001. The monthly newsletter *Bandillo ng Palawan*, which is published by local environmentalists is a good introduction to the preoccupations of the island.

Also on Rizal Avenue, visit the **Culture Shack** and **Karla's Antiques**. Among the souvenirs, look for the excellent *A Musical Journey to the Last Frontier* by Sinika, a group that uses native instruments.

In Puerto Princesa, the **Metrobank** and the **Philippine National Bank** will cash travelers' checks and foreign exchange; elsewhere on the island you won't find this service easily.

TRAVEL ADVISORY

Malaria is known in the Palawan region, especially if you visit during the monsoon season between July and August. Malarial mosquitoes tend to decline in numbers during the dry season, reducing the risk. The malaria-carrying breed of mosquito, known as anopheles, is the culprit. According to a Japanese representative of the El Nido Pangulasian Island resort, the mosquito is most active between 10 PM and 2 AM and within mainland coastal villages near stagnant water rather than on outlying islands. He based this conjecture on a scientific study on malaria risk by a Japanese

Large outriggers, used commercially and as passenger boats, in the harbor at Puerto Princesa.

team commissioned by the Ten Knots Development Corporation.

Make sure you are well-prepared by covering up legs and arms after dark and by following your antimalarial medication dosage carefully. Larium, for example, requires that you begin treatment a week before arriving in a potentially malaria-prone place, that you continue taking tablets throughout and then for four weeks after you leave. Resochin and Fansidar are commonly prescribed, yet the mosquitoes in Palawan seem to have developed a resistance to Resochin. If you do suspect you might be coming down with malaria, with its telltale signs of persistent fever and chills, go straight to the hospital at Puerto Princesa, where local doctors are familiar with both symptoms and treatment. Mosquito repellent and nets are clearly useful.

WHERE TO EAT

Puerto Princesa has a good reputation for its seafood specialities, as well it should, with access to so many varieties of fresh fish. **Kalui's**, opposite the Badjao Inn, on Rizal Avenue, is considered to be the city's best restaurant. Its friendly and knowledgable owner and chef, Louis Olieva, also brightens the occasion. Also recommended is **Casa Linda's**.

WHAT TO SEE AND DO

Located between Puerto Princesa and Iwahig, the **Irawan Crocodile Farming Institute**, a Japanese-financed crocodile farm, aims to preserve and advance international research studies on the endangered Philippine crocodile. Somewhat alarmingly, this farm has allegedly exported some of the beasts in the inanimate form of shoes, belts and handbags. The farm is open Monday to Friday from 1 PM to 4 PM and on Saturday and public holidays from 8 AM to noon.

Iwahig

In Iwahig, which lies 23 km (14 miles) south from Puerto Princesa at the foot of Mount Stavely, there is an unusual prison "commune," in which inmates live in relatively unguarded villages, without walls, tending

crops, orchards and coconut plantations set in 386 sq km (149 sq miles). It was established in 1904 and is perhaps the only prison without bars in the world. Tourists are welcome at the prison shop which sells handicrafts made by the prisoners, who are called "colonists." Palawan has a remarkably low incidence of repeat offenders and perhaps this experiment in criminal psychology is one of the reasons. The penal colony is entirely self-sufficient and is not funded by the state. You can hire a tricycle from Puerto Princesa for a half day to take you to both of these destinations, which are about a half hour's journey from Puerto Princesa. Otherwise ask about buses at the City Tourist Office. It is unlikely, however, that you have made the journey to Palawan only to see crocodiles and prisoners.

Honda Bay

The islands that pepper Honda Bay, about 12 km (seven miles) from Puerto Princesa by boat, are rewarding to visit and it is possible to stay overnight on some of them. While divers wax lyrical about the underwater panoramas, less ambitious activities —such as snorkeling, lazing on the beach, or exploring coastal tracks — are equally sublime. Majestic mountain scenes dominate the view — in the distance, Mount Cleopatra Needle rises 1,590 m (5,220 ft). The Honda Bay islands include the following: **Pandan**, **Snake**, **Cowrie**, **Starfish**, **Bat**, **Meara Marina** and **Loli**. Most of these islands have inviting, shallow reefs and good beaches for picnics. Pandan Island is the best known, yet Snake Island, despite its name, is probably the most pleasant for a day's visit. There is a small resort on Meara Marina Island. Bat Island on the other hand, is home to more than a thousand bats, which hang off the mangroves by day, and by night flap off in search of fodder.

WHERE TO STAY

Moderate

Asiaworld Resort Hotel ((4821) 2111 or 2022 **(** MANILA (2) 833-9858 or **(** (2) 834-1354, National Highway, Barangay San Miguel, is Puerto Princesa's largest and most modern hotel, formerly part of the Hyatt chain. It has a good swimming pool and Chinese and Japanese restaurants, as well as nightly live entertainment at its disco.

Inexpensive

Emerald Plaza Hotel (VIA OPERATOR (4821) 2611 or 2263, Malvar Street Puerta Princesa, is a good choice for an inexpensive stay, with quiet clean rooms and a swimming pool. **Badjao Inn (** (4821) 2761 or 2380 FAX (4821) 2180, 350 Rizal Avenue, is very popular with divers and has either fan-cooled or more expensive air-conditioned rooms, with

Around the island, boats are used to make coast-hugging journeys to regions inaccessible by jeepney, bus or car.

St. Paul Subterranean National Park

Also known as the "Underground River," St. Paul Subterranean National Park encompasses 39 sq km (15 sq miles), with spectacular mountains, limestone caves, white sand beaches and lush forest. The river itself flows through the underground cave for about eight kilometers (five miles), emerging into

refrigerator and television. The hotel has a pleasant garden and restaurant.

How to Get There

Two daily Philippine Airlines flights arrive from Manila and take 70 minutes to reach Puerto Princesa. Philippine Airlines also flies to nearby Coron town on Busuanga, north of the main Palawan Island. From here, it is practical to see the rest of Palawan from boat. Pacific Airways Corporation and Aerolift also have flights to and from Cuyo and Coron in Palawan. Interisland boats ply regularly from Manila to Puerto Princesa and make stops along the route via the Cuyo islands and Panay, in the Visayas.

the sunlight where it meets the South China Sea at St. Paul Bay. The majestic **St. Paul Mountain** soars for 108 m (354 ft) above the cave's entrance.

Before you visit the Underground River, you will need to get a permit from the parks' main station, at **Malipien**, **Cabayugan**, an hour's walk away from the river's entrance. This formality also allows you to get acquainted with the sights you are about to see. The station has very basic lodging and a camper's kitchen. Check with the Provincial Tourist Office in Puerto Princesa for details.

There is much to smile about in Puerto Princesa. The city has won awards for its orderliness and policies towards development. OVERLEAF: Part of the spectacular St. Paul Subterranean National Park.

From the station, you follow the **Monkey Trail** over the headland (or around the beach at low tide). Onwards, the track passes a bamboo bridge through dense jungle, echoing with cries of native birds. It's not at all uncommon to see wild monkeys, lizards and vividly plumed birds. As the fee to visit the park is minimal, make sure you show your appreciation to your guide, along with a tip or donation at the station.

After you board the boat at the cave's entrance and set off, your eyes take a while to get used to the pitch-black passageway.

You'll hear strange sounds in an otherwise uncanny silence: bats mewing and flapping, drips of moisture from the ceiling some 15 m (49 ft) above your head and the growl of the boat's motor as you glide on, past awesome glistening, glass- or marble-like colorful stalagmite and pillared stalactite formations. The way is lit by your guide, who carries a carbide or kerosene lamp. About halfway into the cave, you can land on a small muddy underground beach, which is usually a cue to turn around and return. It is possible to go farther, as the river extends another two kilometers (one and one quarter miles). The local guides have sound instincts about the conditions that you will be encountering and it is best to defer to their wisdom.

How to Get There

The park is reached most easily from the township of Sabang, by four-wheel-drive vehicle along the relatively new road from Puerto Princesa, a fairly effortless 90-minute -or-so journey in the dry season, but it takes longer during the monsoon season.

The whole trip can be arranged through the Provincial Tourist Office in Puerto Princesa and costs P500. There are several inexpensive places to stay overnight in Sabang, including the **Villa Sabang**, **Mary's Cottages**, the **Bambua Jungles Cottages** or at the park ranger station itself.

Another route is to travel to **Baheli**, also about 90 minutes' drive from Puerto Princesa, where outrigger bancas make the three-hour voyage to the river's starting point. This option is only recommended during the dry season, as heavy rains during the monsoon can create treacherous conditions. Generally, you'll be discouraged from visiting the park during rough weather or storms, which tend to occur during June to November.

TRAVELING SOUTH

Traveling farther south, the region around the city of **Quezon**, 157 km (97 miles) southwest of Puerto Princesa, reveals another of Palawan's remarkable natural gems: the network of 200 or so warrens that make up the **Tabon Caves**. Since their discovery in 1962, only 29 have been explored and only seven are open to the public. The caves have been a rich site for finds of fossilized prehistoric remains — called "Tabon Man", carbon-dated to 50,000 years, the oldest trace of homo sapiens in the Philippines. **Diwata Cave** the most beautiful, 30 m (100 ft) above the sea. The best way to arrange your visit is to ask at Quezon's small and interesting **National Museum** for a guide to lead you around the caves—a tour which takes about half an hour. From Puerto Princesa, it is a five-hour jeepney ride to reach the caves.

Note, too, that Quezon is the venue for two colorful annual festivals: the **Feast of our Lady of Lourdes** and **La Naval de Manila** (see FESTIVE FLINGS, page 42).

About four kilometers (two and a half miles) northwest of Tabon, the **Tabon Village**

Resort has simple, inexpensive and comfortable cottages and is a good base from which to explore the surrounding waterfalls and dense jungle. Located on Tabon Beach, it is managed by a Belgian, Theo. Tabon Village is a beautiful place, although the rocky shore can make swimming difficult. The resort's restaurant, **Mutya ng Dagak**, "Pearl of the Sea," is on an artificial island which is connected by bridge and is an unusual place to dine.

On the southeastern point of Palawan, **Brooke's Point** was where British explorer Sir James Brooke lived, and the watchtower he built stands here. The small township of Brooke's Point has a backdrop of gigantic ranges, dominated by **Mount Matalingajan,** at 2,086 m (6,843 ft), the island's largest mountain, which lies 25 km (16 miles) away. If you have come this far, you must go to **Mainit Hot Springs**, 10 km (six miles) northwest of Brooke's Point. Near forest and mangroves, the waist-deep hot sulfuric springs look onto a waterfall. Heavenly.

The nearby uninhabited **Ursula Island** used to attract thousands of nesting birds, but it seems many have been frightened away to far-off Tubbataha Reef by the presence of shotgun-toting hunters. It is still home to the rare *sieste colores* ("seven colored") bird, which is unfortunately prey to poachers. At sunset, there is a spectacular display as the birds swoop and wheel to their nests. You can reach Ursula Island by hiring a pumpboat from Brooke's Point or **Bataraza**. Another notable destination is **Balabac Island**, off the southern tip of Palawan. This isolated island is home to the Muslim tribal Molbogs and has rare conus seashells. From here, vintas make frequent excursions across to the Malaysian islands.

TRAVELING NORTH

From Puerto Princesa, if you have already reached St. Paul Subterranean National Park and wish to travel farther, you will have to pass through **San Rafael**, a settlement that is close to an area populated by the nomadic Batak tribes. Reluctant to have much contact with outsiders, the Batak have unfortunately had to contend with the incursions of determined tourists, sometimes led by Philippine-organized tour groups. As in many situations

throughout the Philippines, the issue of whether or not to encroach on the private lives and customs of many tribal groups is an extremely sensitive one.

The Bataks are considered to be the most "primitive" and colorful of Palawan's tribal people, with their trinket adornments, flying squirrel tails on their backs and flowers in their hair. Traditionally, men wear G-string-like garments and women are bare-breasted. To reach the Batak village involves a two-hour drive from Puerto Princesa to **Tanabao** and then a three-hour trek through jungle.

Farther north, the pleasant seaside village of **Roxas** looks out across a sweeping bay, ringed by a coral reef and a number of beautiful small islands, including **Pandan Island** which has a resort, Coco-Loco. As you follow the coast-hugging road farther up, you pass vistas of breathtaking jungle, with hints of the exotic creatures — including crocodiles — found inland. **Taytay** was Palawan's original Spanish capital, with the ruins of a fort built in 1622. From Taytay, the rugged adventurer can explore by outrigger banca the many surrounding islands, some of which have small bungalows to rent. In the area,

OPPOSITE and ABOVE: Palawan is still home to a number of primitive tribes, one of which, the cave-dwelling Tau't Batu, was only discovered in 1978.

Paly Island is where giant hawksbill turtles come ashore to nest and lay their eggs from November to December.

WHERE TO STAY

The **Coco Loco Beach Resort (**/FAX (4821) 2388, Pandan Island, Roxas, PO Box 18, Puerto Princesa and the **Club Noah (** (4821) 501 **(** MANILA (2) 522-2911 FAX (2) 583323, Apulit Island, Taytay, are two resorts that are popular with divers in search of a moderately priced base for exploring the beautiful Taytay Bay area.

EL NIDO REGION

Tucked within the northern reaches of Palawan, the El Nido region is difficult to reach from the southern part of the island, unless you are prepared for a long land and boat journey. Many visitors to El Nido come to stay at one of the two Ten Knots Development Corporation resorts located here, the El Nido Miniloc Island and Pangulasian Island resorts and so arrive by charter aircraft. As the small plane circles to land around the grass strip near El Nido township, you will glimpse the majesty of the landscape you are about to enter. The grass strip airport is charming and tiny, with iced tea and snacks served to guests of the resorts. From here, you are ferried by an outrigger boat across the deep emerald sea to either island, past hovering giants of stone, craggy coves and slivers of white sand.

El Nido gets its name from *nido*, the prized *balinsasayaw*, or swiftlet's "nest", the essential ingredient for the region's famous, supposedly curative bird's nest soup. Visiting ornithologist Paul Baker described, in 1927, the nests as "of pure white semi-translucent saliva half cups stuck against the sloping roots of small caves, like a half saucer of fine strings of glass, all matted together." Witnessing the dexterous Palawanese *boceadores*, as the nest gatherers are called, climb into the vertiginous heights of the limestone caves to harvest the swiftlet's nests is an impressive sight. Boceadores, who risk their lives each time they scale these jagged crags, acquire their right to gather nests by bidding for a concession granted by the municipal

government and are always worried about opportunistic poachers, for one kilogram (two and a quarter lbs) of top quality birds' nest can be sold for more than US$3,000.

Within the El Nido region, some of the more spectacular places to see include the **turtle sanctuary** at **Inalula**, the black marble **Pinasil Cave** at **Bigan**, and the giant rock formations at **Dilumacad**. **Matinloc Island** is one of the most beautiful islands, with its hard-to-find Secret Beach, which has to be reached by swimming through a wide rock crevice that only experienced guides will be able to bring you to.

WHERE TO STAY

Expensive
Miniloc Island Resort lies in a tiny cove dwarfed by grand outcroppings of limestone. Its row of stilt cottages and terraced bungalows are prettily set into the hillside. Small enough to feel intimate — especially surrounded by so much rampant nature — it has also been devised to allow as much freedom as possible to explore outlying islands and dive sites, as during any reasonable time of day, you can be ferried to your destination of choice for a stay of a few hours. For idle snorkelers, the resort's lagoon attracts a surprising number of exotic fish. The resort is geared for serious divers, and if you come on a diving holiday, the package includes two dives a day, all equipment, as well as all meals. When making reservations, ask for a stilt water bungalow or a cliffside cottage, either of which are more atmospheric than the beach cottages. Accommodations are pleasantly furnished, with ceiling fans and good hot water pressure — almost a miracle in such a remote location. Service is friendly and eager to please and the buffet-style food is good.

The **Pangulasian Island Resort** won the 1995 Kalakbay Award as Resort of the Year by the Philippine Department of Tourism for its "outstanding contribution in ecotourism." Located on a spectacular wide beach, it is ringed by a coral reef that teams with fish. Somewhat less expensive than its sister version at Miniloc, this resort is equally beautiful, located in a more open setting, with

Perfect snorkeling waters around Miniloc, El Nido.

30 air-conditioned cottages and duplexes in a beach row, all with private verandahs. Room-only rates are available, but it is best to take the package which includes all meals, an introductory dive for non-divers with an experienced instructor and daily offshore snorkeling. For licensed divers, the deal is two dives a day inclusive of a boat, equipment and diver guide and use of all marine sports equipment.

Reservations for both Miniloc Island and Pangulasian Island resorts should be made in Manila through **Ten Knots Development Corporation** ((2) 894-5644 or (2) 894-5734 or (2) 893-0606 FAX (2) 810-3620, Ground Floor, Exchange Corner Building, 107 Herrera Street, Legazpi Village, 1229, Makati.

Both resorts are run by a joint venture between A. Soriano Corporation and Nissin Sugar Ltd. of Japan, with the stated aim of developing awareness about conservation and protection of the El Nido region, cooperating with and employing the local community. The company has initiated an environment education campaign, beach cleanup and tree planting projects and a mooring buoy project to protect El Nido's coral reefs.

Inexpensive

There are several small bungalow cottages in El Nido town, which will appeal to travelers and rugged individualists who want to experience the "real" Palawan. **Mariana Cottages**, located at the quiet end of the town's beach, is peaceful and pleasantly decorated. **Malapacao Island Resort** has simple bungalows.

El Nido town

Typical of a southeast Asian village, whose residents depend on the reefs for much of their food and income, El Nido town snuggles around a wide bay at the foot of a dazzling line of limestone mountains. Its residents appear to be civic-minded and churchgoing, and the small but bustling **market** is the town's main focus. Signs dotted throughout the town point to an information campaign by the El Nido Foundation to raise environmental awareness, with instructions for

"Zero Waste Management through Total Recycling of Domestic Wastes: You Can Adopt This Technology for Your Household Benefits." Notices pinned on trees advertise upcoming fiestas and band practices. Many of the men here make a living by fishing with fine nets on shallow reefs and seagrass beds and collecting sea urchins by hand. Spiky lobsters are a prized catch, relished by locals and visitors alike; recently their value has soared, so the bulk of the catch goes to restaurants.

General Information

The **El Nido Tourist Office**, found on the main street, is helpful for advising on local walks. They have produced little maps of the town and the region, with suggestions for visiting ancient burial caves, adventurous hikes, marble cliffs and other spots for those in the know. Local fishermen often hire themselves out as guides, escorting you by banca. The Tourist Office likes you to register in their visitor book, since visitors are still a novelty. This also allows them to keep track of guests while they are in the area.

How to Get There

You can reach the El Nido region either by charter flight or by a land and boat journey from Puerto Princesa. From Manila, Ten Knots Development Corporation runs daily charter flights by Dornier plane, a 90-minute journey.

The other alternative is to fly to Puerto Princesa and take a jeepney to Roxas, which takes seven hours, then take a pumpboat from Taytay to El Nido. During monsoon season, the pumpboat service goes from Abongan. The amount of time all this can take depends on weather conditions and making these connections. It is an arduous trip.

ISLAND HOPPING THROUGH THE CALAMIANS

There are several smaller, wonderful strings of islands to explore, including the Calamian group, with its main islands of **Busuanga**, **Culion** and tiny **Coron**. The largest port town and diver's base is on Coron Island. Spectacular coral gardens and submerged vessels sunk during World War II are some of the rewards to those who venture into the depths here. Names of these islands and the names of some of the towns are the same and so confusion often occurs. Note that there is a Busuanga Island, with both a Busuanga town and a Coron town, while there is also a small separate island, to the south, called Coron. It is in the bay to the south of this in a triangle, between the islands of Busuanga and Coron, and the island of Culion, that lie some 24 Japanese naval wrecks, 12 of which are charted. It is the Philippines' premier wreck diving site.

WHERE TO STAY

Expensive

Club Paradise (MANILA (2) 816-6871 to 75 FAX (2) 818-2894, Dimakya Island, Coron, is located off the northern side of Busuanga Island, on Dimakya Island. The resort has 40 native-style comfortable, non-air-conditioned cottages with verandahs and tiled bathrooms, tucked into a palm-landscaped cove which is lovely for swimming. It is a good choice for action-seeking visitors who don't necessarily want to concentrate only on diving. It has a pleasant seaside lounge, a tennis court, swimming pool, game room, and it arranges island hopping excursions. There are a variety of water sports on offer, including fishing, and the resort has full facilities for diving. The rate includes all meals, an introductory dive and full use of all the sports facilities. It is reached from Busuanga via boat — a ride of an hour and 10 minutes. The luxury resort of **Amanpulo** (see below) is located nearby on Pamalican Island, and this can be reached from Manila by chartered plane. You can also visit Calauit Island from Busuanga.

Inexpensive

An inexpensive option popular with divers is the **Sea Breeze Guest House (** MANILA (2) 922-9750 or (2) 980937, located in the town of Busuanga.

CALAUIT ISLAND

Within the Calamian group is the very special Calauit Island. Founded in 1976, this

unusual wildlife island sanctuary is home to many African animals, a dramatic sight in such a radically tropical terrain. The island spans 3,700 hectares (9,100 acres) and the animals roam free. There are giraffe, zebra, eland, impala, bushbuck, gazelle and waterbuck from Kenya. From the original stock of 58, the population has increased some 400, of which most are island-born. Also, the island is home to several indigenous species endemic to Palawan, such as Calamian deer, scaly anteater, wild pig, monkey, monitor lizard, bear cat, squirrel,

Palawan porcupine, mouse deer and the Palawan peacock pheasant as well as other bird species. The seas surrounding the island abound with fish and coral, while giant turtles come ashore to lay their eggs and the unusual *dugong,* or sea cow, grazes in its seaweed beds.

To visit Calauit Island, you must first get permission from the **Conservation and Resource Management Foundation (** (2) 78581 to 89, Ground Floor, IRC Building, N° 82 Epifanio de los Santos Avenue, Metro Manila. When calling, ask for Dr. Francisco Panol.

TUBBAHTAHA REEFS NATIONAL MARINE PARK

Lying in the middle of the Sulu Sea, about 150 km (93 miles) from Palawan, the **Tubbataha Reefs** are world famous. The best known of all Philippine dive locations,

Fragile though it may appear, the outrigger *banca* is a most stable vessel, ideally suited for travel through the waters of the archipelago.

the reefs were declared a marine park in 1988. Despite the region's isolation, dive boats are frequently booked up for months in advance by avid Japanese, European and American divers. This is partly because diving is only possible between mid-March to mid-June when the monsoon winds no longer blow.

The eight-kilometer (five-mile)-long and one-kilometer (half-mile)-wide reef is bounded by a pair of rocks, its deep blue lagoon ringed with shallower light green waters, which vary in depth from knee to waist high. Many varieties of coral, fish and spectacular drop-off points make this a stunning place to explore.

Tubbahata Reef is home to some 300 species of coral and nearly 400 species of fish (including six shark species), the two main reef sites are frequently visited by hawksbill and green turtles. Black and white-tip sharks, small jacks, barracudas, mackerel and schools of vibrantly colored tropical pelagic fish are easily sighted, as well as the unusual dugong. Vast communities of migrating seabird colonies also visit the nesting sites within the Tubbataha Reefs National Marine Park, with more than 1,000 brown boobies nesting here every season. Giant turtles lay their eggs on the reef's shores and baby sharks often doze on its rocky shallows.

Yet sadly, since the marine park was established, the reefs have noticeably deteriorated. An estimated quarter of the corals are now damaged, in part because of the illegal dynamite fishing practices, but mostly because of the regular visits by dive boats. Dive boats often anchor directly on reefs, a problem that becomes compounded by repeated visits to the same sites.

In 1989, a controversy over the management of this precious marine resource erupted when a group of sport divers observed that a large-scale seaweed farm was being set up with government permission within the Tubbahata Reefs. The seaweed entrepreneur behind the venture was in the throes of constructing an entire stilt house village, to which he planned to bring some 6,000 families to work as his employees. Finally, months later, after the Philippine conservation groups rallied to prevent the farm,

President Aquino ordered the removal of the farm. Although it was ultimately successful, the incident jaundiced Philippine and international conservationists, who realized the extent to which industry could take priority over the protection of what was an already apparently shielded environment.

The marine reserve is managed with the assistance of the Tubbahata Foundation, a collection of conservationists and dive operators, and only diving by tourists and sustainable fishing practices by the nearby Cayancillo islanders are permitted.

THE CUYO ISLANDS

Remote, scarcely touched, this pristine Cuyo Archipelago, lies between the sea boundary of the Visayas and Luzon. Its islands are on the ancient trading routes from China to Borneo. They were explored by Miguel Lopez de Legazpi in 1568 and 1569 as he traveled the route that led to the conquest of Manila. The Spanish made the Cuyos part of their strategic defence against the Moro raiders during the seventeenth, eighteenth and early nineteenth century and built a string of forts that jut out along the eastern coast of Palawan and Cuyo. This was again repeated during World War II, with the incursions by the Japanese. The people of the Cuyo have remained secluded, living mainly from fishing and seaweed gathering.

AMANPULO

Amanpulo, or "peaceful island" was created for travelers seeking the idyllic beauty of a tropical island. It is set on a private island, Pamalican, part of the Quiniluban group of Cuyo Islands, within the Sulu Sea. Amanpulo, part of the Amanresort chain, is dreamlike, with a tropical perfection in every detail that can not fail to soothe even the most finicky jetsetter. It is already a favorite with Hollywood movie stars and elite Asian travelers. But everyone is treated like royalty at Amanpulo.

The Resort
Surrounded by white sand beaches, turquoise waters and a coral reef set 300 m

(984 ft) from shore, Amanpulo (MANILA (2) 532-4040 FAX (2) 532-4044 or (LONDON 0171 349-9233, PO Box 456, Pasay City 1300, Metro Manila, provides a variety of water sports and beach activities.

There are 40 pavilions, 29 on the beachfront and 11 set amongst landscaped fragrant frangipani and bougainvillea plants. Gracefully and eclectically-designed, touches of Zen elegance but unabashed hedonism are everywhere. All of the 40 casitas are spacious, modern versions of the traditional Filipino bhay kubo house. Small carts are parked outside each pavilion if you can't be bothered to walk, although it is possible to jog and walk around coastal paths. It is the most sophisticated resort in the Philippines, with the added advantage of having expert diving tuition, facilities and equipment to explore several renowned dive sites in the surrounding reef.

All pavilions make the best possible use of natural light, and watching the constantly changing skyscape becomes addictive. Strategically-placed hammocks and verandah deck chairs are poised for perfect sunset viewing. Each pavilion has air conditioning, a rather regal kingsize bed, sliding glass panels that open out onto a wraparound wooden terrace and hushed lighting that gives a lantern effect. Facilities include a telephone, a bar, a television and compact disc player. Bathrooms are splendid, accented by wooden slats and marble. Fresh flowers are placed throughout the pavilion daily. There is an enticing restaurant and bar, with all the sophistication you could want, but you can dine, if you prefer, on your own balcony overlooking the bay.

If all this perfection becomes a bit too much, you can patronize an establishment owned by an islander by the name of Gary, who has set up a small bar, the Amangary which caters mostly to the hotel staff. It is much cheaper and has equally lovely views of the sunset.

The rates for the beach and hillside casitas are US$425 and the treetop casitas are US$350 per night. An extra person charge of US$50 is applied for all casitas accommodating more than two people. Baby cots are provided free of charge, and as many as two children under 16 years old

traveling with their parents stay free of charge. A four-day PADI diving course will cost you US$400.

How to Get There
Two charter flights a day service Pamalican Island from Manila airport. If you are transferring from an international flight, a car will meet your arriving flight and ferry you to the Amanpulo lounge, where you can leave any surplus luggage, should you wish. The cost is US$250 per person round trip and US$125 for children under 11 years. The air-

craft is a 12-seat, pressurized Super Kingair 200; the flight takes 50 minutes. Space is on a first-come, first-served basis, when the scheduled flight is full, but additional flights are sometimes added.

El Nido takes its name from the Spanish for "nest". Here, in this beautiful part of northern Palawan, swiftlets produce nests from saliva, and these are collected as a culinary delicacy. Capitalizing on the unique natural environment of northern Palawan, a couple of award-winning resorts have been developed so that tourists may live as closely as possible to the environment while still enjoying a certain level of luxury.

Mindanao

DESPITE ITS REPUTATION as a somewhat turbulent hotbed of insurgency, Mindanao should not be missed by adventurous travelers. The region is rich in extraordinary natural scenery — promiscuous splashes of exotic plants and blossoms, exquisite beaches and pristine waters and a fascinating amalgam of Muslim and tribal cultures. With its striking mulong-clad women, the geometrical, colorful, sails of the local *vintas*, or boats, and the presence of the Badjaos, or sea gypsies, amongst many of the fiercely independent tribes native to this region still clinging to the beliefs and traditions of their ancestors, Mindanao is a world away from the heavily touristed and somewhat anodyne pleasures to be found in beach resorts of, for example, Cebu.

Located northeast of Borneo, Mindanao is the second largest and southernmost principal island in the Philippines and has a complicated medley of tribes, only a small proportion of which are mentioned in any detail here. The Christian majority and the Muslim minority, along with the main Muslim coastal tribes — Samal, Tausug and Yakan — had lived together peacefully for years. Although most of the Philippines were converted to Roman Catholicism by the Spanish missionaries in the sixteenth century, many of the southernmost islands remained staunchly Islamic.

Ethnically, the Philippine Muslims (who number about 1.5 million) are slightly less Malay than the rest of the island's population, and their faces are suggestive of Arab ancestry. During the 1970s, Mindanao became the center of a Muslim rebellion led by the Moro National Liberation Front (MNLF), the largest Muslim organization in the country, which waged a bloody insurgency against the dictatorship of President Marcos. Moros in general have always been resistant to the idea of centralized government and their insurgency has paralleled that of the New People's Army (NPA) in Northern Luzon. In 1976, under considerable pressure, Marcos agreed to bestow upon the Moros a large amount of regional autonomy, including a separate judiciary and security force, yet little was actually done to achieve this. In 1989, the MNLF declared a ceasefire after the Aquino-led government pledged

to honor some of its demands. The same issues have remained unresolved in real terms and sectarian strife continued. Nevertheless, in August 1996, President Ramos and the head of the MNLF, Nur Misuari, brokered a complex agreement that many say may be the key to lasting peace in the region. But both the Christian majority and some Muslim factions have denounced this agreement, leaving open the possibility of further fighting. More than 150,000 people have been killed in the secessionist rebellion in the past 26 years.

Today, as the government negotiates with the moderate leadership of the MNLF for a limited regional autonomy, another rebel movement has emerged from Mindanao as the frontline disrupter of peace. The Abu Sayyaf organization reflects the younger, increasingly radical generation of Filipino Muslims, whose ideology has been influenced by Saudi Arabia and Libya. Their strident call for a *jihad*, or holy war, against the government and what they refer to as the "Christian settlers" on southern Mindanao make them the Hizbollah of the Philippines.

Operating from their main jungle camp base in the densely forested island of Basilan, about 27 km (17 miles) off the coast of Mindanao's Zamboanga del Norte, the Abu Sayyaf rebels are believed to be responsible for many bombings, grenade attacks, kidnappings and murders in the southern Philippines. Many of its numbers are

OPPOSITE: Vibrant color plays an important part in the dress of the T'boli tribe from South Cotabato Province, Mindanao, one of the most prestigious tribes in the Philippines. ABOVE: T'boli children.

Muslim Filipinos who initially fought alongside mujahidin rebels in Afghanistan and some disgruntled Moro Front members. What used to be a loosely affiliated group has become the nation's most violent rebel movement. Their presence is especially strong in Basilan, and for this reason it not safe to travel there.

Yet despite these rather alarming hazards, Mindanao remains well worth visiting and fairly safe if you keep to the main tourist resort areas, such as Davao and Dakak and especially avoid the autonomous zones of Basilan Island and the Sulu Archipelago. Zamboanga City itself is somewhat unstable and periodically suffers random bomb attacks and shootouts. Foreign journalists often brave this region, yet bear in mind that even if you are not an American Christian missionary, as a foreigner you may still be a likely target if you stray off the beaten track.

The denizens of Mindanao and the Sulu Archipelago are a diverse mixture of tribes.

Among the Muslims, the Moros were so named by the Spanish, because of their perceived resemblance to the Moors of North Africa, even though at that time, they were an amalgam of distinct ethnic groups, each under their own leadership by local sultans or *datus* (chieftains). Photographs dating back to 1898 give an impression of the extraordinary appearance of Mindanao's aristocracy, dressed in exotic, gaudy silk costumes, elaborate sarongs, turbans and headdresses, with curving swords tucked jauntily at the waist. Headdress was indicative of a strictly-observed social hierarchy between tribes, functioning as a prestige ornament and only those who had killed many enemies could wear the most elaborate variety, ranging from scarlet and gold silk to bark or rattan matched with cock feathers. High-ranking women traditionally wore their hair in Chinese-style kowtows and painted their faces. Perhaps the most fashion conscious were the Bagobos, who wore heavily beaded, woven tinalak or abaca fiber lined with brass bell trimmings, which tinkled with their movements and who had their teeth cut to spiky triangles. The Bagobos were — and still are — considered among the most elaborately dressed and adorned tribal people in the Philippine Archipelago.

The Samal, a group of Islamic traders, seafarers and fishermen are famous for their villages built on stilts around the shallows of Mindanao's shores. For a tribe adept at sea, the watery expanses offered protection against intruders. Linked together by plank walkways, these land and sea villages near Zamboanga are a remarkable sight. With a similar way of life, the Tausug dominate the most attenuated part of the Sulu Archipelago. The smaller number of some 30,000 Badjaos wander up and down these

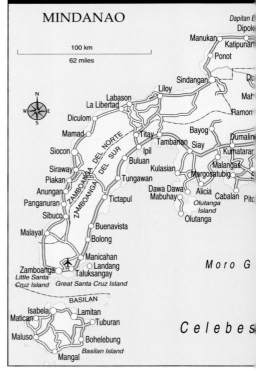

coasts eking out a waterborne lifestyle, and at Sitangkai they have constructed entire floating villages; their lives are completely at the whim of tides and typhoons. It would be interesting to speculate what these sea dwellers — who only come ashore to visit markets and ultimately to be buried — would think of the Hollywood movie, *Waterworld*, with aspects of the movie's futuristic vision resembling their daily life. The Sulu Archipelago has been and continues to be regarded as a dangerous area, both in the past and now, with its notorious Moro pirates and smugglers.

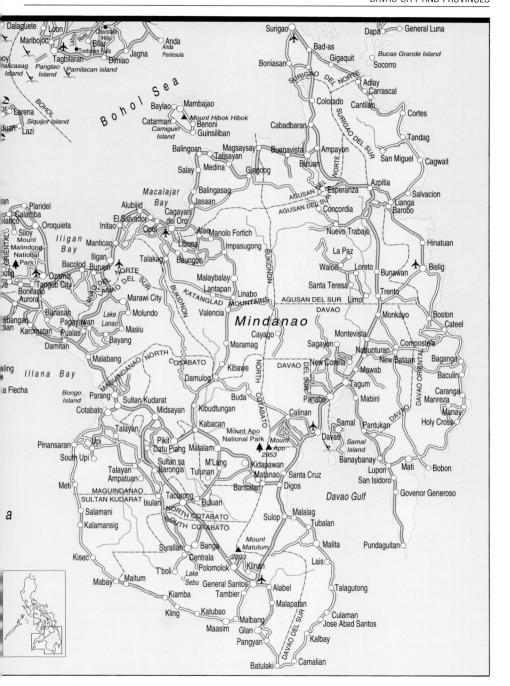

DAVAO CITY AND PROVINCES

Located on the southeastern side of Mindanao, Davao City is flanked by three provinces, Davao del Sur, Davao del Norte and Davao Oriental. Davao City, in the province of Davao del Sur, is Mindanao's largest and most industrialized — and one of the largest human settlements not only in the Philippines but in the world, spanning

2,400 sq km (927 sq miles) — with many fruit and flower orchards on its perimeters. Its wide sweeping bay overlooks Davao Gulf and Samal Island and is fringed by elaborate stilt villages. Hints of geological instability are sometimes felt — the city lies 60 km (37 miles) from the archipelago's most active fault line.

Within the Davao provinces live a number of indigenous tribes, who to a large extent preserve their culture, way of life and dress. They are the Bagobos, the Mandayas, the Mansakas, the Atas, the Kalagans, the

Tagakaolos and the Mangguangans.

The region rather than the city itself is what is most worth seeking out. After you've sampled Davao City, venture on to more exciting scenic spots found within the **Mount Apo National Park** and the **Philippine Eagle Research and Nature Center** as well as the special resort of **Pearl Farm Beach Resort**.

GENERAL INFORMATION

The **Department of Tourism** office ((82) 221-0070 or (82) 221-6955 FAX (82) 221-0070 is at Door N°7, Magsaysay Park Complex, Santa Ana District 8000, Davao City. It is located beside the Apo View Hotel. The office is very helpful and is well-stocked with information

about local tours, guided walks, inland resorts and city lodgings. They can also let you know if your visit has coincided with any festivals, such as the **Christmas Festival**, parades or special other events.

WHAT TO SEE AND DO

Davao is a rewarding place to be if you are interested in flowers, especially orchids.

The MINFLO market (Mindanao Federation of Cutflower and Orchid Grower's Association) has a wide selection, ranging from the indigenous waling-waling, to the colorful hybrids vanda, mokara and kagawara. Outside the city, it is glorious to visit the orchid plantations, especially from April to September, when the ethereal and delicate blossoms are at their most beautiful, before being plucked, packaged and flown off to some far-flung, flower-starved destination. The well known plantations are the **Derling Worldwide Orchid Corporation** in **Dumoy**, **Yuhico Orchid Gardens** in **Greenhills**, and the **Puentespina Orchid Gardens** along JP Cabaguio Avenue. Elsewhere, fruit orchards bulge with export produce,

ABOVE LEFT: Elaborate beaded T'boli headdress. ABOVE RIGHT: Davao orchids. RIGHT: Mt. Apo — 2,953 m (9,685 ft), the country's highest peak.

including Cavendish bananas, the small Davao papaya, hairy rambutan, sweet pomelo, green mandarins, mangosteen, prickly durian and other citrus fruits.

In Davao City, you must see the **Dabaw Etnica** at the Mandaya Weaving Center. Hailing from the eastern coast of Mindanao, a community of indigenous Mandaya have set up here, in a nipa weaving village, where they live and work, weaving the handicrafts that they sell here. Dressed in their customary tribal garb, both men and women fashion bags, wallets, purses, wall hangings and

marble temple with interior wood carvings depicting the life of Buddha. It is located off J.P. Cabaguio Avenue. On the other side of the ecumenical coin is the **Shrine of the Holy Infant Jesus of Prague**, located six kilometers (three and three quarters miles) from the city center in **Matina**, which has an open air replica of the holy image of Prague. Every January 14 and 15, the Santo Niño de Praga Festival is held. The **San Pedro Cathedral**, within the city center, is unusual for its blend of Moorish and traditional Christian influences. Outside the city, the beaches of **Talomo**,

rugs out of the root- and bark-dyed abaca fabric, with the pattern known as *dagmay*, embellished with beads and embroidery. The village is behind the Insular Century Hotel Davao (see below). Before or after your visit, see the collection of tribal artifacts, costumes and native fabrics at the **Dabaw Museum**; the artifacts on display there are similar to the work created today. The museum, in Insular Village, Lanang District, also has fascinating dioramas, musical instruments, ethnological maps, weaves, burial, wedding and war implements.

Davao City's large community of Filipino-Chinese is reflected in the flamboyant scale of the **Taoist Lon Wa Buddhist Temple**, a well-patronized, atmospheric, black veined

Talisay, Salakot and Guino-O have interesting fishing villages. **Talomo Beach** was where the Japanese landed their vessels in 1942, followed by the Americans in 1945. Wartime shipwrecks are submerged at various points around the bay.

Farther afield, there is much in the Davao region to explore. The **Mount Apo National Park** has as its centerpiece the country's highest mountain, which soars 2,953 m (9,688 ft) above sea level. Mount Apo ("grandfather of mountains") straddles the borders of Davao, North Cotabato and Bukidnon and its 72,796-hectare (180,000-acre) extent goes as far north as the provinces of Agusan del Sur and Misamis Oriental. Within the park's forested slopes are hot springs, waterfalls, geysers, sulphur formations, freshwater lakes, rivers and cascades. As well as these grand scale attractions, you may be equally entranced by beauty here on a tiny scale, with many varieties of native wildflowers, showers of orchids, including waling-waling, overhanging ferns and rare birds and animals. A good way to explore the park's environs is to take a Department of Tourism organized climb from **Kidapawan City** in North Cotabato, 107 km (66 miles) from Davao City, where you can hire a tour guide to lead you through what can be a four-day trek through

enous tribal people of the Philippines, they weave the unusual t'nalak abaca cloth and forge brass utensils you might see in Davao.

In a large forest reserve, and also home to other rare plants and birds, the **Philippine Eagle Nature Center** is a nurturing base for rare and endangered Philippine eagles, which are endemic to the archipelago's forests but have been adversely affected by the widespread destruction of their habitat. With its unusual crested feathers and quizzical face, the Philippine eagle is irresistible. At the Center, a 30-minute film introduces you

some of the nation's most sublime landscapes, including the **Agko Blue Lake**, which is in sections both icy cold and simmeringly hot, the **Marbel River**, a milky river flowing from Mount Apo's crater, **Lake Vanado** and the **Mount Apo Crater**, with its breathtaking views and dramatic smoky plumes emanating from the volcano's fiery innards. This trail, for which you must register in the municipal mayor's office, is one of the most manageable of the park's longer scenic trails.

Much farther inland, en route to South Cotabato, in the shadow of Mount Matutum, the reclusive and artistic T'boli tribe live in a settlement along the shores of **Lake Sebu**. Isolated and somewhat at the mercy of encroaching civilization, like other indig-

to the breeding and incubation of Pag-sa (which means "hope"), the first Philippine eagle to be born and bred in captivity. The center is located in Calinan, about 36 km (22 miles) northwest of Davao City. Ask at the Department of Tourism office for details of how to visit — they sometimes run tours. Another interesting bird sanctuary is found at **Caroland Farms**, in **Bago**, 13 km (eight miles) south of Davao City, which is home to wild native ducks, known as "whistling ducks" for their strange shrill calls.

OPPOSITE: Exotic and rare orchids grown in Davao City. ABOVE LEFT: Tropical fruits, such as the coconut, abound. ABOVE RIGHT: A Philippine Hawk Eagle. OVERLEAF: The Philippine Eagle Center shelters this endangered species.

The unusual practice of horse fighting can be witnessed during the summer months from March to May in **Malita**, 150 km (93 miles) south of Davao City. The fighting stallions are trained by Tagakaolo and B'laan tribesmen and transported down from their villages to the Malita arena. One of the more fiesta-style events connected with horse fighting occurs on January 28, with a celebration staged by the Tagakaolo, B'laan and Manobo associations, who also stage ethnic dance and music performances, along with the horse skirmishes.

seamlessly with the surroundings. Cottages have unforgettable vistas as do the restaurant and sea pavilion bar. The resort lies within some 14 hectares (35 acres) of gardens and is now developing a recreation center.

Aside from its penchant for tedious musak, the resort's only drawback is that to reach the it involves a 90-minute plane flight from Manila to Davao which takes off at the unsociable hour of 4 o'clock in the morning. That, combined with a 45-minute boat transfer from Davao, makes for a fairly gruelling

Pearl Farm Beach Resort

Despite its relative remoteness, **Pearl Farm Beach Resort (** (2) 832-0893 FAX (2) 832-0022 or (DAVAO (82) 62749 FAX (82) 234-7581 on **Samal Island** is, for some, the entire point of coming to Mindanao. This extraordinary resort is, at about US$155 a night (US$195 for suites), significantly less expensive than the more famous Amanpulo resort, but it is comparable in some ways. Formerly a pearl farm, the resort's design uses native materials. Bamboo, rope, stone, coral and native wood are the themes along with arts and crafts of the tribes of Mindanao. The stilt cottages and suites are built over the water, in a luxury version of the stilted houses found in the region, and they meld

journey. But the sunrise here is lovely, and when you arrive you can settle in for a morning nap in your delightful room or suite. After recovering, you can devote the rest of your time to serious hedonism, with plenty of opportunity to windsurf, sail, SCUBA dive, snorkel or work on your tan. The restaurants are good and the swimming pool is sublime, with views of the surrounding sea. Make sure you reserve waterside accommodation, as the longhouse on the hillside (US$115) doesn't have the atmosphere available elsewhere on the resort. All the rooms have air

ABOVE: The odd practice of horse fighting attracts visitors to Malita. OPPOSITE TOP and BOTTOM: The luxurious Pearl Farm Resort, Samal Island.

conditioning, and all have views over the ocean. Pearl Farm is connected to the rest of the world by radio only, so you will have to reserve through either its Manila or Davao office (see above) or through the resort's London contact, **Cambrick Trading** ((0171) 357-6390 FAX (0171) 357-6353.

Elsewhere around **Samal Island**, there are many enticing beaches and diving possibilities to delve into, as well as Christian and Muslim fishing settlements to explore.

WHERE TO STAY

Moderate
Insular Century Hotel Davao ((82) 76051 to 61 FAX (82) 62959 (MANILA (2) 810-6907

and 812-4953 FAX (2) 815-1930, PO Box 144, Lanang, is the city's top resort, with well-furnished rooms, good facilities and various restaurants. Its views across the Davao Gulf and to Samal Island are stunning. The swimming pool, with coconut trees set all about it, is quite pleasant. Less expensive than the Insular, the **Apo Beach Hotel** ((82) 221-6430 FAX (82) 221-0748, J. Camus Street, is a large, serviceable hotel with a swimming pool, poolside bar and a very popular discotheque.

Inexpensive
D'Fabulous Venee's ((82) 76026, MacArthur Highway, Matina, is the choice for those on a budget.

WHERE TO EAT

Davao is a place where you can eat simply and well, with its abundance of fresh fish, fruits and exotic culinary cross-currents. Stroll along **F. Torres Street** to browse: **Harana** ((82) 73937, has good Mindanaon cuisine and a pleasant bamboo verandah. **Tsuru Japanese Restaurant** ((82) 72896, Door N° 3, Don Rafael Castillo Building, Legazpi Street, serves excellent Japanese dishes, including sushi. The seaside cafés at **Luz Kimilaw Place** on the Santa Ana Wharf have a good reputation for their sizzling, freshly caught and freshly cooked fish dishes. Rows of *bariles* (yellowfin tuna) grill over hot coals. Also excellent are the *sugpo*

(large prawns) and *pusit* (squid), served with steamed rice and *toyomansi* (lemon soy sauce).

SHOPPING

Another place in the region to sample tribal wares is the **Aldevenoc Shopping Center**, which will give you an idea of the range of crafts available. Across the road from the airport, **Nieva's Arts and Crafts** is an excellent, comprehensive showcase of the work by local and regional craftspeople and certainly worth visiting.

HOW TO GET THERE

Davao City is the international gateway to the southern Philippines. Philippine Airlines runs flights to the region twice each day from both Manila and Cebu, with the flight from Manila taking one hour and 35 minutes and from Cebu, 55 minutes. Philippine Airlines connects Davao with Cagayan de Oro and Zamboanga. From Manado in Indonesia, Bouraq Indonesia Airlines runs flights to Davao and Cagayan de Oro twice weekly and Hong Kong to Davao via Cebu and vice versa also twice each week. Many shipping lines connect Davao with neighboring southern island provinces.

In Mindanao, the opening of General Santos International Airport has created a new gateway to the south, with regularly scheduled flights from Indonesia and Borneo. General Santos is located in South Cotabato province, which flanks the province of Davao del Sur.

NORTHERN MINDANAO

LANAO PROVINCES

The hilly provinces of Lanao have much natural beauty, with their profusion of forested lakes, springs and natural falls. **Iligan** is the provincial capital of Lanao del Norte and close by, the legendary **Maria Cristina Falls** —30 m (100 ft) higher than the more famous

Dazzling white sand at White Island, an uninhabited sandbar favored by tourists, off Camiguin Island.

Niagara Falls of North America—are breath-taking. **Lanao del Sur** province, ranged around the beautiful and gigantic Lake Lanao, is considered the Islamic cultural capital of the Philippines. This is where you'll find the **Mindanao State University**, the **King Faisal Center for Arabic Studies** and the Aga Khan Museum. Since there has been an advisory warning from the United States State Department that traveling in this inland region can be risky, you may wish to check the situation out with your embassy while you are in Manila before setting out.

Initao, the caves are the home of a highly unusual species of bat, with odd, cauliflower shaped noses. A good time to visit Cagayan de Oro is during the **Kagayhaan Festival**, when the Cagayanons throw a colorful Mardi Gras-style street fiesta to honor their patron saint, Augustine.

Where to Stay
The best place to stay in Cagayan de Oro is the **Pryce Plaza Hotel** (63-8822) 721791 FAX (8822) 726687, Carmen Hill, which is modern, comfortable and moderately priced.

MISAMIS ORIENTAL PROVINCE

Across Mindanao, the province of Misamis Oriental is worth visiting as an entry point for reaching the remarkably beautiful island of **Camiguin**. The city of **Cagayan de Oro** is the province's main city, and it has a friendly, hospitable atmosphere. It is prettily ranged around Macajalar Bay, with a backdrop pineapple plantations and green mountains. The proximity to some remarkable beaches, caves, springs and dive locations make this an understated, but special place. In the city, see the **Xavier University's Museo de Oro**, which has a collection detailing the tribes of Mindanao. Within the outlying Tubigan Hills, near the village of

CAMIGUIN

A tiny, tear-shaped island off the northern coast of Mindanao, Camiguin would be spectacularly beautiful even if it wasn't unusual for its number of forested volcanoes, which add to its dramatic scenery. One of the island's seven volcanoes, Mount Hibok Hibok, is active, yet peaceful at present, aside from the occasional rumble. Empty curves of alternating white and black sandy beaches, clear seas, solidified lava flows, hot and cold springs tucked away in trails leading through tropical forest, touches of Spanish colonialism and ancient archaeological treasures make this an idyllic island to visit, and tourists are still rare.

Most of the island inhabitants are broadly of Visayan descent. They survive on farming and fishing and live in bamboo stilt homes built over mangroves. Camiguin is especially fun to visit in October when the islanders celebrate the **Lanzones Festival** for two ornately costumed, fiesta-filled days (see FESTIVAL FLINGS, page 50). Stay at least a few days in Camiguin, longer if you can.

What to See and Do

It is possible to explore the island from tip to tip within several hours by jeepney, bus

and tricycle, but you could linger on its beaches or walk its forested tracks for hours. **Mount Hibok Hibok** dominates the skyline, with its 1,250-m (4,100-ft)-high summit. In the Philippines, this is regarded as one of the more challenging mountains to climb. Trails around its perimeter allow you to appreciate its low-lying scenery. About four kilometers (two and a half miles) from the main town of **Mambajao** (which has some pretty Spanish colonial mansions and a church), the **Katibawasan Falls** are impressive, cascading 50 m (164 ft) to a natural pool surrounded by wild orchids and ferns, boulders and forest. Other beautiful scenic places within the island are the **Santo Niño Cold Spring**, in **Caterman** and the

Esperanza Ardent Spring, a free flowing hot spring which is heated by geothermal activity from Mount Hibok Hibok, nestled amongst trees and boulders. If you manage to be here alone, it is heavenly. Elsewhere on the island, **White Island** is the main beach strip, an uninhabited sandbar, reached by banca from **Barangay Agohay**. Evidence of the destructive power of the volcano is suggested by the huge **white cross** placed out in the bay, marking what was once a small town that collapsed into the sea when Mount Hibok Hibok erupted in 1871.

Where to Stay

By and large, making reservations is not easy in Camiguin, which doesn't yet have much of a tourist infrastructure, let alone an efficient telephone network. There is hope this will be remedied soon. Stay at **Tia's Beach Cottages** ((8822) 871045, in **Mambajao**, or the **Mychelin Beach Resort** ((8822) 874005, on the coast west of Mambajao, which has simple cottages facing the sea and decent food served in a beachside restaurant. It is geared to divers who are keen to explore the coral reefs that ring the island. To get here,

OPPOSITE: Colorful roofs in Mambajao, Camiguin. ABOVE LEFT: The Katibawsan Falls drop 50 m (170 ft) into a beautiful natural pool. ABOVE RIGHT: Fishing is the chief occupation for the Camiguin islanders.

ask the *motorella,* or tricycle, driver for Turtle's Nest Beach, close to Mahayahay Beach. At **Bolokbolok**, one kilometer (half a mile) west of Mambajao, you can stay in a novel "tree hotel" at the **Tree-House**, which has a café and tennis court nearby. If you are seeking something a bit more modern, try **Caves Beach Resort (** (8822) 879040, at **Agoho**, near Mambajao, which has more conventional bungalows, a dive shop and a reasonable beach. In Manila you can enlist the help of **Blue Horizons Travel and Tours** (see TRAVELER'S TIPS, page 250) for reserving accommodation.

How to Get There

There are ferries on alternate days between the island's principal port at **Benoni** from Cagayan de Oro, and the 10-km (six-mile) journey takes a long, long time. The ferry terminal in Mindanao is at **Balingoan**, on the main highway between Butuan and Cagayan de Oro. The curiously named Bachelor Express runs between these two towns every 30 minutes. Or you can take the ferry from Cagayan de Oro proper to the other port on Camiguin, **Guinsiliban**, more convenient, but an hour longer, and the service is less frequent. Adventurous travelers have been known to charter fishing bancas to take them across the Bohol Sea from either port and even farther afield, to Tagbilaran on Bohol and nearby Panglao Island.

DIPOLOG AND DAPITAN

Farther across the northwestern coast is Dipolog, the main gateway to western Mindanao, which is encircled by a series of exquisite sheltered beaches and is the location of the exceptional **Dakak Beach Resort**. The surrounding forest is a haven for native birds and deer and has some spectacular walking trails for energetic hikers.

The nearby town of **Dapitan** remains largely untouched since the days when José Rizal lived in exile here for four years from 1892, banished from Manila for founding the *Liga Filipina,* the Philippine League. With ancestral houses and shady plazas fringed by acacia trees, it was described then by Rizal as "especially made for isolation from the vulgar world," which remains an accurate

description. During his stay here, Rizal set up a medical clinic and a school, showed the local fishermen how to use modern equipment and experimented with growing fruit and coffee. He painted, sculpted and even sent rare plant and insect specimens to naturalists in Europe. He also met Josephine Bracken, the American woman who became his common-law wife, then 18 years old and accompanying her blind adoptive father on a tour of the archipelago. A **shrine** in memory of Rizal lies along the seashore of the town of Talisay.

Dapitan is also the site of the annual **Kinbayo Festival**, held in July, a flamboyant re-enactment of the Battle of Covadonga fought between the Spanish and Moors (see FESTIVE FLINGS, page 48).

Where to Stay

MODERATE TO EXPENSIVE

Situated on the ruggedly beautiful northwestern tip of Mindanao, off the mainland near Misamis Occidental, **Dakak Beach Resort (** MANILA (2) 721-0450 or (2) 721-0447 FAX (2) 721-2463, State Financing Center,

ABOVE: Holding tight to the family's prize fighting cock, Mambajao, Camiguin. RIGHT: Ingenious treehouse, complete with moored boat, in Camiguin.

Ortigas Avenue, Metro Manila, is located at **Taguilon**. The resort is a lush, 50-hectare (120-acre) elegant hillside hideaway, with 80 air-conditioned, marble-floored, thatched nipa cottages secluded beneath a tropical forest of palms, frangipani and fruit trees. The huts face the 700-m (766-yd)-long white sand beach cove with a view across Dapitan Bay. Dakak is owned by flamboyant Filipino television producer Romie Jalosjos and thus popular with the country's actor glitterati — with its seaside restaurant and bar, water sports, tennis, horseback riding and wonderful sunset views from each bungalow's private verandah. Dakak has the sort of modern conveniences that make rustic isolation that much more comfortable, such as satellite television, a large swimming pool, a Jacuzzi and sauna and a discotheque, as well as simple hammocks strung up under trees. It is reached by a coach ride from Dipolog — a 70-minute direct flight from Manila flown five days a week by Philippine Airlines — and then a 20-minute boat ride from Dapitan. They have a well-equipped diving center and offer SCUBA instruction. Encircled by large islands, Dakak manages to avoid the otherwise stormy winds of the typhoon season.

The **Dapitan Homestay Association** is quite active and has a number of welcoming homes on its books. The town is small enough that it is possible to make inquiries once you arrive.

How to Get There

Philippine Airlines flies to Dipolog via Cebu, with a flight time from Manila of two hours; and 45 minutes from Cebu, five times weekly. Other connections from the Visayas and Mindanao can be made via Cebu's Mactan International Airport.

ZAMBOANGA

With its sixteenth century Spanish fortress, pink-tinged sand beaches and ethnically-mixed population, the bustling waterfront city of Zamboanga, located on the tip of the Zamboanga Peninsula, is distinctly exotic. Like the city's main language, Chabacano, which is a babel of pidgin Spanish, Visayan and tribal dialects, Zamboanga is also an

unusual blend of Christians, Muslims and some five tribal groups, including the Samal, Tausug, Yakan, Badjao and Subanon. Zamboanga is an important regional fishing and trading port town and is also the gateway to the Sulu Archipelago and Basilan Island.

Arabic and Muslim influences are clearly reflected in the city's architecture, with its qutab-topped mosques and curvilinear roofs. The Moro men put on their traditional best for special occasions — sarongs with braided waistcoats and cumberbunds, with a fez or a turban, many armed with a decorative dagger tucked at the hip — while the women wear harem-type trousers with silk sheen brocade jackets.

Spanish influences preside here in the widespread Christianity, smatterings of the language in the local dialect and in a diaspora of Spanish colonial forts, watchtowers and buildings.

GENERAL INFORMATION

The **Department of Tourism** office ((62) 991-0128, is at the Lantaka Hotel, Valderosa Street.

WHAT TO SEE AND DO

In the somewhat bland, modern city center, there are several places to see before you venture out to the more traditional stilt villages lying on Zamboanga's perimeters.

Currently under renovation and being made into a museum, **Fort del Pilar**, which dates from 1635, was built by the Spanish as a bastion against all their potential foes — the Moros, Dutch, British and Portuguese. Reeking of early imperial power, with its sturdy one-meter-thick walls and its cannons, this was the southernmost outpost for the Spanish, who made their capital around this fort. It was occupied by the Americans in 1899 and then by the Japanese in World War II. On the outside of the east wall, the shrine of Nuestra Señora del Pilar, the city's patron saint, draws devotees to pray and light

ABOVE: Access to the stilted Taluksangay Muslim Village, in Zamboanga.

candles here, especially on Saturday evening and Sunday.

In the curious **Salakot House**, which is built in the shape of a large, wide-brimmed salakot hat, an extensive collection of Moro brassware is on display, giving you the chance to see the evolution in design of many beautiful but functional utensils used throughout the centuries. Other buildings in the compound are intriguing, such as the vinta-shaped cabin and a house built from shells. At the time of writing, the house was closed, but it may reopen in the near future. The

At the harbor near the Lantaka Hotel (see below), the beach and the sea are the site of a **floating market**, with local boatmen operating vintas laden with reed mats, hand-woven textiles, wood carvings, Muslim brassware, unusual ceramics, coral and shell trinkets — some of which are locally made and some of which are imported from Indonesia, Malaysia and China.

Keep an eye out especially for the colorful, geometric, handwoven Samal and Yakan mats and cloth as well as the famous T'boli nalak woven patterned cloths. If you are still

Pansonaca Park has beautiful botanical gardens and is where Zamboangans come to picnic.

A trip to see the unique stilt villages of **Rio Hondo** and **Taluksangay**, approximately 19 km (12 miles) east of Zamboanga, is also worthwhile. It is here that a mixture of Samal, Tausug and Badjao live, with the settlements connected by bamboo and wooden causeways, dominated by a mosque with ochre-tinted minarets. The arched bridge near the village is a good place to keep a polite distance. The residents aren't impressed with amateur anthropologists or curious foreigners wandering around their living space with cameras, but will respect you if you respect them.

in a bazaar mood, you should take a visit to the fish market near the wharves and see the fabulous daily array of ocean creatures and the adjacent public market. Zamboanga is proud of its unusual seafood delicacy, locally grown in fish farms, called *curacha*, a hybrid cross between a crab and a lobster. Another local variant you should try are fresh lotus leaves.

The **Santa Cruz Islands**, reached after a 25-minute boat ride from the city, have remarkable pink sands, created from the centuries-long erosion of pink coral in the

ABOVE: The vivid colors and patterns of Zamboangan woven fabric. RIGHT: A Yakan tribeswoman demonstrates traditional weaving in Zamboanga.

surrounding reefs. The Great and the Little Santa Cruz islands have been declared a national park and their beaches and waters are popular swimming, diving and snorkeling spots close to the city. There is a cemetery on Great Santa Cruz with small smiling figures and miniature wooden boats marking the grave sites of the Badjaos. You can hire a banca to make the 15-minute journey, from near the Lantaka Hotel.

Back in town, the **Zamboanga Golf and Country Club** is going to seem quite tame after all this immersion in tribal culture.

WHERE TO STAY AND EAT

Moderate
Garden Orchid Hotel ((62) 991-0031 to 33, Governor Camins Road, is the most luxurious hotel in Zamboanga, with a decent restaurant, travel agency, shop, swimming pool and well-equipped health club. It is, however, located by the airport and thus not convenient for getting around.

Inexpensive
The **Lantaka Hotel** ((62) 991-2033 to 35, Valderosa Street, is a very popular hotel, the old queen of Zamboagan hotels and located right on the water. If somewhat worn, it has charm, friendly staff and reasonable facili-

ties. The outdoor bar here is a great spot for sundowners.

Lotus Restaurant is a recommended spot for Chinese meals, while the **Vista del Mar** serves local specialities.

HOW TO GET THERE

Daily Philippine Airlines flights link Manila with Zamboanga, with a flight time to Pagadian Airport of 90 minutes. Connecting flights are also available from Cebu and other regional airports in the Visayas and

Mindanao, including Dumaguete, Davao, Bacolod, Iloilo and Cagayan de Oro. Interisland ferries connect with both provincial and regional ports.

There are also boats to and from Sandakan, in Malaysian Borneo.

LEFT: Scarecrow on guard in the rice paddy. ABOVE RIGHT: Red snapper and other fish in the Zamboanga Fish Market. RIGHT: Young girls of the T'boli tribe, from South Catabato Province, don their traditional beaded finery for fiesta days and for occasional visits to town.

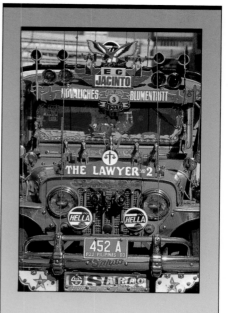

Travelers' Tips

GETTING THERE

BY AIR

Most visitors arrive in and depart from Manila's Ninoy Aquino International Airport (NAIA), with more than 200 scheduled flights by international carriers arriving each week from some 30 countries. Increasingly, Cebu's Mactan International Airport is becoming a well-patronized hub for carriers such as Philippine Airlines and for international charter flights, notably from Sydney, Tokyo, Hong Kong and Singapore. In Luzon, Laoag International Airport has air links with Taiwan, while Subic Bay International Airport is gaining profile. Meanwhile, General Santos Airport and Davao Airport in the southern province of Mindanao are becoming popular for scheduled flights from Indonesia and Borneo.

Airlines which fly to the Philippines are Air France, Air Nauru, Air Niugini, British Airways, Bouraq, CAAC, Cathay Pacific, China Airlines, Continental/Air Micronesia, EgyptAir, Garuda, Gulf Air, Hang Khong Vietnam, Japan Airlines, KLM, Korean Airlines, Kuwait Air, Lufthansa, MAS, Northwest Orient, Philippine Airlines, PIA, Qantas, Royal Brunei Airlines, Saudi Arabia Airlines, Singapore Airlines, Swissair, Thai International and United Airlines. In addition to Philippine Airlines, Cebu Pacific Air and Grand Air offer scheduled flights to several destinations within Asia.

It may be useful to know some background on the national carriers. Thirty years ago, the best known international airline in Asia was not Cathay Pacific, Singapore Airlines (which had yet to be formed) or Thai Airways. It was PAL, Asia's oldest airline, which made its first Pacific crossing in 1946. Under Ferdinand Marcos, the state-owned airline's reputation sank. It was privatized in 1992, six years after Marcos was kicked out.

Despite operating in Asia, the world's fastest growing market and having a ready made market of millions of Filipinos working abroad, PAL accumulated losses of P10.7 billion (US$410 million) over the past decade. Meanwhile its safety record was not impressive. Now that a wealthy Chinese-born businessman — Mr. Tan — has gained majority control, he promises to pump in five million pesos of capital into the airline and to purchase US$4 billion worth of new aircraft from Boeing and Airbus, things may be looking up. The airline is already being called "New PAL." PAL's international flights cover some 34 destinations in 18 countries, including Los Angeles, San Francisco, Honolulu, Hong Kong, Tokyo, Osaka, Taipei, Jakarta, Kuala Lumpur, Singapore, Ho Chi Minh, Paris, Frankfurt, Dubai, Abu Dhabi, Jeddah, Dhahran, Sydney, Melbourne and Brisbane.

PAL offers a (somewhat chauvinistically termed) "Flying Sportsman Card," which allows golf, SCUBA diving and bowling enthusiasts an extra baggage allowance for their equipment on all PAL international and domestic flights. You need to apply for the card as you purchase your ticket.

Gradual deregulation of the airline sector means that more overseas airlines are now being granted access to Manila and, importantly, to the main regional centers of Cebu, Luzon and Mindanao. Some of the country's newer airlines, such as Cebu Air and Grand Air (which was started by a disgruntled group of former PAL managers), will be allowed to compete on international routes as well, including those to Hong Kong and South Korea.

If you are planning to visit several countries in Asia, you may get the best value for your money if you purchase a ticket package at your starting point that allows you to

OPPOSITE: Aerial view of North Palawan and its scores of islands. ABOVE: El Nido airport.

stop off at several regional destinations. Alternatively, you can book a ticket with a stopover in Hong Kong or Bangkok and purchase your onward ticket at one of these Asian gateways. However, if you are flying from Australia, New Zealand or the Pacific islands, where few discounted short-haul fares are available, this advice will probably not apply. In general, you will find that the fares you are quoted by travel agencies are relatively similar. If you are quoted a significantly lower price by an individual travel agency, be wary.

Sailboat

The Philippines is a popular destination for sailing and as a stop-off en route from Hong Kong to Australia and within the Pacific Rim. If you are interested in joining a crew while in the Philippines, one of the best places to inquire is the Manila Yacht Club, where you can also use the notice board. The season generally runs from December through May. Note, however, that the Philippines is listed as one of the world's most dangerous sailing regions (along with Indonesia, Somalia, Djibouti, Brazil, China, Hong Kong and

BY SEA

Freighters

Manila's busy port is served by legions of international vessels, yet few of these offer passenger services. You can inquire about passenger services on **American President Lines**, 1950 Franklin Street, Oakland, CA 94612, USA, or **Lykes Bros., Steamship Co.**, Lykes Center, 300 Poydras Street, New Orleans, LA 70130, USA, both of which call in at Manila and other Far East ports between the United States Gulf Coast and Singapore. Nevertheless, freighter passage is typically more expensive than air fare — not really surprising given that passengers spend many nights and take many meals aboard.

Macao) because of piracy. The area between Hong Kong and Luzon in the Philippines and China's Hainan Island is especially risky. Increasing numbers of vessels have been hijacked; pirates are usually armed with guns, pistols and knives.

VISAS

If you are coming from the United States, Asia, Oceania, or Europe you need only have a valid passport and an onward ticket to a destination outside the Philippines. You will be given a visa valid for 21 days. If you wish to stay longer, you must apply for a visa extension either from a Philippine Embassy or Consulate in your home country prior to your departure, or from the Commission of Immigration and Deportation (CID), Magallanese Drive, Intramuros, Manila, after you arrive in the Philippines.

CUSTOMS AND DEPARTURE TAX

Visitors are entitled to bring in two cartons of cigarettes, or two tins of pipe tobacco and up to one liter of alcohol. Returning Filipinos — *balikbayans* — fall under a different set of rules and, therefore, should check with their embassies or consulates. You may bring

July (but can start in June) and lasts until November. Temperatures during this season sometimes reach 32°C (90°F). You are in the tropics after all, where high humidity is a fact of life, especially during the monsoon season. "Winter" — with its comfortable temperatures of around 25°C (78°F) — is the most pleasant season in which to travel. Filipinos may tell you that it is cold, but if you are used to northern winters, you will find it a delicious, not-quite-sweater weather. Nevertheless, if you are traveling into mountainous regions, be prepared to dress warmly.

in unlimited amounts of currency, but you cannot take more than P5,000 out of the country. Any antiques you have purchased must be accompanied with a certificate from the National Museum. It is a good idea to keep receipts for any major purchases. Departure tax is P250, which is payable in Philippine pesos only.

WHEN TO GO

The best time to go to the Philippines is between December and early May, during the dry season; January is the perfect month to visit. May can be hot, averaging 28°C (83°F). The rainy season — the commencement of the southwest monsoon — begins around

Typhoons frequently assail the archipelago, often more than a dozen squalling annually across the high seas and half that number descending on the islands. They are unpredictable, sometimes beginning in late summer, and the season usually lasts through November.

WHAT TO TAKE

The answer is — as little as possible. Light and loose clothes are the most practical and comfortable when walking or traveling. At

OPPOSITE: An inter-island ferry setting off from Cebu City, Visayas. ABOVE: A flotilla of Samal Boat People, Zamboanga.

an island resort, a shirt or shorts or a sarong over your swimwear take you anywhere. Hats and sunglasses are essential as the tropical sun can be extremely hot. Bring a sweater, long trousers and socks if you are traveling into the mountains and good walking shoes if you are planning to explore mountain trails or caves.

At formal gatherings, appropriate attire for women is a matter of personal discretion. For men, if you attend any event which would normally require a jacket and tie (a curse in this weather) you can opt for a *barong tagalog* — an embroidered shirt that is considered formal dress, usually worn with black trousers. They cost about P1,000.

Otherwise, general necessities include any prescription medications you may need (although, department stores and pharmacies do stock patent medicines and prescription drugs in addition to well-known brands of toiletries), sunscreen lotion, mosquito repellent, a first aid kit, a raincoat or poncho, a flashlight (torch), a Swiss army knife, a travel alarm clock, a sleeping bag for overnight ferry trips and a padlock.

TOURIST INFORMATION

OFFICES OF THE
PHILIPPINE DEPARTMENT OF TOURISM

Asia Pacific
SYDNEY Philippine Department of Tourism ((61 2) 2996815 or 2996506 FAX (61 2) 2996817, Consulate-General, Wynyard House, Suite 703, Level 7, 301 George Street, Sydney, Australia.

TOKYO Embassy of the Philippines ((81 3) 3464-3630 or 3396-2209 FAX (81 3) 3464-3690, 11-24 Nampeidai Machi, Shibuya-ku, Tokyo, Japan.

OSAKA Philippine Tourism Center ((81 6) 5355071 to 72 FAX (81 6) 5351235, Second Floor, Dainan Building, 2-19-23 Shinmachi, Nishi-ku, Osaka 550, Japan.

HONG KONG Philippine Consulate-General ((852) 866-6471 or 866-7859, 866-9097 FAX (852) 866-6521, Room 602 United Centre, 95 Queensway, Hong Kong.

SINGAPORE Embassy of the Philippines ((65) 235-2184 FAX (65) 733-9544, 20 Nassim Road, Singapore.

SEOUL Philippine Convention and Visitor Center ((82 2) 525-1709 FAX (82 2) 598-2293, 403 Renaissance Building, 1598-3, Socho Dong, Socho-Ku, Seoul, Korea.

TAIPEI Manila Economic and Cultural Office (/FAX (886-2) 778-4969, Fourth Floor Metrobank Plaza, 107 Chung Hsiao E. Road, Section 4 Taipei, Taiwan ROC.

In the United States
NEW YORK Philippine Center ((212) 575-7915 FAX (212) 302-6759, 556 Fifth Avenue, New York, NY 10036.

LOS ANGELES Philippine Consulate-General ((213) 487-4525 FAX (213) 386-4063, 3660 Wilshire Boulevard, Suite 825, Los Angeles, CA 90010.

SAN FRANCISCO Philippine Consulate-General ((415) 956-4060 FAX (415) 956-2093, 447 Sutter Street, San Francisco, CA 94108.

In Europe
FRANKFURT Philippine Department of Tourism ((49 69) 20893-95 FAX (49 69) 285127, Kaiser Strasse 15, 60311 Frankfurt Am Main, Germany.

LONDON Philippine Department of Tourism ((44 171) 499-5443 FAX (44 171) 499-5772, 17 Albermarle Street, London W1X 7HA, United Kingdom.

PARIS Ambassade des Philippines ((33 1) 42-65-02-34 or 42-65-02-35 FAX (33 1) 42-65-02-38, Department of Tourism, Bâtiment B, 3 Faubourg Saint Honoré, 75008 Paris, France.

CURRENCY AND TIPPING

The local currency (peso) is used everywhere. It is divided into 100 centavos. Bank notes are available in denominations of 5, 10, 20, 50, 100, 500 and 1000 pesos. Coins are 1, 2 and 5 pesos and 1, 5, 10, 25 and 50 centavos.

Most hotels and restaurants, however, automatically add this charge to your bill, in which case additional tips are optional. Five to 10 pesos is sufficient for bell boys and porters, though if your luggage is heavy, pay more. Taxi drivers are usually tipped. Of course, tipping largely depends on the rapport between you and the person on the receiving end.

GETTING AROUND

Travel throughout the Philippines is generally easy and fairly cheap. Until recently, the

Foreign currency can be changed at banks or hotels, most large department stores and authorized money-changing shops. United States dollar transactions, as well as major credit cards, are widely accepted. Hotels, foreign exchange dealers, private dealers and major department stores authorized by the Central Bank change most international currencies. Travelers' checks are usually accepted for change. Avoid unauthorized dealers. ATMs (Automatic Teller Machine) are fairly easy to find throughout the Philippines, particularly in Manila and the major cities.

At press time a United States dollar was worth approximately 40 pesos.

Tipping is standard practice in the Philippines. Ten percent of the bill is the usual rate.

air networks — which are extensive — have been dominated by Philippine Airlines. Overbooking used to be a major problem, especially in the peak season. However, several new airlines have now stepped onto the scene offering additional flights on popular routes, as well as creating new flights to more remote destinations.

Equally, the island nation's ferry infrastructure has seen dramatic improvements over the past year, as well as the launching of a luxury cruise ship service around the islands. With ferries, try to avoid traveling during inclement weather or if the vessel

ABOVE: A brilliantly decorated porch celebrating Pahiyas, the Rice Harvest Fiesta, Lucban, Quezon.

appears to be overcrowded. And also avoid taking small pump boats or bancas at night when they risk being run down by larger vessels.

Because of the distances between islands, it is usually better to start and end most journeys by airplane. Long-distance buses are the main overland option, although there is a railway line from Manila to southern Luzon. A combination of bus and banca usually completes the journey to your destination. Car rental is also available and international agencies have offices in most major cities.

BY AIR

Manila is the major hub for internal flights within the Philippines, while Cebu also functions as a minor hub. Philippine Airlines (PAL), the nation's main domestic carrier, flies to 43 destinations within the archipelago, covering the major places, but also servicing such remote points as Basco in the Batanes Islands and Jolo in the Sulu Archipelago.

Round-trip flights on the interisland Philippine Airlines, which can be booked from overseas, are about US$150. But PAL doesn't fly to the more remote outer islands, where many of the best resorts are located. To reach these resorts, you must travel on small charter planes — best booked through your travel agent or hotel — and their rates are much higher.

The emergence of small regional airlines is helping to improve the situation for traveling on domestic routes. Previously Philippine Airlines, the national carrier, had a virtual monopoly on internal air travel and often struggled to provide adequate capacity.

Aerolift Philippines, Pacific Airways, Grand Airways, Asian Spirit, Cebu Pacific and Air Philippines are among the smaller carriers which service more remote islands with both scheduled and charter flights.

Domestic Carriers

PHILIPPINE AIRLINES ((2) 816-6691 FAX (2) 816-6938, Fourth Floor, PAL II Building, Legazpi Village, Makati, Manila 1229.

AEROLIFT PHILIPPINES ((2) 812-6711 FAX (2) 819-0386, Fourth Floor, JAKA II Building, 150 Legazpi Street, Legazpi Village, Makati, Manila.

AIR PHILIPPINES ((2) 526-4747 FAX (2) 521-2603, Seventh Floor, Ramon Magsaysay Building, Roxas Boulevard, Manila.

GRAND AIRWAYS ((2) 831-2774 FAX (2) 891-7667, Eighth Floor, Philippine Village, Airport Hotel, Airport Road, Pasay City 1301.

PACIFIC AIRWAYS ((2) 832-2731 FAX (2) 832-7692, 3110 Domestic Airport Road, Pasay City 130.

ASIAN SPIRIT ((2) 840-3811 to 16 FAX (2) 813-0183, Ground Floor, LPL Towers, Legazpi Street, Legazpi Village, Makati, Manila.

Travelers with limited time can investigate the seven-day "flightseeing" package offered by **Philippine Air Safari**. This is an island hop around the country's major attractions, allowing you to see as much of the archipelago as possible within a limited amount of time. The voyage is adventurous — with an itinerary that includes soaring over the active volcano of Mount Mayon, exploring Sohoton Caves National Park and Bohol's Chocolate Hills, staying overnight on the beautiful island of Camiguin and experiencing Palawan's El Nido, Busuanga Reefs and Calauit Island. Flights are seldom longer than 90 minutes — on twin-engine aircraft — and nights are spent in comfortable selected hotels. The package includes such activities as paddling outrigger canoes, sampling coconut wine and riding water buffalo. Contact **Blue Horizons Travel and Tours** ((2) 876071 to 76 FAX (2) 815-4825 or 876632, Ground Floor, Peninsula Manila, Ayala Avenue, Makati, Manila, an established Filipino- and Swiss-owned and managed company, which also offers a range of other tours.

ABOVE: Philippine Airlines Airbus at Zamboanga Airport, Mindanao. OPPOSITE TOP and BOTTOM: Malacañang of the North, Ilocos Norte.

By Boat

Intrepid island-hopping travelers may find much to appreciate about the ferry system in the Philippines. Such a comment may seem out of place given that Filipino ferries have long had a reputation for being near-derelict craft, often dangerously overcrowded and seldom keeping to a schedule. Often this reputation is well-deserved. However, a new breed craft — super-ferries — has emerged — some as modern as jetliners and quite

Of the many interisland shipping companies which provide service to points within the archipelago, **WG&A SuperFerry** and **Suplicio Lines** (see below) have the largest network and are the most intent on improving their craft. Cabins range from deluxe to economy. Together, these two companies cover most of the destinations you may wish to visit by boat, including Bohol, Cebu, Davao, Dipolog, Dumaguete, Iloilo, Leyte, Kalibo, Masbate, Surigao, Palawan and Zamboanga.

The voyage from Manila to the Visayas — the most popular trip — usually lasts about

comfortable. These ferries present a safe, viable mode of transport to and from island destinations.

It is also possible to opt for the most luxurious alternative — the Philippine's first luxury cruise ship — the MV *Mabuhay Sunshine*, which offers four-day, three-night cruise packages to destinations such as El Nido, Sicogon Island, Iloilo and Cebu. A four-day cruise costs approximately US$479 per person, including all meals, entertainment activities, land transfers in Manila, service charges and taxes. For reservations contact WG&A Philippines (see below), which also offers tour packages to Cebu, Iloilo and Puerto Princesa, along with participating hotels.

20 hours. The popular Cebu–Bohol WG&A SuperFerry trip, however, is considerably shorter at two and a half hours.

Interisland Ferries

WG&A SUPERFERRY **Manila (** (2) 635-3495 or 635-3497 FAX (2) 635-3496, Fifth Level, Building B, SM Megamall, Mandaluyong City, Manila. **Cebu (** (32) 72821 to 28 FAX (32) 253-2917 Sergio Osmena Boulevard, North Reclamation Area, Cebu City.

SUPLICIO LINES **(** (2) 252-6271 to 85 FAX (2) 265-858, Pier 12, North Harbor, Tondo, Manila. SUN CRUISES **(** (2) 831-8140 FAX (2) 834-1523, PTA Cruise Terminal (Old Hoverferry Building), Cultural Center of the Philippines Complex, Roxas Boulevard, Manila.

BY RAIL

There is only one operating railway line, from Manila to Naga City in southern Luzon. The Philippine National Railway's 478-km (300-mile) Southern Line extends to Legazpi City in Albay, a 14 hour journey. All trains have air-conditioned coaches as well as standard economy class.

BY BUS

Buses are the most common form of public transport in the archipelago. If not the most comfortable option, they at least guarantee a taste of authentic Filipino life — and they are one of the cheapest ways to see the Philippines. Several principal bus companies are franchised to operate throughout the country; they include **Philippine Rabbit** and **Victory Liner**.

It is possible to travel overland by bus to the Visayas and Mindanao via the Pan Philippine Highway and then link up with connecting ferry services to Sorsogon, Samar, Leyte and Surigao. Buses to outlying islands in the Bicol region also connect by ferry to Masbate and Catanduanes.

Major Bus Lines

PHILIPPINE RABBIT ((2) 711-5819, 819 Oroquieta Street, Sampalac, Manila.
VICTORY LINER ((2) 833-0293, Epifanio de Los Santos Avenue, Pasay City, Manila.

IN THE CITIES

Airport Transfers

Taxis are available at the airport. It is advisable to hire a taxi to travel into the city, on a prepaid basis, from the government stands you will see inside the airport on arrival. You can also arrange a taxi or bus shuttle with your hotel before arrival or through hotel representatives at designated counters in the arrival lobby. A nominal fee is charged for each piece of baggage.

Taxis

Taxis are the easiest and most comfortable way of getting around in the cities. Air-conditioned taxis cost P3.50 per kilometer, and an additional P12.50 charge is added to the final cost. Regular taxis cost P2.50 per kilometer and then add P7.50 to the final charge. Hotel air-conditioned taxis tend to be far more expensive, and since they charge about P100 an hour, they are more useful if you have a series of locations to cover. Usually, unless you are taking a long trip or traffic is unusually dense, taxi rides come to less than P100.

Rental Cars

Several major rental car agencies, including Avis, Budget and Hertz have offices in

Manila and offer a full range of vehicles from jeeps to limousines as well as the most conventional cars. Vehicles can be rented with or without a driver. A valid foreign or international driver's license is essential.

Jeepneys

In Manila and elsewhere, jeepneys are a way of life. Lovingly decorated, these elongated trucks are the principal mode of transport for most Filipinos. Successors to United States Army jeeps which were converted into minibuses after World War II, these silver bullets live up to their epithet: "folk art on wheels."

OPPOSITE: En route for the capital, Tagbilaran, Bohol. ABOVE: Dried fish on sale in Laoag, Ilocos Norte.

Jeepney's are festooned with items such as fighting cocks on their hoods, horses prancing on the fenders, scantily-clad women, loud landscapes painted on the sides which juxtapose with depictions of Christ's bleeding heart and slogans redolent of Sunday School: "Sacred Heart," "God is Love" or "Praise the Lord" and a plethora of patron saints.

Holding up to 20 people, they ply Manila's secondary and even some major roads. Although there are regular stops, you can flag one down and hop on: Call out "Bayad!" and pay the driver as you embark.

Tell the conductor where you are going and he will tell you how much you owe. You should keep your receipt as proof that you have paid.

The Light Rail System
This is the fastest, cheapest way to explore Metro Manila. Six pesos takes you from **Monumento** (the northern end of Epifanio de los Santos Avenue, EDSA) to **Baclaran**, first along Rizal Avenue and then Taft Avenue. Most tourist maps have the route of the LRT (Light Rail Transit) marked.

If you are too far back, pass your P1.50 down to him. When you are ready to get off, call out "Para!", wait until he slows down and hop off.

The smaller, ubiquitous version of the jeepney is the other urban staple: the tricycle. These smoke-belching motorbike-powered taxis have gaudy oversize sidecar cabins, wide windshields and vinyl-padded hoods and often have kamikaze drivers.

Buses
Both air-conditioned and non-air-conditioned buses travel all the major routes in Metro Manila except Roxas Boulevard. On an air-conditioned bus, the fare starts at P6. Non-air-conditioned bus fares start at P1.50.

Calesas
These horse-drawn carriages are seen all around **Binondo** (Manila's Chinatown), where they are used by schoolchildren, as well as at Intramuros and the entrance to Rizal Park, where you will be solicited. Calesas are common elsewhere in the Philippines, notably Cebu and Vigan. Sadly, the horses often look like they are on their last legs, although there are some examples of good practice.

ACCOMMODATION

The peak season in the Philippines is from November to May. Make sure you have accommodation booked before arrival or be prepared to take your chances. Check with your travel agent, and shop around for special package deals that may be offered — it is possible to find considerable discounts this way.

In this book, accommodation categories are divided into **luxury** (US$120 and above), **expensive** (US$80 to $120), **moderate** (US$40 to $80) and **inexpensive** ($US40 and below).

Service is included in most hotel and restaurant bills (see CURRENCY AND TIPPING, above). Unless room rates are specified as a net price, calculate your total bill by adding on a 10-percent service charge and the

Malaria can be a problem in parts of the archipelago, such as Palawan, where the female anopheles mosquito is the culprit. You are therefore advised to protection yourself by covering up after dark and by taking antimalarial tablets. These days, with some controversy over side effects, Larium is considered the most effective of the array. Resistance to the historic antimalarial standby, quinine, has long been outmoded by quinine's synthetic form, Cloroquine and the malarial parasite has also become resistant to Fansidar, the next generation drug.

government tax of between 13.7 percent and 14.6 percent.

HEALTH

The Philippines is not a high-risk destination, but like most tropical Asian countries, there are precautions to take. Unless you have recently been to a cholera-infected or a yellow fever region, no vaccinations are required. You should make sure you have booster shots (if necessary) for cholera, typhoid, tetanus (especially for divers and snorkelers) and hepatitis. Although not essential, it a good idea to be immunized against smallpox, polio, diphtheria and measles. Ask your doctor.

Pregnant women especially should seek advice before taking antimalaria drugs.

Although tap water in the Philippines is generally suitable to drink, you may wish to stick to bottled water or use purification tablets. Sampling raw (unwashed and peeled) fruit and vegetables, unpasteurized dairy products and patronizing unsalubrious-looking restaurants, may be asking for trouble. Make sure you have antiseptic cream for treating cuts and scratches, especially from coral. Be wary of walking barefoot (except on the beach), since the

OPPOSITE: *Calesas* in Chinatown Manila. ABOVE LEFT: Slices of watermelon on sale in Quiapo, Manila. RIGHT: Carbon Market, Cebu City.

Philippines has its share of microscopic parasites and worms, which burrow into the skin.

Given the scale of sex industry in the Philippines — which the government has been trying to crack down on — the grim statistics about the AIDS boom in Asia are worth bearing in mind. According to the World Heath Organization, the Philippines has been relatively unscathed thus far, with an estimated 18,000 infected, a fifth of the infection rate of Thailand, for example. Epidemiologists think the estimate is low and health workers believe the Philippines could

be headed for an AIDS disaster because of rampant prostitution and because of the opposition of the Roman Catholic Church to educational programs about AIDS.

Medical facilities are fairly good for emergencies, diagnostic tests and dispensing medication; most general hospitals are private. Health insurance is best arranged before you depart your home country.

BUSINESS AND BANKING HOURS

Private and government offices are open either from 8 AM to 5 PM or from 9 AM to 6 PM, Monday through Friday. Some private companies are open on Saturday from 9 AM to noon. Most shopping centers, department stores and supermarkets are open from 10 AM to 7:30 PM daily. Banks are open from 9 AM to 3 PM, Monday through Friday.

TIME

The Philippines clock is set at Greenwich Mean Time (GMT) plus eight hours.

ELECTRICITY

Voltage is 220 AC, 60 cycles. Most hotels in Manila, and the main hotels throughout the Philippines, have 110 and 220 volt outlets.

COMMUNICATIONS

The country code for dialing the Philippines from outside the country is 63.

The Philippines is upgrading its telecommunications system, with digital link-up almost completed. Local phone calls can be made from public, coin-operated booths, which are either 75 centavos or P2, red or silver-colored respectively. There are specially-marked pay phones which allow you to make regular, domestic and international collect calls. Most hotels have IDD or DDD (Direct Distance Dialing) phones in the room. Calling overseas on Sunday can save as much as 25 percent and these rates also apply if you call between midnight and 6 AM. USADirect is a 24-hour service that lets you call the United States mainland and Alaska collect without passing through a local operator. The code is 105-11 to reach an AT&T operator.

MAIL

The Philippine postal system is generally reliable, although cash and valuable items should not be sent through the mail. The main post office in Manila is on the south bank of Pasig River; there is also a branch at Rizal Park, next to the Manila Hotel.

MEDIA

There are more than 24 morning papers to choose from, most of them in English, including the *Manila Bulletin*, *Philippine Daily Inquirer*, *Manila Chronicle*, *Manila Times* and the

Philippine Daily Globe. There is also a wide selection of magazines. You can get most major English newspapers and magazines — *International Herald Tribune, Newsweek, Time, Asiaweek, Far Eastern Economic Review* and regional newspapers at major hotel bookshops and large stores.

Television programing runs from approximately noon to midnight, showing quantities of American-produced shows as well as Filipino. In some areas it is possible to receive CNN and ABC as well as other channels on the STAR satellite system.

NATIONAL HOLIDAYS

January 1   New Year's Day
April 9   Day of Valor
May 1   Labor Day
June 12   Independence Day
November 1   All Saint's Day
November 30   Bonifacio Day
December 25   Christmas Day
December 30   Rizal Day

During Holy Week Maundy Thursday and Good Friday are holidays.

AM and FM radio stations broadcast throughout the day and night, with primarily Tagalog on the AM stations and English on the FM stations.

DUTY-FREE SHOPPING

Duty-free shops are located at the departure and transit areas of the NAIA (Ninoy Aquino International Airport) in Manila and the MIA (Mactan International Airport) in Cebu. Just across from the NAIA is the **Duty-Free Fiesta Shopping Center**. It is the country's largest duty-free outlet which carries quality items ranging from international imports to selected Filipino export products.

EMERGENCIES

For immediate assistance, dial 166 or 168.

HOSPITALS

Philippine General Hospital ((2) 521-8450
U.S.T. Hospital ((2) 731-4697
Makati Medical Center ((2) 815-9911

SAFETY

As a rule, crime in the Philippines is not directed at travelers. All the same, it is wise to

OPPOSITE: Herbal medicine for sale outside Quiapo Church, Manila. ABOVE: Newsstand in Chinatown, Manila.

be alert, especially in Manila. Kidnappings and murders are not uncommon in the Philippines, and although armed insurgents in the south of the country no longer pose the threat they did in past eras, it is useful to realize that the Philippines is by no means a docile place.

Gang thefts are the most common crimes reported by tourists to the police. These thieves modus operandi is to befriend the potential theft victim in a bar, restaurant or other tourist spots, with offers of hospitality, and then to drug them with a strong seda-

tive such as ativan; although, police say that victims are rarely harmed. Tourists should be on the lookout for thieves and tricksters (such as fake policeman and immigration officers wanting to impose on-the-spot fines) especially around Ermita and Malate.

Having said all that, by and large, expect Filipinos to be warm, friendly people, who with even the slightest encouragement will go out of their way to be helpful.

ETIQUETTE

To show proper respect, always begin an inquiry with, "May I ask a question?" Keep in mind that Filipinos hate to say no. Above all, avoid public confrontation or criticism. Filipino pride demands that once a confrontation starts, there is no backing down.

LANGUAGE

Although there are over 100 regional languages in the Philippines, the national language is Tagalog, with the second most widely spoken language being English. All business, governmental and legal transactions are conducted in English. Although you can easily get by in the Philippines with English, you may wish to endear yourself by trying to speak Tagalog. Even if your accent is wrong, most Filipinos will be pleased that you are attempting to speak their language.

Mabuhay, the word tourists frequently encounter, means welcome, or long life. *Po* and *ho* are traditional expressions of respect still used widely, especially when addressing elders. *Salamat* or "thank-you," as in many cultures, is always appreciated. The Spanish influence is ever-present in the language of the Philippines, especially for basic words like *cuchara* (spoon), *ventana* (window) and *guapo* (handsome).

BASIC EXPRESSIONS

yes   *opo*
no   *hindi po*
How are you?   *Kumusta po sila?*
Good morning.   *Magandang umaga po.*
Good afternoon.   *Magandang hapon po.*
Good evening.   *Magandang gabi po.*
Good-bye.   *Palaam na po.*
Please come in.   *Tuloy po kayo.*
Please sit down.   *Maupo ho kayo.*
I'm well, thank-you.   *Mabuti po naman.*
Please drive slowly.   *Dahan-dahan po lang.*
May I take a photo?   *Maari po ba kayong kunan ng retrato?*
I cannot speak Tagalog.   *Hindi po ako nagsasalita ng Tagalog.*
What do you call this in Tagalog?   *Ano pong tawag dito sa Tagalog?*
Where do you live?   *Saan po kayo nakatira?*
where   *saan*
left   *kaliwa*
right   *kanan*
straight   *derecho*
Slow down.   *Dahan-dahan.*
Stop here.   *Dito lanf.*
Be careful.   *Konting ingat lang.*
entrance   *pasukan*
exit   *labasan*
enough   *tama na*
too much   *masyadong marami*
hot   *mainit*

cold   *malamig*
water   *tubig*
delicious   *masarap*
sweet   *matamis*
hungry   *nagugutom*
thirsty   *nauuhaw*
sleepy   *inaantok*
old   *matanda*
young   *bata*
big   *malaki*
small   *maliit*
to like   *magustuhan*
I want to go to…   *Gusto kong pumanta sa…*

Brazil ((2) 810-9421 or 851878, Sixth Floor, RCI Building, 105 Rada Street, Legazpi Village, Makati.
Canada ((2) 815-9536, Ninth Floor, Allied Bank Center, 6754 Ayala Avenue, Makati.
China ((2) 853148, 4896 Pasay Road, Dasmarinas Village, Makati.
France ((2) 810-1981, Sixth Floor, Pacific Star Building, Makati Avenue corner Senator Gil Puyat Avenue, Makati.
Germany ((2) 864906, Sixth Floor, Solid Bank Building, 777 Paseo de Roxas Street, Makati.

Do you have?   *Meron ba kayong?*
I want more…   *Gusto ko pa ng…*
Bill, please.   *Ang bil nga.*

EMBASSIES AND CONSULATES IN MANILA

Arab Republic of Egypt ((2) 880-3962, 229 Paraiso Street, Dasmarinas Village, Makati.
Argentina ((2) 875655 or 886091, Sixth Floor, ACT Tower Condominium, 135 Senator Gil Puyat Avenue, Makati.
Australia ((2) 817-7911, G/F Dona Salustiana S. Ty. Tower, 104 Paseo de Roxas, Makati.
Belgium ((2) 876571, Sixth Floor, Don Jacinto Building, De la Rosa corner Salcedo Street, Legazpi Village, Makati.

Indonesia ((2) 855061, 185 Salcedo Street, Legazpi Village, Makati.
Italy ((2) 874531, Sixth Floor, Flr. Zeta Building, 191 Salcedo Village, Legazpi Village, Makati.
Japan ((2) 818-9011, 375 Senator Gil Puyat Avenue, Makati.
Jordan ((2) 818-0731, 3502 Golden Rock Building, 168 Salcedo Street, Paseo de Roxas, Legazpi Village, Makati.
Netherlands ((2) 887753, Ninth Floor, King's Court Building, 2129 Pasong Tomo, Makati.

OPPOSITE and ABOVE: Faces from Ilocos Sur Province.

New Zealand ((2) 818-0916, Third Floor, Gammon Center Building, 126 Alfaro Street, Salcedo Village, Makati.

Norway ((2) 880469, 69 Paseo de Roxas, Makati.

Russian Federation ((2) 810-9614, 1245 Acacia Road, Dasmarinas Village, Makati.

Singapore ((2) 816-1764, Sixth Floor, ODC International Plaza Building, 217-219 Salcedo Street, Legazpi Village, Makati.

Spain ((2) 818-3561, Fifth Floor, ACT Tower, 135 Senator Gil Puyat Avenue, Makati.

Switzerland ((2) 819-0202, Eighteenth Floor,

Solid Bank Building, 777 Paseo de Roxas, Makati.

Sweden ((2) 819-1951, Sixteenth Floor, PCI Bank Tower II, Makati Avenue, corner de la Costa, Makati.

Thailand ((2) 815-4219, 107 Rada Street, Legzapi Village, Makati.

United Kingdom ((2) 816-7116, 15-17 Floors, LV Locsin Building, 6752 Ayala Avenue corner Makati Avenue, Makati.

United States of America ((2) 521-7116, 1201 Roxas Boulevard, Ermita.

Recommended Reading

On Manila bookshelves, look for the Philippines' most eminent contemporary writer, F. Sionil José. His novels include *Three Filipino Women* and *Sins*. Nick Joaquin, a well-known Filipino writer and commentator, is also worth reading. Filipina American Jessica Hagedorn, a poet and performance artist, has written a spirited novel about Manila, *Dogeaters*. *For Every Tear a Victory* by Hartzell Spence is a good yarn about former President Ferdinand Marcos, while *The Rise and Fall of Imelda Marcos* by Carmen Navarro Pedrosa is a breathless romp through the life and times of Imelda. Teodoro Agoncillo's *A Short History of the Philippines* is a charming, personal view of Philippine history. *The Culinary Culture of the Philippines* by Gilda Cordero Fernando is worth taking home.

BURUMA, IAN, *God's Dust — A Modern Asian Journey*, New York, Farrar Straus Giroux, First Edition, 1989.

DE LA COSTA, HORACIO, *Readings in Philippine History*, Manila, Bookmark, 1965.

FENTON, JAMES, *All the Wrong Places: Adrift in the Politics of the Pacific Rim*, Boston, Atlantic Monthly Press, 1988

HAMILTON-PATERSON, JAMES, *Ghosts of Manila*, New York, Vintage Press, 1988.

HAMILTON-PATERSON, JAMES, *Playing With Water — Alone on a Philippine Island*, New York, Sceptre Books, 1987.

JOAQUIN, NICK, *A Question of Heroes*, Manila, Ayala Museum, 1977.

KARNOW, STANLEY, *America's Empire in the Philippines*, New York, Random House, 1989.

REID, ROBERT H. AND GUERRERO, EILEEN, *Corazon Aquino and the Brushfire Revolution*, Baton Rouge, Louisiana State University Press, 1995.

SHERMAN, HAROLD, *Wonder Healers of the Philippines*, London, Psychic Press, Ltd., 1967.

ABOVE: Hanging around a pedicab, in Taluksangay Muslim Village, Zamboanga. OPPOSITE: Loboc Church, Bohol, Visayas.

Quick Reference A–Z Guide
to Places and Topics of Interest with Listed Accommodation, Restaurants and Useful Telephone Numbers

A accommodation, categories of *254*
Abra de Ilog *158*
Alaminos *133*
  accommodation
    Hidden Valley Springs Resort ((2) 840-4113 to 4114 or 818-4034 FAX (2) 812-1609 *133*
Amanpulo (MANILA (2) 532-4040 FAX (2) 532-4044 or LONDON 0171 349-9233 *36, 214–215*
American Cemetery and Memorial *110*
American colonialization *78*
American landing, 1944 *192*
Angeles City *140*
  access
    Clark International Airport *141*
  accommodation
    Derby Inn ((45) 2074 *140*
    Holiday Inn Clark Field ((45) 599-2246 FAX (45) 599-2248 *140*
    Sunset Garden Inn MOBILE ((097) 378-1109 *140*
    Swagman Narra Hotel ((45) 30157 *140*
  attractions
    International Hot Air Balloon Festival *140*
    Mount Pinatubo *141*
  general information
    car rental, Avis MOBILE ((45) 301-1885 *140*
  restaurants
    Maranao Grill Restaurant MOBILE ((45) 202-5847 *141*
Angono *136–137*
  attractions
    artists' commune *137*
    Gigantes Festival *50*
Anilao *129–130*
  attractions
    diving *129, 130*
    water sports *129*
  environs
    Taal *130*
anting-anting (amulets) *104*
Antipolo *44, 137*
  attractions
    Easter crucifixions *44*
Apalit *46, 139*
  attractions
    Apung Iru River Festival *46*
Apo Island *181*
  attractions
    diving *181*
B **Bacalor** *139*
  attractions
    old churches and houses *139*
Bacolod *178–181*
  access *181*
  accommodation
    Bacolod Convention Plaza Hotel ((34) 83551 to 9 FAX (34) 83392 *180*
    Bascon Hotel ((34) 23141 *180*

    Goldenfield Garden Hotel ((32) 83541 *180*
    L'Fisher Hotel ((34) 82731 FAX (34) 819-2502 *180*
  attractions
    Bacolod Plaza *178*
    Buglas Collection *178*
    Hofilena Art Collection *180*
    Masskara Festival *49*
    Patag *180*
    San Sebastian Church *178*
    Santa Clara *178*
    Silay *180*
    St. Joseph the Worker Chapel *179*
    Torres Antique Collection *178*
    Vega Antique Collection *178*
  environs
    Calumangan *180*
    Canlaon Volcano *180*
    Mambocal Mountain Resort *180*
    Victorias Milling Company *179*
  general information
    Department of Tourism Office ((34) 29021 *178*
  shopping
    markets *179*
    Philippine Antiques and Artwares *179*
    Recuerdos de Bacalod *179*
    Woodshave Shop *179*
Baguio *145–147*
  access *147*
  accommodation
    Baguio Hotel Ambassador ((74) 442-2746 *147*
    Baguio Midtown Hotel ((74) 442-7164 *147*
    Burnham Hotel ((74) 442-2331 or (74) 442-5117 *147*
    Swagman Attic Inn ((74) 442-5139 *147*
    Vacation Hotel Baguio ((74) 442-4545 FAX (74) 442-3108 *147*
    Woods Place Inn ((74) 442-4642 *147*
  attractions
    Baguio Arts Festival *50*
    Baguio Botanical Gardens *145*
    Baguio Cathedral *145*
    Baguio Christmas Festival *50*
    Baguio City Market *145*
    Baguio Mountain Province Museum *146*
    Burnham Park *145*
    Dominican Hill *146*
    Easter Weaving School *146*
    golfing
      Baguio Country Club golf course *146*
      Camp John Hay golf course *146*
  general information
    Tourist Information Center ((74) 6708 or (74) 7014 *145*
  restaurants
    Café by the Ruins *147*

shopping
  Good Shepherd Convent   146
  Narda's   146
Balabac   209
Balanga   142
Balicasag   176
Banaue   32, 60, 147–150
 access   150
 accommodation
  Banaue Hotel ((73) 386-4087 to 88
   FAX (73) 386-4088 or (MANILA (2) 812-1984
   FAX (2) 812-1164   150
  Banaue Youth Hostel ((73) 386-4087 to 88
   FAX (73) 386-4088 or (MANILA (2) 812-1984
   FAX (2) 812-1164   150
 attractions
  Batad Village   149
  Cambulo   149
  Guihon Natural Pool   150
  Ifugao tribal villages   149
  rice terraces   149
  Tam-An Village   149
barong tagalog national dress   56
basketry   56
Basey   195
Bataan Peninsula   141–142
 access   142
  Sun Cruises ((2) 831-8140   142
 accommodation
  Montemar Beach Club (MANILA (2) 815-8306
   FAX (2) 818-8544   142
 attractions
  Bataan Day, honoring WW II casualties   44
  WW II sites   142
Batac   154
 attractions
  Balay Ti Ili, Marcos memorabilia   154
  Malacañang del Norte museum   154
Batangas Province   129–130
 access   129
 accommodation
  Aquaaventure Reef Club ((2) 816-7461 to 72
   FAX (2) 813-1967   130
  Bonito Resort (MOBILE (912) 306-1696
   FAX (2) 819-1157   130
  Dive South Marina Resort ((2) 724-1129
   or (2) 812-7073   130
  Maya Maya Reef Club Manila ((2) 810-6865
   FAX (2) 815-9288   130
  Punta Baluartes ((2) 894-1466 to 68
   or (2) 894-5793 FAX (2) 893-4491   131
 attractions
  dive sites   130
  Taal Church   130
Bataraza   209
Bird Island   195
birdwatching   33–34
Boac   159
Bocaue   47
 attractions
  Pagoda sa Wawa Festival   47
Bohol   176–177
 accommodation
  Balicasag Island Dive Resort
   (MANILA (2) 812-1984 or 810-3655
   FAX (2) 812-1164   177
  Bohol Beach Club ((32) 211091 or (32) 211543
   or (32) 211544 FAX (32) 211545 or
   (MANILA (2) 522-2301 FAX (2) 522-2304   176

  Crystal Coast Villas ((32) 3179 or
   (MANILA (2) 828-0441   177
 attractions
  Anda Peninsula   176
  Baclayon Church   175
  Bilar   175
  Bohol Provincial Museum   175
  Bool Barrio   175
  Busay Falls and Laboc River   176
  Chocolate Hills   17
  diving   176, 177
  offshore islands, excursions to   176
  Punta Cruz Watchtower   176
  Sandugo Festival   47
  Tagbilaran   174
 general information
  Punta Cruz Diving Club
   (/FAX (32) 54114   174
 shopping
  city market   175
Boracay   12, 184–192
 access   190–191
 accommodation
  Club Panoly Resort ((2) 536-0682
   FAX (2) 582628   187
  Coco-Mangas Hotel Beach Resort
   ((2) 521-9443 FAX (2) 817-9978   189
  Family Cottages   189
  Friday's ((2) 892-7443 FAX (2) 819-0281   187
  Galaxy Beach Resort   189
  Jony's Place (VIA OPERATOR 3119   189
  Laguna de Boracay (VIA OPERATOR 3603   189
  Lorenzo Main (VIA OPERATOR 3808 or 3204   188
  Lorenzo South ((2) 990719 or 926-3958
   FAX (2) 961726   188
  Mika's Place, Diniwad Beach   189
  Mona Lisa White Sands ((36) 288-3205
   FAX (2) 924-7052   188
  Palm Beach Resort and Lanai
   (VIA OPERATOR 3408   188
  Paradise Lodge Beach Resort
   (/FAX (2) 833-7908   189
  Pink Patio ((2) 812-9551 FAX (2) 810-8282   188
  Sandcastles ((2) 500-906 FAX (2) 504967   188
 attractions
  flea market   186
  horseback riding   186
  Laurel Island   186
  Puka Beach   186
  water sports facilities   186
  White Beach   186
  Yapak Beach   186
 general information
  bike hire   186
  Boracay Dateline newspaper   186
  Boracay Sand Paper   186
 nightlife
  Coco-Mangas Hotel bar   189
  Kon-Tiki Bar   191
  Moonshiners Bar   191
  Music Garden   191
 restaurants
  Avenhja's Fruitshakes   191
  barrio market   191
  Friday's   191
  La Reserve   191
  Puka Beach Café   186
  Severo de Boracay   190

Brooke's Point, Palawan *209*
Bulacan Province *139*
Busuanga Island *212*
C **Cagayan de Oro** *232*
  accommodation
    Pryce Plaza Hotel ((8822) 721791
      FAX (8822) 726687 *232*
  attractions
    Initao village *232*
    Kagayhaan Festival *232*
    Xaxier University's Museo de Oro *232*
Cainta *137*
Calamba *132*
  attractions
    Birthday of José Rizal ceremony *46*
Calapan *158*
Calbayog *195*
Caluit Island *213*
  attractions
    Caluit Island Wildlife Sanctuary *34, 213*
  general information
    Conservation and Resource Management
      Foundation ((2) 78581 to 89 *213*
Caliraya Lake *136*
  accommodation
    Lake Caliraya Country Club
      (MANILA (2) 485151 TO 59 *136*
  environs
    Paete *136*
    Pakil *136*
Camiguin *18, 232–234*
  access *234*
  accommodation
    Caves Beach Resort ((8822) 879040 *234*
    Mychelin Beach Resort ((8822) 874005 *233*
    Tia's Beach Cottages ((8822) 871045 *233*
    Tree-House *234*
  attractions
    Esperanza Ardent Spring *233*
    Katibawasan Falls *233*
    Lanzones Festival *49, 233*
    Mambajao *233*
    Mount Hibok Hibok *233*
    White Island *233*
Canlaon Volcano *32*
Capul Island *195*
Cardona *137*
  attractions
    Morong Church
Catbalogan *195*
Cavite Province *127–128*
  accommodation
    Banyan Tree Nasugbu Evercrest Golf and
      Country Club ((43) 473-4411 or
      (MANILA (2) 712-9293 *128*
    Ridge Resort and Convention Center *128*
    Taal Vista Hotel ((19) 223226 or (19) 712-7525
      FAX (19) 109225 (MANILA (2) 817-2710
      FAX (2) 818-8208 *128*
    Villa Adelaida (MANUAL EXCHANGE 267 or
      (MANILA (2) 810-2016 TO 19 *128*
  attractions
    Aquinaldo Shrine *127*
    Kawit *127*
    People's Palace in the Sky
      ((46) 413-1295 *128*
    Taal Lake and Volcano *128*
    Tagaytay Ridge *127*

Cebu City and Province *13, 168–172*
  access *172*
  accommodation
    Alegre Beach Resort ((32) 311231
      FAX (32) 214345 *171*
    Argao Beach Resort ((32) 72620
      (MANILA (2) 522-2301 *171*
    Badian Island Beach Club ((32) 253-6364 or
      (32) 253-6452 FAX (32) 263-3385 *171*
    Cebu Beach Club
      (MOBILE/FAX (32-912) 501-2610 *170*
    Cebu Club Pacific ((32) 79147
      FAX (32) 231-4621 *171*
    Cebu Green Island Club ((32) 95935
      FAX (32) 231-1269 *171*
    Cebu Midtown Hotel ((32) 253-9711
      FAX (32) 254-6363 *170*
    Cebu Plaza Hotel ((32) 311231
      FAX (32) 312069 *170*
    Centrepoint International Cebu ((32) 254-7111
      FAX (32) 253-0695 *171*
    Coral Reef Hotel ((32) 211-1191
      or (32) 211-1193 to 4 FAX (32) 211-1192 *170*
    Costabella Tropical Beach Resort ((32) 210828
      or (32) 210838 FAX (32) 314415 *170*
    Hotel de Victoria ((32) 254-1331 *171*
    Maribago Bluewater Beach Resort
      ((32) 211260 or (32) 217617 *170*
    Montebello Villa Hotel ((32) 313-681
      FAX (32) 314455 *171*
    Park Place Hotel ((32) 253-1131
      FAX (32) 211131 or (32) 210018 *170*
    Plantation Bay ((32) 340-5900
      FAX (32) 340-5988 *170*
    Shangri-La Mactan Island Resort ((32) 310288
      FAX (32) 311688 *60, 170*
    Swiss Chalet (EXTEL
      CELLPHONE (097) 323-0086 *170*
    Tambuli Beach Club ((32) 211534
      or (32) 211544 *170*
  attractions
    Argao *168*
    Badian Island *168*
    Basilica Minore del Santo Niño *167*
    Carbon Market *168*
    Carcar *168*
    Casa Gorordo *167*
    Cebu Capitol *168*
    Cebu City Museum *167*
    Fort San Pedro *167*
    Mactan's Bahug-Bahugan Sa Festival *44*
    Magellan's Cross, remains of *167*
    Moalboal *168*
    Naga *168*
    Olongo Island *168*
    Osmena Residence *167*
    Pescador Island *168*
    Sala Piano Museum *167*
    Santo Niño de Cebu (Sinulog) *42*
    Sogod *168*
    Taoist Temple *168*
    University of San Carlos *168*
  general information
    Department of Tourism
      ((32) 254-2811 FAX (32) 254-2711 *167*
  nightlife
    Bai *172*
    Balls *172*

Bigwig   172
Caruso Music Bar   172
casino in Cebu Plaza Hotel ((32) 311231   170
Frankfurter Hof   172
Motion   172
Music Concourse Outback Lounge   172
Our Plaza   172
Pards   172
St. Moritz   172
Thunderdrome   172
restaurants
Alavar's Seafood House ((32) 96120   171
Anton's, Mactan   172
Café Adriatico ((32) 217366   171
Chateau de Busay   172
Crab House ((32) 231-5165   171
Ginza ((32) 281419   171
Govinda's   171
Lumpia House   171
Seafood City ((32) 213795   171
seafood market cafés, Mactan   172
Swiss Chalet   172
shopping
Carbon Market   168
Mactan furniture factories   168
colonization of the country   72
conquistadores   72, 73
Coron   212
attractions
diving   212
Corregidor   19, 124–126
access   126
accommodation
Beach Cottages   126
Corregidor Inn   126
attractions
Malinta Tunnel sound and light show   126
Suicide Cliff Buddhist shrine   126
Topside, Middleside, Bottomside and
the Tail sites on the island   126
general information
Sun Cruises ((2) 831-8140   126
cruising in the Philippines   27
Culion   212
Cuyo Islands   214–215
access   215
accommodation
Amanpulo (MANILA (2) 532-4040
FAX (2) 532-4044 or
LONDON 0171 349-9233   36, 214–215
attractions
Amanpulo island   215
diving   215
D **Dapitan**   234
accommodation
Dapitan Homestay Association   236
attractions
Kinbayo Festival   47, 234
shrine to José Rizal   234
wildlife and nature   234
Davao City and Province   220–231
access   231
accommodation
Apo Beach Hotel ((82) 221-6430
FAX (82) 221-0748   230
D'Fabulous Venee's ((82) 76026   230
Pearl Farm Beach Resort ((2) 832-0893
FAX (2) 832-0022 or (DAVAO (82) 62749
FAX (82) 234-7581   228

attractions
Araw ng Dabaw festival   42
Caroland Farms, Bago   225
Dabaw Etnica weaving center   224
Davao Orchids and
Fruits Festival   48, 224
Festival of Santo Niño de Praga   224
fishing villages   224
Malita horse fighting   228
Mount Apo National Park   224
orchid growing plantations   222
Paskuhan Festival   50, 222
Philippine Eagle Nature Center   225
San Pedro Cathedral   224
Shrine of Holy Infant Jesus of Prague   224
Taoist Lon Wa Buddhist Temple   224
general information
Department of Tourism office ((82) 221-0070
or (82) 221-6955 FAX (82) 221-0070   222
restaurants
Harana ((82) 73937   231
Tsuru Japanese Restaurant ((82) 72896   231
shopping
Aldevenoc Shopping Center   231
Nieva's Arts and Crafts   231
Dipolog   234
access   236
accommodation
Dakak Beach Resort ((2) 721-0450
or (2) 721-0447 FAX (2) 721-2463   18, 38, 234
attractions
wildlife and nature   234
diving   21–23, 128–129, 143, 156, 168, 171, 180, 184,
186, 210, 215, 228, 236, 240
contacts
Batangas, Dive South Marina Resort
((2) 724-1129 or (2) 812-7073   130
Bohol, Punta Cruz Diving Club
(/FAX (32) 54114   174
Manila, Philippine Commission on Sports,
SCUBA Diving (PCSSD) ((2) 503735   143
dive sites
Amanpulo   215
Anilao (various)   129
Apo Island   180
Apo Reef National Marine Park   157
Batangas   24
Bird Island   195
Boracay   186
Busuangas   157
Cathedral Island   143
Cathedral Rock Marine Sanctuary   130
Cebu (various)   24
Coron Island   212
Devil's Island   143
El Nido   210
Hundred Islands area   143
Mactan   168
Marinduque   159
Mindoro   24
Moalboal   168
Nasugbu   130
Palawan   25
Pescador Island   168
Puerto Galera   24
Quezon Island   143
Siquijor   180
Sombrero Island   130
Sumilon Marine Park   180

Tubbataha Reefs National Marine Park   24, 213
wreck diving   26
Verde Island   130
Visayas (various)   24
Dumaguete   180
access   181
attractions
Anthropological Museum   180
diving   181
Silliman University   180
general information
JMC International Travel and Tours
((2) 873109 FAX (2) 817-5556   180
Magnum Marine Corporation ((2) 813-1696
FAX (2) 818-5043   180

E ecological and environmental issues   23
ecotourism   33
El Nido region and village   12, 210–212
access   212
accommodation
Malapacao Island Resort   212
Marina Cottages   212
Pangulasian Island, c/o Ten Knots
((2) 894-5644 or (2) 894-5734 or (2) 893-0606
FAX (2) 810-3620   212
attractions
Bigan black marble cave   210
Dilumacad giant rock formations   210
edible birds' nest collection   210
Inalula turtle sanctuary   210
general information
Tourist Office   212
electricity   256

F festivals
All Saints' Day   50
Apung Iru River, Apalit   46
Araw ng Dabaw, Davao   42
Ati-Atihan, Ibajay   42
Ati-Atihan, Kalibo   13, 41, 61, 184
Baguio Arts Festival, Baguio   50
Baguio Christmas Festival, Baguio   50
Bahug-Bahugan sa Mactan, Mactan   44
Bamboo Organ Festival, Las Piñas   42, 127
Bataan Day remembrance, Bataan   44
Binirayan–Handuyan, San José and others   45, 51
Birthday of José Rizal, Manila and Calamba   46
Carabao, Pulilan   45
Davao Orchids and Fruits Festival, Davao City   48
Dinagyang, Iloilo   42
Feast of Our Lady of Candelaria, Iloilo   42
Feast of Our Lady of Lourdes, Quezon City   42
Feast of St. John the Baptist   46
Feast of the Black Nazarene   41
Fertility Rites Festival, Obando   45, 139
Fiesta of St. Martha, Pateros   47
Fiesta sa Bora-Boracay-cay, Boracay   187
Flores de Mayo   45
Giant Lantern Parade, San Fernando   51, 61, 139
Gigantes, Angono   50
Gigantes, Quezon   61
Independence Day   46
International Hot Air Balloon Festival,
Clark Field   140
Kaamulan, Malaybalay   48
Kagayhaan, Cagayan de Oro   47, 232
Kalighawan Festival, Iba   143
Kamundagan, Naga City   51
Kinbayo, Dapitan City   47

La Naval de Manila, Quezon City   49
Lanzones, Mambajao   49, 233
Lem-Lunay T'Boli, Lake Sebu   48
Manila Day, Manila   46
Masskara, Bacolod City   49
Maundy Thursday, Good Friday and
Easter Sunday   42
Moriones, Marinduque   42, 61, 159
Pagoda sa Wawa festival, Bocaue   47, 139
Pahiyas Festival, Quezon Province   45
Pahiyas Festival, in Lucban and Sariaya   137
Parada ng Lechon, Balayan   46
Pasko sa Tanjay Christmas Festival, Tanjay   50
Paskuhan, Davao City   50
People Power Days   42
Penafrancia, Naga City   48
Sandugo, Tagbilaran   47, 175
Sunduan, Paranaque   48
Thanksgiving parade, Balayan   130
Turumba, Pakil   45
Zamboanga Hermosa, Zamboanga   49
fishing and game fishing   27
foods   52
fruits   54

G **Gasan**   158
geography   69
golf   35–36, 94, 110, 129, 131, 142, 146, 154, 170, 240
Guagua   139
attractions
Betis Church   139
Guimaras Island   183
accommodation
Costa Aguada Island Resort ((33) 831-2261
FAX (33) 833-0357   184
Isla Naburot Resort ((33) 76616
or (33) 75867   184
Nagarao Island Resort ((33) 78613   184
attractions
diving   184
Tiniguiban Puland Payasan Beach   184

H handicrafts   54
history   69–89
American colonialization   78
American landing WW II, 1944   192
British occupation of Philippines   76
conquistadores   72, 73
ilustrados, the rise of   77
independence   83
Katipunan secret society   78, 134
Japanese invasion   82
Marcos years   85
Spanish, colonization by the   93
World War II   80
Honda Bay   204

I **Iba**   143
attractions
Kalighawan Festival   143
Ibajay   42
attractions
Ati-Atihan Festival   42
Iligan   231
attractions
Maria Cristina Falls   232
environs
Lake Lanao   232
Ilocoon Island (Lakawon)   180
attractions
diving   180